AF540763

Hospitality and Cruise Ship Management

Hospitality and Cruise Ship Management

Ravindra Ahuja

RANDOM PUBLICATIONS
NEW DELHI (INDIA)

Hospitality and Cruise Ship Management

ISBN 978-93-5111-934-0

Published in 2016 in India by

RANDOM PUBLICATIONS

4376-A/4B, Gali Murari Lal, Ansari Road
New Delhi-110 002
Phone : +9111-43580356, 011-23289044, 011-43142548
e-mail: sales@randompublications.com,
info@randompublications.com, randomexports@gmail.com

Type Setting by : Friends Media, Delhi-110089
Printed at : Sanat Printers

Preface

The Hospitality and Cruise Industry is one of the fastest growing and most dynamic industries in the world, but shortage of qualified and experienced professionals still exist. Cruise Ship Hospitality industry has one of the most exciting careers imaginable. Hospitality isn't limited to the world class hotels. It includes luxury resorts, premiere casinos, exciting outdoor venues, fun theme parks, CRUISE LINES and much more.

It is projected to continue to grow and as it expands, employers around the world, increasingly demand qualified, skilled managers. You need skills and professional training to succeed in the fast paced, international field of hospitality. Currently there are more than 200 million positions available in the hospitality industry.

By 2013, it is predicted to reach 250 million worldwide. With the growth in tourism industry, more and more people are traveling abroad as well as within the country, thus leading to big demand for professionals in the field of hospitality and tourism management.

One of the fastest growing leisure industry sectors, the cruise industry faces many challenges. While supply continues to grow at double-digit levels, demand struggles to keep pace. Given the demands on infrastructure and the risk of an eroding on-shore experience, fewer ports are in a position to accommodate the cruise lines as supply grows. At the same time, the public sector's scrutiny of industry practices related to the environment, taxation, security, safety and labour mounts. Despite these challenges, many cruise lines report record levels of profitability.

The cruise ship industry has experienced an enormous growth in terms of popularity, size and variety of destinations in the last years, with bigger and more luxurious ships designed to meet the also growing demand for cruising as a holiday option that offers beauty, adventure, relaxation and entertainment to passengers from across the world.

– Author

Contents

1

Introduction

HOSPITALITY INDUSTRY

The hospitality industry is a broad category of fields within the service industry that includes lodging, event planning, theme parks, transportation, cruise line, and additional fields within the tourism industry. The hospitality industry is a multibillion-dollar industry that depends on the availability of leisure time and disposable income.

A hospitality unit such as a restaurant, hotel, or an amusement park consists of multiple groups such as facility maintenance and direct operations (servers, housekeepers, porters, kitchen workers, bartenders, management, marketing, and human resources etc.).

Usage rate, or its inverse "vacancy rate", is an important variable for the hospitality industry. Just as a factory owner would wish a productive asset to be in use as much as possible (as opposed to having to pay fixed costs while the factory is not producing), so do restaurants, hotels, and theme parks seek to maximize the number of customers they "process" in all sectors. This led to formation of services with the aim to increase usage rate provided by hotel consolidators.

Information about required or offered products are brokered on business networks used by vendors as well as purchasers.

In looking at various industries, "barriers to entry" by newcomers and competitive advantages between current players are very important. Among other things, hospitality industry players find advantage in old classics (location), initial and ongoing investment support (reflected in the material upkeep of facilities and the luxuries located therein), and particular themes adopted by the marketing arm of the organization in question (for example at theme restaurants).

Also very important are the characteristics of the personnel working in direct contact with the customers. The authenticity, professionalism, and actual concern for the happiness and well-being of the customers that is communicated by successful organizations is a clear competitive advantage.

CRUISE

One of the fastest growing leisure industry sectors, the cruise industry faces many challenges. While supply continues to grow at double-digit levels, demand struggles to keep pace.

Given the demands on infrastructure and the risk of an eroding on-shore experience, fewer ports are in a position to accommodate the cruise lines as supply grows.

At the same time, the public sector's scrutiny of industry practices related to the environment, taxation, security, safety and labour mounts. Despite these challenges, many cruise lines report record levels of profitability. To help our clients meet these and other challenges, PwC teams provide advisory services to cruise companies, industry associations, governments, destinations, prospective investors and lenders.

HOW PWC CAN HELP YOU

PwC has a team of dedicated professionals with cruise operations, finance and technology experience. Our relationships with the major cruise line companies, combined with the experience of our specialists and the resources of our renowned Hospitality and Leisure practice, provide unparalleled industry services for our clients.

Our cruise services include:

- Supply and demand analysis
- Our professionals develop a census of cruise vessels and identify new ship deliveries for the industry as a whole or various tiers, such as the contemporary, premium or luxury segments; address the size and type of cabins, including those with ocean views and private balconies, ancillary amenities and other facility considerations; analyze historical cruise demand; and estimate future demand.
- Surveys
- We develop surveys to gather data regarding customer preferences and satisfaction, specific cruise performance, itineraries, ports of call, shore excursions and other passenger experiences.
- Facility programmeming
- Our specialists analyze a vessel's facility programme, including number and mix of cabins, and food and beverage outlets and amenities, as well as study potential pricing strategies, to position a ship for value enhancement.
- Financial analysis
- Our teams prepare prospective financial analyses for a proposed or existing cruise entity. These analyses also include assisting entities with joint venture agreements, management contract negotiations, the overall capital structure with lenders and investment bank

negotiations. Other services include tax consulting and valuation expertise.

- Economic impact studies
- Our professionals estimate the economic consequences associated with the cruise industry for specific destinations, including incremental tax revenues, capital investment, and increases in direct employment and tourism, as well as the related multiplier effects of induced economic activity.
- Strategy and planning
- We identify client objectives, then recommend and foster the implementation of a course of action designed to meet those objectives.

SOLVING COMPLEX BUSINESS PROBLEMS

PwC has made a long-term commitment to the cruise industry. Our global perspective and operational knowledge provide unmatched value for our clients, and our indepth experience allows us to help manage the critical challenges you face in the cruise industry today.

Cruise tourism is a globalized phenomenon that experts and tourism scholars have studied from multiple perspectives. A general overview is needed to expand the current understanding of cruises in our modern societies. As the industry has grown so too has the scientific interest in it. Sociologically speaking, one of the aspects that historically characterized this form of tourism has been isolation; travelers seek cruise-tourism as a mechanism of escapement (Wood, 2000; Wilkinson, 1999).

The lack of commitment of cruise-tourism consumers to local economies and habits produces troubling points, discussed in specialized literature. Cruise-tourism specialists have evaluated the industry in terms of its impact on local economies (Dwyer and Forsyth, 1996; Peisley, 1992; Forsyth and Dwyer, 1995; Lester and Weeden, 2004). From 90s decade onwards, the concern for economic multipliers and economic impacts set the pace regarding the question of sustainability. From this viewpoint, cruise shipping helps communities to preserve their natural resources. Ecological destinations such as Antarctica and Australia have been offered to provide international demand of ecological consciousness (Dowling, 2006; Stewart and Draper, 2006; Klein, 2006; Dobson and Gill, 2006).

However, in the last years, to be more exact after the attacks on New York's World Trade Center, cruise related tourism has been seen as one of the safest ways to experience foreign travel. The current period has been challenging to the tourism industry. From virus outbreaks to terrorism, the onset of this new millennium produced many problems for the tourism industry. Under such a context, many policy makers insisted on the need to improve the sense of safety at tourist destinations. The intervention of national governments, in this process, was of paramount importance by identifying and tracing those elements that jeopardize the societal order. Starting from the premise that cruise consumption mirrors the feeling and political contexts of societies, this conceptual review essay emphasizes on cruises as modern dispositive where travelers are protected.

Security has been commoditized and is offered as a product. Cruises combine not only aspects of security and curiosity, but also represent a valid alternative to integrate hospitality and mobilities, but unless otherwise resolved, cruise tourism in case of accidents may become a trap. From Titanic to Costa Concordia the degree of vulnerability of passengers may actually be higher in cruises than other means of transport (first and foremost whenever a strange virus surfaces and expands rapidly on board) (Miller et al, 2000; Lois et al, 2004).

This chapter provides readers with an all-encompassing view of risk and practical suggestions to be followed to mitigate the risk on the high seas. Particularly, the question of technological mobility engenders new threats to be seriously reconsidered. Safety related studies of cruises seem to be in their infancy. To fill this academic gap in the literature this review examines not only the historical roots of megacruise accidents, but also the conceptual discussion of risk re-production in sociology.

PRELIMINARY DEBATE

Beth J. Harpes writing for the Associate Press notes that 1912 the sinking of the Titanic was one of the world's great tragedies. Today, one hundred years later the Titanic's sinking is a form of "dark tourism". Harpes writes: "A hundred years ago, the sinking of the Titanic was a tragic disaster. Today, this disaster has become nothing more than an entertaining family outing. There are replica ships in Tennessee and Missouri, graveyard tours in New York and Nova Scotia, traveling exhibits from Las Vegas to Atlanta, and two brand new museums in Belfast, Northern Ireland, and Southampton, England. Hotels and restaurants are serving Titanic dinners, and ships are even heading to the disaster site — including an anniversary cruise that slashed prices last-minute from nearly $5,000 to $1,000." (Newslader com, 2012).

The facts surrounding the ill-fated maiden voyage permeate popular culture. The disaster has spawned countless books, television specials and movies — perhaps none more famous than James Cameron's Oscar-winning film "Titanic," one of the highest-grossing movies of all time. To coincide with the anniversary the epic film has been re-released in 3-D. The Titanic tragedy has even spawn reproductions. Thus, not only is there a museum in Belfast, Northern Ireland, but there are also sister Titanic attractions in places far from the sea such as Branson, Missouri, and Pigeon Forge, Tennessee, catering to the fascination of American audiences. What is it that makes the Titanic so intriguing and universal to so many people? What fascinates us to the point that Northern Ireland is using the sinking of the Titanic as a centerpiece for its tourism promotion? Although cruise problems and tragedies are not new and have been with us, perhaps since the beginnings of recorded history, the Titanic's sinking acts as not only a metaphor for cruises but also as a metaphor for tourism risk and dangers.

Even a superficial study of perhaps the world's most famous cruise tragedy reveals much about the tourism industry and its sociology. Recently the cruise ship population has increased by leaps and bounds. Despite increased safety and security measures, as the number of cruise ships has grown so too has there been an increase in cruise ship incidents.

This chapter seeks to discuss some of the theory behind cruise risks and dangers. We present our material against an historic backdrop and then move into theory and recent cruise history.

This chapter then seeks to open the topic of cruise risk management, dangers and disasters for discussion and to encourage further research in this area. The chapter then seeks to tie the ideas or danger and risk to the concepts or dark tourism and to human being's fascination with daring the vastness of that part of the planet which remains its last unexplored and least well understood frontier (Timothy, 2006).

CRUISE LINE

A cruise line is a company that operates cruise ships. Cruise lines are distinct from passenger lines which are primarily concerned with transportation of their passengers: instead, cruise lines are primarily in the leisure entertainment business, some of which occurs at the destination but a great deal of which takes place aboard ship. Cruise liners typically have two separate staffs: the crew under the captain and a hospitality staff under the equivalent of a hotel manager. Among cruise lines, some are direct descendants of the traditional passenger lines, while others were founded from the 1960s on specifically for cruising.

The business is extremely volatile; the ships are massive capital expenditures with very high operating costs, and a slight dip in bookings can easily put a company out of business. Cruise lines frequently sell, renovate, or simply rename their ships just to keep up with travel trends.

A wave of failures and consolidation in the 1990s has led to many lines existing only as "brands" within larger corporations, much as a single automobile company produces several makes of cars. Brands exist partly because of repeat customer loyalty, and also to offer different levels of quality and service. For instance, Carnival Corporation owns both Carnival Cruise Lines, whose former image were vessels that had a reputation as "party ships" for younger travellers, but have become large, modern, and extremely elegant, yet still profitable, and Holland America Line, whose ships cultivate an image of classic elegance.

CRUISES AND MODERNITY

One way that we live the "tourism gaze" is through the relatively modern phenomenon of cruises. In fact the modern cruise acts a unifier of many of the forms of the tourist gaze about which Urry and Larsen write. We go on cruises, then, to gaze at others and to be gazed at, to see unique sights, and to see categories of sites, to gaze at the ordinary lives of people whose lives are different from ours, and to gaze at unique experiences. Both classical tourism and cruises for the rich existed prior to World War II, however, the middle class phenomenon that we know as "mass tourism" only began in the years after the close of the second Word War.

Delp writes: "Cruises as we know them today are really only about 50 years old, but the tradition goes back more then a hundred years when passengers started booking travel on mail ships crossing the Atlantic." (News Travel, 2012)

Although cruises existed in many parts of the world, the modern cruise is principally a North America phenomenon that reflects the ideals, strengths and weaknesses of US middle class society of the 1960s and 1970's. By this point in history, cruises for the masses had become so accessible for North Americans in the late 1960s, that they were also cannibalizing other forms of tourism. For example, New York's Catskill Mountains resorts, known as the Borsht Belt and famous for being the launching pad for many comedians, was not able to withstand the onslaught of the Caribbean Cruise industry. The modern middle class cruise was highly comparable to the all-inclusive Catskill Mountain resorts and offered the additional advantages. As in the case of the Catskill Mountains, cruises offered unlimited food, snacks, in many cases, liquors and non-stop entertainment.

The Caribbean tourism region also provided relatively tranquil and romantic waters upon which to gaze, a variety of ports-ofcall to see, social status in which to be seen, and a sense of adventure and danger. The Caribbean's chronic problems of crime turned the ordinary into the extraordinary by harkening back to its history of piracy.

Thus, quoting Schroeder (2002:73) Urry and Larsen note: "there are many examples of the attraction of tourists for criminals, for muggings, prostitution, pickpocketing (sic) and illegal businesses relating to the addictions of visitors. Part of the allure of the Caribbean is the said to be that 'danger' is just around the corner, just beneath the veneer. Tales of Pirates, Rastas, drugs and Yardies all contribute to the performing of 'dangerous tourism' in these paradise islands of the Caribbean (Urry and Larsen, 2011, 220). Last but not least, the French philosopher, George Amar (2011), argues that humankind is experienced a new paradigm respecting to mobilities where freedom and security converge. The technological advances, enrooted in modernity, have created mobile hotels (cruises), which focused on the social bonds of travelers. Most certainly, the old paradigm of mobility as an alienable mechanism of indoctrination is being radically altered. Today, thousand of people select these transports to connect with partners, and new friends.

REVIEW OF THE THEORETICAL LITERATURE

Maximilliano Korstanje has written extensively about the sociology of dangers, threats and risks (Korstanje, 2009; 2010; 2011 and Korstanje and Tarlow, 2012). Korstanje notes that scholars have long asked the question: how do we define the notion of threat and what determines that something (or someone) is a risk? Defining threats and risk is not a simple matter. Authors have long sought to define the concept and to determine when and how a risk becomes a threat. What are the cruise industry's risks and at what point to these risks become threats?

To complicate the issue, Korstanje notes that threats carry risk and risks may produce threats. Thus, there is a cybernetic interaction between risk and threat. Furthermore, there is no agreement on what conditions produce a risk. In our highly complex world composed of real, partial and false information both the scholar and the cruise passenger rarely are sure of reality. In the case of cruises, as in other areas of tourism we note that there are threats judged to be external, such as piracy, a terrorist attack or even a hurricane, others that are internal, such as the norovirus or the threat of passenger on passenger, crew on passenger or passenger on crew sexual assault. The threat of illness is so great that the Los Angeles Times ran a headline on February 4, 2012 stating: "2 Florida cruise ships riddled with norovirus, Anyone surprised?" (Nation Now, 2012). Korstanje (2011) notes that currently we lack a theory that permits us to understand when a risk becomes a threat and/or a threat becomes a risk. He further notes that we do not have a clear demarcation between these concepts.

This problem is best analyzed by reviewing the literature of several scholars in the filed of risk/threat. We begin by analyzing the work of the German sociologist Niklas Luhmann (2006).

Luhmann argues that society is not constructed from a collection of individuals, but rather through the communicative processes that interact between these individuals. He further posits that society cannot function without articulating mediating elements that produce uncertainty such as love, money and power. Cruises are symbols of this articulation, thus, the cruise is a sign of danger; it is often portrayed as a place of romance, and it symbolizes a certain level of both wealth and power. Lehmann argues that a society does not maintain itself by repressing these emotional symbols, but by interaction complexities that interlock a society's subgroups. Thus, the cruise represents a place where the unstated emotion becomes signs of an interlocking transient society that exists at the ephemeral level. From Luhmann's perspective, the cruise's potential risks then permits societal agents uniting in such a manner that they produce institutional confidence.

For example, the lifeboat symbolizes confidence and the belief that the crew will be the last to abandon ship acts both as a confidence building measure and as a means to establish a social order. As in other social systems, the cruise system's own complexity is framed by the notion of trust and the exercise of authoritative power. Based on the contributions of structuralism, Luhmann understands that without power (which he defines as a chain of sub-codes) the subject (in this case the passenger) cannot communicate nor form links with its institutions (the cruise liner). Unlike other sociologists, Luhmann openly questions an agent's rational reasoning by taking into account that agents often act in ways other than what they rationally believe but rather act on instincts, outside influences or their gut reactions.

Following this approach, risk is not based on the possibility of damage but rather it is a rational outcome from the subject's thought process. Risk can then only come into being when there exists a previous decision on the part of the involved party in which this rational reasoning permits the capability of avoiding a decision's consequences (the principles of self-restraint). All risks imply the possibility of avoiding the risk at the same time that it calls upon (other) faculties to predict the risk.

For this reason it is not possible to consider chance risks when the victims do not have: 1) participation in the event's creation 2) the possibility of avoiding it, or of reversing its impact. For example, a cruise accident or terrorist attack must not be considered risks but rather dangers. To claim, as does Beck (2006) that we can create a fictitious bridge between predictability and risk is a clear defect that results in "alarmism." Risk does not come about as a probability but as a communicative quality of those who assume authority in a society's power structure.

Luhmann further argues that as a general principle, those who create risks rarely suffer the risk's consequences. It is not the cruise's staff that creates the risk, but those who control the cruise from afar. We can then define the conceptual division between risk and danger. The cruise tragedies noted above are not risks for those on board but rather dangers (for the passenger and crew). These incidents, however, represent risks for the cruise line's corporate management or for the builder of the boats.

Examples are: the cruise ship sinks, the passengers are robbed or assaulted, or a passenger dies not due to Divine Providence, but because those who direct the company did not provide proper oversight (Luhmann, 2006). For there to be risk then, there must have been a calculation of future loss and/or benefits measured against the probability of an occurrence (that is to say, that the danger was seen as avoidable) (Korstanje, 2009; 2010; 2011). Likewise D. D'Andrea (2011) suggests that threats become real when there is the danger of not taking counter measures to stop them.

Seen from this perspective, risk refers to the potential danger brought about by a decision (or a decision not to make a decision). Can it be argued that not to make a decision implies a danger; to make a decision implies a risk? Luhmann argues that "with a threat, something must occur (and we do not know if it will happen) in such a way that what has been produced or may be produced may never occur. A threat refers to the idea that something is inevitable unless something else occurs or interrupts the process that has already begun" (D´Andrea, 2011: 90).

A Giddens (1991) offers another perspective. Giddens argues that modernity contains a dilemma in which the process of reflective thought is tied to risk.

According to Giddens, the issue of risk does not lie in its effects or in the decision making process, but in the level of the social agent's knowledge. For Giddens, then, the problem of risk starts from the organization between the agent and its primary security basis, the relationship between the agent's caretakers or in the case of the cruise, its crew. From this perspective the tragedy of the Costa Concordia is not only in the loss of life and property but also in the breaking of a covenant between the crew and its passengers. From Gidden's perspective order is based not only in rationality but also in doubt. Security then depends on how a problem is understood and what the calculus is for its solutions. These two indicators carry the original idea that trust becomes "defensive cloak" in our social life.

The nexus between a passenger and his/her caregivers (the crew) produces trust-ties where the passenger is supplied with the adequate tools (lifeboats, information etc.) so as to be able to confront potential threats. When there is a lack of discipline and proper information then doubt enters into the equation and thus accelerates risk. This acceleration blurs the boundaries between the passengers' sense of past, present and future. Giddens (1991, p. 4) writes on one hand that, modernity lessens risk in certain aspects of life, but in other areas of life it generates new risks.

The modern world, results in an aplitic tendency not necessarily due to the inevitability of risk, but because it introduces new risks for which the past does not provide us guidance from which to find solutions. From this perspective, modernity' tendency to produce rapid change and with it to introduce ever more challenging risks has greatly changed the role of the tourism security expert.

The classical order of control, as seen on a cruise ship, is based on the fixing of clear boundaries within time and space. Space permits the monopolizing of force and legal coercion. Thus, a ship's captain is often isolated from the cruise's passengers and to sit at the captain's table is not only a sign of prestige but of social stratification.

The cruise's staff, like all bureaucracies is oriented towards controlling interpersonal special and temporal relationships.

Giddens argues that post-modernism has begun a process of reflection where time and space relationships are not only clarified (connecting absences with being present) but also that demonstrates a crisis of jurisdictions and legitimacy that invades all aspects of life on the cruise. For example, the cruise company offers us the chance for relaxation and rejuvenation coupled with fun almost as if the traveler were to find him/herself in a medical situation. The cruise staff "sees" us for a certain price, and just as in the case of risk management these "experts in relaxation" try to capture of mitigate outside risks within societal limits.

From one perspective, this risk mitigation is positive because it gives the traveler autonomy but it also generates new risks. Thus, the freedom to be oneself on a cruise may lead to the risk of socially unacceptable behaviour in the eyes of another, and as such promote conflict within a confined world of both space and time.

The excessive increase in perceived risk, Giddens admits, is a product of societies based on industrial consumption. Does this concept of consumption apply to the leisure world of cruises and travel?

From the perspective of this chapter we can note that Gidden's contributions are as follows: a) Scientific advances permit the reversal of exterior risks, but generates new risks that can lead to a system wide collapse as undermines the system's functionality; b) The modern world is not only rationally complex but is tied exclusively to the future. The cruise passenger travels not only in the present but also in the hope of obtaining memories in which the past intersects with the future.

As in Hebrew grammar, the past is in reality a future; c) Risk facilitates the conditions necessary for the introduction of rationality in an individual's life as it obliges that person to make decisions or to permit others (experts, staff members, and travel professionals) to decide for him/her; d) The process of reflexive thought generates a lack of authority during a crisis; each person may challenge the staff's decision; e) The cruise industry must take into account that modernity is an irreversible phenomenon that impacts the subject's identity isolating him from institutions and making him more vulnerable; f) With the passage from hierarchical logic based on authority to reflexive thought used by both crewmembers and passengers there is a systematic increase of new risks. Thus the passengers on the Costa Concordia chose not to believe crewmembers and made what they considered to be rational decisions; g) In modernity there is no option of non-decision.

SEA TRAVEL IN HISTORY

Ever since Biblical times human beings have been traveling. At times these travels have been for specific purposes such as business or to flee an advancing army. Later humans began to travel for pleasure. We may argue that tourism began only after the age of urbanization had begun. People in agricultural societies had neither the leisure time nor the resources to for pleasure travel, but with the dawn of urban centers travel for reasons such as spirituality and then pleasure became possible. While travel by ship is an ancient form of travel it is only with the dawn of the nineteenth century that tourism, as we know it, came about.

This new phenomenon was unique in that it was born of an urban perspective. Tourism has often sought to emulate or mimic the dominant elite's lifestyle. As such in the world of tourism, economic status subordinated territoriality. For most of world history tourism merely "was"; it was rarely a subject of a serious academic study. As scholars began to study tourism they noted two consisting sets of values that produced one of tourism many social divides. Just as the Biblical text often subliminally divided the world between the world of agriculture and nomadic herders, the tourism literature often demonstrated a divide between "the intelligent well-to-do" and the "less sophisticated common folk "whose spending habits were far from desired.

Scholars then have noted that tourism slowly transformed itself from an elite pleasure to one of mass consumption. For example, Cursak describes the transformation of the Irish coast into a place of tourism. Cursak demonstrated how Anglo-Saxon ideals infiltrated the local norms, often by means of conspicuous consumption, thus generating a "locale-within-a-locale" thus reducing opposition to Anglo-Saxon principles to a minimal. Cursak argued that tourism produces norms and codes that govern multiple aspects of life. From this perspective classical tourism acted as an agent connecting the local aristocracy to the foreign aristocracy in a place ritualized by luxury and eccentricity that stood far removed from the practical necessities of most common people (Cusack, 2010).

As noted above not all travel has been land based. In fact multiple sea images have crept into our land based vocabulary, thus the camel is called the ship of the desert, and an economic rescue package is called a bailout. Despite the inherent dangers in sea travel human beings have been fascinated with the sea and have set sail upon it since the dawn of time. From the Biblical literature to the Icelandic Sagas, human beings have shown a fascination with the sea. For many the sea was and still is a symbol of eternity, of unbridled power, of adventure and at test of man against the elements. The sea has become a symbol of our love-hate relationship with that which we cannot control. Although the centuries have turned into millennia, humanity's love for the sea and our sense of awe is still very much with us. The ocean's are very much part of what Urry and Larsen (2011) call the tourist gaze. Urry and Larsen write of various forms of tourist gazes including: (1) the unique- object-gaze such as the Eiffel Tower, (2) genre-gaze such as American skyscrapers, (3) the uniqueness-of-the-familiar gaze (visits to museums that tell the story of ordinary people in extraordinary ways), (4) the gaze-of-the-unusual-ordinary, for example seeing how domestic tasks are carried out in another society, and (5) the gaze of the ordinary-extraordinary, such as a rock from another planet of from the moon (Urry and Larsen, 2011, pp.15-16).

2

Cruise Management

A cruise ship is a luxury vessel that is used to take passengers on a pleasure voyage in a journey that is as much a part of the experience as the various destinations on the way. In contrast to an ocean liner that transports passengers from one point on the globe to the other often across the oceans, a cruise ship or a cruise liner as it is known by most, takes the people on board to a round trip that is of varied duration, from a single day to possibly a week and culminates at the originating port. This is a very refreshing mode of enjoyment and recreation, which relaxes the mind and replenishes energies to a great extent.

HISTORY

The present day form of cruising can be traced back to the beginning of the twentieth century when the transoceanic traveling was at its zenith. The only mode of transport was the ships so the different companies that were in this business offered the best services to compete in the market. These ocean liners with luxurious services offered what came to be known as line voyages. But because of the long journey, which at best would be no less than four days, there had to be huge storage for fuel and other necessities and that didn't leave much room for luxuries. With the advent of jet airplanes in the latter half of the last century, there was a shift in passenger preference and the long sea voyages were left for only the ardent sea fans.

Fig. For Representation purpose Only

ADVENT OF CRUISE SHIPS

This situation was ideal for the launch of a cruise ship. It needed something strikingly different and exciting to bring back the interest of the people to sea voyages and this is where these trips gained popularity. Considering the fact that the journey is relatively short with many stoppages at exotic locations, the ships are designed accordingly, thereby making more room and utilizing that space for an open design that exudes extravagance. It would be appropriate to liken a cruise ship to a floating hotel complete with a hospitality unit amongst other crew members.

FACILITIES ON CRUISE SHIPS

The facilities on board these cruise liners include great dining services. Some liners offer open air dining on the deck, where as, there are others that have expensively designed dining halls with mouth watering recipes to leave a long lasting impression on the passengers. In addition to this there are casinos, fitness centers, spas, cinemas, and some ships even have a Broadway like theater.

These cruise ships also boast of swimming pools, hot tubs, lounges, libraries, gyms and clubs. To put it in a nut shell, they pamper the passengers with the best of hospitality and services that can be imagined with some of the choicest natural views along the sea. Over the last decade, cruising has become an integral part of the tourism industry contributing over $25 billion yearly to this booming sector. The major bulk of the business as expected comes from the North American and European regions but the other areas like the pan pacific are also catching up.

THE ELEMENTS OF CRUISING

THE ELEMENTS OF CRUISING

It could be argued that our planet Earth is, in one significant sense, misnamed. This is because 71 per cent of the surface is covered by water (Lutgens, 1992). Air travel has been cited as a major influence on changing leisure activities, yet even a novice can recognize the opportunities for sea and water based vacations using ships as floating resorts. According to Day and McRae (2001), a cruise ship provides easy access to some of the world's most popular destinations, and this simple statement holds the key to the current successes that the industry enjoys.

This can be exemplified by examining below and completing the task that is described.For many tourists, the cruise experience embodies a series of powerful motivators: it is often perceived to be safe, social, customer friendly, and service oriented (Cartwright and Baird, 1999). The ship provides a mobile, consistent, and easily accessible location to act as a home away from home while the tourist samples the port of call. The tourist adapts to shipboard life and learns to relax into a vacationroutine (Gibson, 2003): a routine that can be interspersed with a choreographed range of ship or land activities.As travel expert Douglas Ward says, "Over 10 million people can't be wrong (that's how many people took a cruise last year)! Cruising is popular today because it takes you away from the pressures and strains of contemporary life by offering an escape from reality.

Cruise ships are really self-containedresorts, without the crime, which can take you to several destinations in the space of just a few days" (Ward, 2001).However, the notion of "cruising" also generates negative perceptions. Dickinson and Vladimir (1997) conducted interviews with people who either had not considered or did not want to go on a cruise. They revealed five specific factors that demotivated the potential tourist: Ward (2001) counters this list by highlighting emerging patterns. Cruising is presented as being both cost effective and high in value. The range of cruise types has expanded to include opportunities for all sorts of people. In this way, cruising can be both socially inclusive and exclusive: families can be catered to as a specialty market, as can single tourists, conference delegates, older travelers, active tourists, groups, etc.—the list is endless. Ward recognizes that this type of vacation is appealing to older customers but also notes that the average age of first time cruisers is now well under 40.

ESSENTIAL ELEMENTS OF THE PERFECT CRUISING BOAT

Heading out on a Nordic Tug 54, a well-found cruiser. Two features set a cruising boat apart from the rest, and from those two features come many special elements. A cruising boat must be able to keep you comfortable while aboard for long periods of time, and it must be able to safely take you long distances. A long period of time could mean years or several weeks, but it will be longer than the quick trip out and back on a Saturday afternoon that characterizes most boating. Long distances can mean around the world or just several hundred miles, but it'll be much longer than a trip to a nearby marina or fishing spot and back.

Essential to both of these features is that a cruising boat needs to be self-sustaining. The degree will vary with the type of cruising you do, but being able to comfortably live in your own little world without being plugged in and hooked up is fundamental to cruising. You might think you want to cruise from marina to marina and that this feature isn't so important, but you'll miss some of the very best of the experience if all you do is marina hop. True, good marinas can add greatly to the experience, and most of us really appreciate this part of it, but there's far more.

My wife, Mel, and I have been amazed through the years as people ask: "But you don't eat on the boat, do you?" When we tell them of course we do, they frequently come back with an incredulous, "Well, do you mean you actually cook on the boat?" This gives us the golden opportunity to explain that we've spent months at a time aboard without ever tying at a marina or going shopping. We tell them about getting meat by spearing fish and lobster, about the early days of collecting rainwater and the later days of making water from the sea with a reverse osmosis system. We tell them about generating electricity from the wind, how we grew sprouts and took along 5-gallon containers of wheat and ground it into flour with a stone grain grinder when we wanted to bake bread.

We tell them about making diesel repairs at sea, changing out props over white sandy bottoms in the Bahamas and fixing outboards. At this point people are often trying to politely back away. But it's not just fun telling about it; it's a lot of fun cruising this way. You can cruise the way you want, but missing out on the pleasures of being at anchor at night and the unique feeling of being in control of your life would be a shame. So depending upon how much you want to marina hop — and how much you can afford to — your boat should be able to serve as your very own independent world for the lengths of time you wish. Here are some other elements that will allow you to do this.

Anchoring gear: Many boats are not built to anchor well. If you cruise enough you're going to need to anchor on occasion. The subject of good anchoring gear would fill many pages.

Briefly, good anchoring gear includes an oversized windlass, a good source of power for that windlass, hefty backing plates, oversized strong points to attach rode (backed by hefty plates), well-designed and supported rollers, and space and carrying capacity for enough chain and at least two anchors of proper size. Some boats lack the ability to safely carry this gear because it overloads the bow, causing dangerous trim. These boats, in my view, are not good candidates for cruising.

Storage: Some builders go for the "oh wow" boat show response by opening up areas to make the boat's interior look spacious when they could have built cabinets and bins. This may be fine for marina hopping, but not for cruising. Look for storage space if you're buying. But if you already have a boat, you might be able to build in cabinetry, cut hatches in cabin decking or do other things to give you more places to put stuff. The longer you want to be independent, the more storage you'll need.

More and more, a good turn of speed is expected in a modern cruising boat.

Tankage: How much potable water the boat will have to carry depends on your personal habits, as well as how you cruise. When we went to the Bahamas with our two young daughters, our two 150-gallon tanks would last a month with daily showers. We topped off with rain whenever we could, but this wasn't reliable. If you don't have this much tankage or would need more water, consider an RO watermaker. They're much more reliable than in the early days and don't take up much room. Ours makes 15 gallons an hour, more than enough for daily use, with a few hours of running the generator, which we'd be doing anyway. Adding tanks must be done cautiously because upsetting the balance of a boat can be dangerous.

Fuel capacity is also critical but often manageable. Trawlers and sailboats usually don't have a problem with this. Express cruisers and other planing boats often do. Their tankage is limited because of weight and the builder's assumption that they'll be marina hopping. However, we've seen many of these boats having a great time running for days at displacement speed without refueling. But, as with other issues, you'll need to consider how you want to cruise. We've had weeks go by in the Bahamas out islands with no diesel available because of tanker problems, storms and poor planning. But if your cruising is to be coastal, getting fuel when you need it will be less of an issue.

Household power: You will need to be able to run the gear that makes you safe and comfortable. This usually means a good diesel genset for your on-board power grid. But you need more. It's a drag to run the generator all the time to keep creature comforts such as refrigeration, lights and the television on line. It's particularly a drag when you've found that perfect anchorage and settled in to a beautiful evening in paradise. A cruising boat needs good deep-cycle batteries. We have an auxiliary bank of two 4D Rolles and a house bank of two 8D Rolles wet lead-acid batteries. Both banks are modular. The cells are installed individually and strapped together. This makes it easier to find a place for them and to load them. Rolles now makes AGM batteries, which are said to be even better for cruising boats.

Our banks are charged while under way by a heavy-duty Balmar alternator and smart regulator. During generator time (and shore power time), they're charged with a Xantrex ProSine 2000, which can ramp up to 105 amps DC incoming, but also can be set for the specific batteries and has a smart-charge regulator. The ProSine inverts the battery power to true sine wave AC power when we've shut down the engines. We can lie quietly at anchor, watch television, use all the ice we want from the icemaker, microwave and do many of the other things that require AC power.

But you don't have to use as much electricity as we do. It's your comfort level you're satisfying, not ours. You might be able to get by with a wind generator and/or solar cells. The latter are improving significantly. The new Solbian solar cells are so thin and flexible they can be sewn or fastened with zippers to Bimini tops. Wind generators and solar cells are relatively expensive for their output but nowhere near as expensive as a diesel generator, and they usually require far less maintenance. Some use these for supplemental power.

Creature comforts: The power you consume, the pleasures you enjoy, the time you can stay out — all are affected by the type of equipment you have. Refrigeration is an important example. If you have a standup house-type AC refrigerator, it's going to take a lot of power from the batteries, via the inverter. You'll have to run the generator much more. However, there are relatively low-cost, effective and efficient DC refrigerator/freezer units on the market. The key to any such unit is a well-built and insulated box for refrigeration and freezing. You can get detailed instructions for building these from manufacturers, and most yards are familiar with these projects. There's often ample space, particularly if you take out the "house" fridge that's designed for the shore grid.

On our boat, we have stainless-steel holding plates in well-insulated boxes. This older methodology freezes the eutectic solution in the plates during generator time — or, if set up properly, while running the engine — and the plates maintain the refrigerator and freezer temperatures for long periods of quiet time. Cooking is another good example. Many change their 220-volt kitchen ranges to propane because an inverter won't power it. We used propane for years, but I became increasingly uncomfortable with it. When we got our present boat, we kept the electric range, using it when the generator is on or when we're plugged in. At other times, we use the microwave, an electric frying pan, a crock pot, a toaster and coffee maker with our inverter, though not all at the same time. We also use an Origo single-burner alcohol stove. Our galley serves us perfectly well when there's no generator or shore power.

Overall basic comfort features are fundamentally important. These include head compartments that fit real people, separate showers, well-thought-out galleys, comfortable beds and — perhaps one of the most elusive design features of all —comfortable seats. An enclosed or enclosable, comfortable steering station is also critical.

Not your grandfather's cruising boat: performance, comfort and seaworthiness with the Hunt 52 Express Cruiser. Accessibility: To be self-sustaining and safe at far distances, you must be able to repair and maintain equipment. If you're thinking, Oh, I'll just let yards along the way worry about those problems, then more power to you, and I wish I had your money. If you leave the beaten path — and this is what cruising is all about — you're going to have times when you fix it yourself or it doesn't get fixed. This can involve serious safety issues because if you can't get to it you can't fix or maintain it.

The engine and generator must have access all around, not just that manufacturer-touted mythological side that has "all the parts you need to service." But that's just the beginning.

Air conditioning, through-hulls, freshwater pumps, bow thrusters, water heaters, watermakers, rudders, stuffing boxes and anything else that needs inspection and maintaining must be accessible. This means more than being able to get your hand to all parts; it means you must be able to get both hands, tools and light to the parts and must be able to remove the part, which includes getting it out, and replace it.

Accessibility must be more than what works for a boatyard. A yard repair might involve a very small person who's done it many times with specialized tools, without people living aboard around the job. On our Gulfstar 47, the engine room had reasonable accessibility, but I had to lift up the "living room floor" in order to get there. Family life was disrupted. This is not what you want. Our current motorsailer has a separate engine room

Ventilation: Many boats have few opening portholes and hatches. This increases construction costs, and they aren't needed for marina barges. But you can't run an air conditioner at anchor unless you run the generator. I am strongly opposed to running a generator at night while sleeping unless the boat and the generator (including the installation) were designed, built and maintained for that purpose, and there are multiple alarms for the myriad disasters this could cause. For air conditioning, we open hatches and portholes and use a 12-volt Bora fan that draws almost nothing. Good ventilation also helps with the depressing cave effect that many get when cooped up down in a hull for long periods of time. A simple wind scoop, fixed over a hatch can create amazing ventilation at anchor.

Hunt 52 Express Cruiser

Private spaces: Cruising for lengthy periods without being able to have private times can quickly lead to unhappiness. Your boat may not have this problem, particularly if it has multiple living areas and multiple levels, as with a flybridge. If your boat doesn't have separate spaces, you can solve the problem with a little creativity, such as adding curtains around the chart table or a bunk, establishing "his and her" zones. Transportation: A good dinghy is indispensable. Our 12-foot aluminum dinghy was built to our specifications 23 years ago and has a 20-hp Yamaha. It serves well as a cargo boat, fishing boat, ferry, dive boat and exploring boat. But your cruising boat must have a place and system for quick, easy and safe storage. This usually means well executed davits or a lift, but don't underestimate the "quick and easy and safe" part. We've seen quite a few boats with a nice dinghy mounted on top and very expensive davits, which you can't use if you tie to the wrong side in a marina or if it's rough in the anchorage. Toys: After the first few days or weeks of cruising magic wears off, you'll be looking for diversions.

That dinghy might be your primary escape, but kayaks, canoes, stand-up paddle boards, home entertainment centers (run off the inverter) and good books will be much appreciated. The key here is there must be a place to put them on board. Escape and survival: What you need will depend on how and where you cruise, but there are some minimum standards.

The boat will need a good life raft or at least a dinghy that can be launched in a storm and will survive, although dinghies seldom suffice for true survival rafts. Even if you plan to cruise just coastal waters, you're going to be aboard much more of the time and be more exposed to the potential of storms and fires. Because of this, a critical element is the space to store a life raft or suitable dinghy, safely out of the way of boarding seas and in a place where it can be easily and quickly launched. Our Switlik offshore life raft will deploy automatically if we're sinking. All life rafts must be maintained according to manufacturer's instructions.

Travel the distance ... safely: There are vast differences between boats in the area of safety, but no matter how you cut it, a cruising boat should be tougher than a boat designed to live only in marinas. We all know this, but sometimes have problems sorting it out. If you plan to cross oceans, you'll want to spend your money on a boat like a Nordhavn, which is expressly designed and built for trips like this, or a purpose-built bluewater sailboat. If you only plan to do coastal cruising, you might think you don't need to spend the money for offshore safety features, spending more of the dollar on inshore comforts — maybe a well-aged Hatteras with more open spaces and big windows. But it's not that easy.

Probably the closest we ever came to losing our boat was in Albemarle Sound in North Carolina. Mel and I were in a tough 47-foot motorsailer with our first baby girl, Melanie, who was less than a year old. We were making the short trip from Ocracoke Island to the North River. The summer day was hot, and there were thunderstorm warnings. I looked ahead to see not just clouds and rain racing towards us but a wall of water lifting up into the air from the surface. When it hit us, the dinghy, trailing astern, went airborne and remained airborne for the duration, twisting wildly on its painter. I clung to the wheel using all the strength I had and the muscle of the 160-hp Perkins to keep the bow into the storm. Mel clung to Melanie, huddled below in the saloon, both in lifejackets. We survived. We had a tough boat. If we'd had a marina barge or a light sailboat, we might have been like the ones who didn't make it. So what do you do?

First, try very hard to figure out where and how you will cruise, then get the boat to suit, spending your dollars on your comfort needs but also, more important, on things to keep you safe. Next, get to know your boat intimately. This not only means how to maintain and repair her, but also how she behaves and how to handle her. Next, take great care to cruise well within your boat's — and your — abilities. This not only means where you go and how far you go, but also paying meticulous attention to the weather. A few years ago, some friends made the trip from the Bimini chain in the Bahamas back to the U.S. East Coast. They were in a cruising boat that worked well for them. It was what I call a "box" boat, but it had a lot of room, comfort, access and space. It would also travel reasonably well at hull speed and on a plane in the right circumstances.

As is typical of this type of boat, it had a high, flat stern, which created a lot of room for the spacious master stateroom aft with queen size bed. But this day the wind came up strongly from the east, and the waves from astern began to build as they moved farther away from the lee of the islands. Soon the following seas were pushing that box stern around until the boat was having difficulty answering the helm. They were in danger of broaching or pitchpoling. They decided it would be best to head back to Bimini, but after several attempts they had to give that up. The boat rolled so badly as her beam began to face the waves that they aborted each turn. They had to continue on, trying to keep the boat stable.

Before the trip was over, several of the broad windows in the main saloon — the very ones that they so appreciated because of the light and view that they provided at anchor — had been smashed by boarding seas, and the boat below was awash. They had to call the Coast Guard to keep them afloat. The boat had been perfect for them for years, cruising up and down the ICW and making calm crossings to the Bahamas to anchor in protected harbours. But this day they used it beyond its capabilities. They soon sold it.

You will probably be cruising in unfamiliar waters, so you may need more sophisticated navigation equipment than you'd need for a Sunday afternoon outing — for example, exceptionally good chart plotters (as well as paper charts), depth finders and binoculars. You may also need better communications gear. We have a Digital Antenna cell phone antenna on our mizzen, around 50 feet up. The cable goes to an amplifier below that transmits throughout the boat. This helps to bring the signal in when we're far from cell phone towers. Long-range cruisers might also want a single sideband set or satellite communications gear. It goes without saying that the boat should be well equipped with robust safety gear, such as lights, EPIRBs, PLBs and fire extinguishers. The list goes on and is beyond the scope of this chapter.

The end of the rainbow aboard a North Pacific 43.

Range of speed: Most people think of cruising boats as displacement hull boats, powerful but slow. There are good reasons for this. But after more than 60 years of cruising in all types of boats, I believe there is also much merit to a boat that will cruise comfortably at hull speed, sipping fuel, and will also travel fast, preferably on plane. Getting up on plane can result in more speed more economically than just pushing water aside with brute power.

Speed can add to safety and enjoyment. When you're out on the water and a storm is coming, it's nice to be able to flex your horsepower and get to a safe harbour quickly. Also, it's often important to make a harbour while the light is good so you can read the water, or get from one harbour to the next in a day so you won't have to run at night.

You can utilize shorter weather windows to make time and fuel-saving runs between inlets. Our displacement hull motorsailer will sip fuel and comfortably cruise at around 6 knots or forge along at 10 knots if we push her. Just that small difference can mean a lot.

CRUISE SHIPS AND PASSENGER SATISFACTION

Cruises have become a major part of the tourism industry. Recent passenger figures suggest that although the cruise industry is growing, so is the competition. The industry's rapid growth has seen nine or more newly built ships catering to a North American market added every year since 2001, as well as others servicing European market. Smaller markets, such as the Asia–Pacific region, are generally serviced by older ships. This growth has made it imperative for cruise companies to delight their current customers so that they will return and refer new customers.

Celebrity Cruises	81.2
Royal Caribbean	79.9
Princess Cruises	79.0
Holland America Line	78.7
Carnival Cruise Line	78.1

*Based on social media reviews of all major cruise ship brands

Passenger Satisfaction								
Large Cruise Ships: 2010								
	Embark	Cabin	Service	Dining	Enter-tainment	Public Rooms	Service	Spa & Fitness
Celebrity Cruises	83.2	84.0	86.4	79.4	72.1	87.0	86.4	79.8
Royal Caribbean	82.3	80.1	86.0	76.8	76.0	84.7	86.0	79.9
Princess Cruises	84.2	80.7	83.4	78.2	68.5	84.2	83.4	76.3

Fig. Cruise Ships and Passenger Satisfaction

But achieving a high percentage of loyal customers is new for the cruise industry. Historically, the industry serves a large proportion of first time customers (about 50 per cent in the North American market). As a result, companies are changing their focus from new customer acquisition to better understanding the elements that impact customer retention. Considerable research has demonstrated that the key variable impacting retention is customer satisfaction.

Customer satisfaction includes all elements of the passenger experience, before, during and after a cruise. Providing an exceptional passenger experience can be a key differentiator and increasingly has become a key element of business strategy for the cruise industry.

Here are the brands earning the highest score for passenger satisfaction among large cruise ships for 2010*: Within organizations, customer satisfaction ratings can have powerful effects. They focus employees on the importance of fulfilling customers' expectations. When these ratings dip, they warn of problems that can affect sales and profitability. These metrics quantify an important dynamic. When a brand has delighted customers, it gains positive word–of–mouth marketing, which is both free and highly effective.

Expectations are a key factor behind satisfaction. When customers have high expectations and the reality falls short, they will be disappointed and will likely rate their experience as less than satisfying. For this reason, a luxury cruise might receive a lower satisfaction rating than a mid-priced cruise ship even though its facilities and service would be deemed superior in "absolute" terms. Here are detailed scores for selected areas contributing to passenger satisfaction for the top scoring brands:

Today's ships offer a new generation of onboard features and a world of innovation, including surf pools, planetariums, on–deck LED movie screens, golf simulators, water parks, demonstration kitchens, self–leveling billiard tables, multi–room villas with private pools and in–suite Jacuzzis, ice–skating rinks, rock–climbing walls, bungee trampolines and much more. Today's new ships also offer facilities to accommodate family members of all generations traveling together.

As a result of effectively marketing new feature–rich ships, passenger numbers have increased in record numbers. But the competition is getting more intense, with many new cruise ships entering the market in the next several years (orders through 2012 includes 26 new builds with 54,000 berths at a value of nearly $15 billion). So satisfying customers is becoming the ante just to stay in the game. The biggest success will come to those companies who understand their passengers and can keep all guests – new and returning – delighted with their experience.

With fantastic luxury and top–class entertainment onboard, today's cruises have seen the voyage itself being the attraction rather than the geographic cruise destinations. Gone are the days of catering for the elite – this industry is geared up for the masses and is now one of the fastest growing sectors of the travel industry.

The more demanding cruise passenger will want to engage with all of a ship's features and services. Companies will need to capture and store more data, yet access to it must be faster and more targeted in order to personalize the guest experience. As a result, voice–of–customer programmes are becoming an important strategy for brands, and will receive even more focus in the next few years.

AN ECONOMICAL YACHT WITH TRUE FATHOM QUALITY

The Element utilizes modern CAD, engineering, tooling, and manufacturing techniques that allow unmatched quality, performance, and fuel efficiency. Weight-saving composite materials, a propeller tunnel/s, and an efficient hull design allow the Element to cruise effortlessly with a range of propulsion options, single or twin.

The Element's wide beam provides stability and enormous interior space. Two comfortable staterooms, a spacious head, and roomy salon rival the features of a much larger yacht. The raised pilothouse is distinguished by commanding views from its comfortable helm chair and settee for five. A unique folding transom lowers to expand the aft deck for access and adventure. The Element 40 is 40.4 feet and only requires a 40' or less slip.

STYLING

The styling is modern and distinctive, but maintains a classic profile. The Element is a handsome pilot house motoryacht with unique features not found on other yachts. With design features like the distinctive tailgate, windows in the hull or gracefully curved transom, the Element stands out in any marina or at sea.

DESIGN

The boats are meticulously designed using CAD software resulting in stellar performance, efficiency and ride. CAD also allows better utilization of space and a higher level of fit and finish. Every component and feature was incorporated into the computer design and located for function and ease of use before the boat was built. The interior design and layout is spacious, comfortable and perfect for extended cruising or just a weekend away.

Extensive engineering features and use of particular materials make the Element extremely quiet. Mechanical noise is reduced by the cored hull construction and isolation of the salon and galley sole. The engine noise is dampened by an engine room that is sealed from the living spaces and insulated by a 2" sound barrier. Access to the engine room is through the aft deck eliminating salon sole hatches and the noise they produce. The hull has been intelligently designed by the naval architect, Greg Marshall with a lifting chine that is not inverted and is quieter while underway or at anchor. The generator is located well aft and is separated from the master stateroom by several compartments and bulkheads.

INTERIOR

The Element was designed to provide the comforts of a home in forty feet while maintaining graceful lines. It is truly amazing that a yacht this size can provide a large salon and galley, while still leaving room for two comfortable staterooms and head. Preferences* are plentiful. Entering the salon from the aft deck you instantly feel that you are on a larger boat. The space is cavernous with a settee on the port and two chairs* to starboard. The comfortable settee is perfect for watching the flat screen entertainment system* forward. The beautiful hand built woodwork is stunning. Enormous windows allow good visibility around the boat.

Forward of the settee is the large "U" shaped galley with abundant storage. Below the galley is a large pantry with 105 cubic feet of storage. A central hallway leads forward from the galley and under the pilothouse to the two staterooms and head. On the starboard side is the guest stateroom with a double bed in-hull window.

On the port side is the head with two doors, one into the master stateroom and one into the hallway. The head is molded fiberglass with a central floor drain for easy cleaning. Above the granite topped vanity is another in-hull window. The head includes a linen cabinet, Tecma fresh water head and a large separate shower. The generous master stateroom features a queen sized bed, large opening stainless ports and ample storage including a walk-in closet.

The raised expedition style pilothouse provides a perfect gathering spot with a settee for five which can be used as a bunk. Both the helm chair and raised settee provide excellent visibility around the boat. At the helm are electronic engine controls and levers for the included bow thruster. The dash is designed to accommodate an extensive array of the latest navigation equipment. The starboard pilothouse door provides access to the deck.

EXTERIOR

The covered aft deck is pure genius. The unique folding transom lowers to expand the deck for access and adventure and getting on and off the boat from either a dinghy or dock could not be easier or safer. When the transom is down, the swim step, aft deck and salon are all on one level. The aft deck also features significant storage. The stairs on the aft deck provide easy access to the boat deck and flybridge. The aft deck counter lifts up to provide easy access to the engine room. The boat deck above the salon is large enough to hold a substantial inflatable and incorporates an elegant electronics mast. The optional flybridge* features abundant seating, a helm station, and an viewing level found on much larger yachts. Wide walk around decks on the foredeck provide a safe area to handle lines or sit and enjoy the view. The anchor windlass includes a capstan and is mounted in a well that drains directly overboard, keeping your decks clean. A deck hatch opens for access to the chain locker and storage.

CONSTRUCTION

The Element is a totally new design utilizing sophisticated tooling and materials. The result is a yacht with superior quality, features, and performance. The use of composite materials and infusion lamination construction reduces weight and increases strength resulting in better efficiency.

Infusion lamination is a technique that uses vacuum pressure to penetrate resin into a laminate. Materials are laid into a mold and a vacuum is applied before resin is introduced. Once a complete vacuum is achieved, resin is literally drawn into the laminate via carefully placed tubing. The part then cures within the vacuum resulting in much higher fiber-to-resin ratio. A controlled amount of resin is metered resulting in greater strength and less weight. Typical hand lay-up construction suffers from excess resin being used and does not have the infusion pressure to help bond the laminate. Excess resin will actually weaken the part. The Elelment by Fathom is one of the few builders utilizing infusion lamination to build its hulls, decks and all other fiberglass components.

Extensive use of composite materials for bulkheads and other surfaces further reduces weight. The hull below the waterline is solid infused fiberglass. The hull sides and deck are cored with synthetic Core-Cell which provides incredible rigidity, thermal insulation, and sound attenuation. Four major bulkheads divide the hull into compartments and providing great strength to the hull and structure above. The hull and deck are mechanically fastened and bonded with a material that is stronger than fiberglass.

MECHANICAL

Element is powered by a full authority common rail diesel. Tankage for approximately 400 gallons of fuel are located outboard of the main and are on the center of buoyancy so the trim of the boat will not change with different amounts of fuel onboard. The bright white two inch acoustic barrier insulation far exceeds the industry norm for keeping the Element quiet. The sole of the engine room is white molded fiberglass and is easy to keep clean. The quality of the Element is apparent throughout the boat and particularly in the engine room. Mechanical and electrical systems rival any yacht on the market. All equipment is chosen for its longevity and quality. The different systems and components are installed in the boat so they can be easily maintained.

Elements are designed to exceed ABYC, NMMA and CE construction guidelines. Safety at sea is paramount and the Element makes no compromises. With advanced engineering and manufacturing, combined with North American quality, the Element reaches a new level of quality and safety setting a new standard to compare all yachts presently available.

A BRIEF HISTORY OF THE PASSENGER SHIP INDUSTRY

The earliest ocean-going vessels were not primarily concerned with passengers, but rather with the cargo that they could carry. Black Ball Line in New York, in 1818, was the first shipping company to offer regularly scheduled service from the United States to England and to be concerned with the comfort of their passengers. By the 1830s steamships were introduced and dominated the transatlantic market of passenger and mail transport. English companies dominated the market at this time, led by the British and North American Royal Mail Steam Packet (later the Cunard Line). On July 4, 1840, Britannia , the first ship under the Cunard name, left Liverpool with a cow on board to supply fresh milk to the passengers on the 14-day transatlantic crossing. The advent of pleasure cruises is linked to the year 1844, and a new industry began.

During the 1850s and 1860s there was a dramatic improvement in the quality of the voyage for passengers. Ships began to cater solely to passengers, rather than to cargo or mail contracts, and added luxuries like electric lights, more deck space, and entertainment. In 1867, Mark Twain was a passenger on the first cruise originating in America, documenting his adventures of the six month trip in the bookInnocents Abroad. The endorsement by the British Medical Journal of sea voyages for curative purposes in the 1880s further encouraged the public to take leisurely pleasure cruises as well as transatlantic travel. Ships also began to carry immigrants to the United States in "steerage" class. In steerage, passengers were responsible for providing their own food and slept in whatever space was available in the hold.

By the early 20th century the concept of the superliner was developed and Germany led the market in the development of these massive and ornate floating hotels. The design of these liners attempted to minimize the discomfort of ocean travel, masking the fact of being at sea and the extremes in weather as much as possible through elegant accomodations and planned activites. The Mauritania and theLusitania, both owned by the Cunard Line of England, started the tradition of dressing for dinner and advertised the romance of the voyage. Speed was still the deciding factor in the design of these ships. There was no space for large public rooms, and passengers were required to share the dining tables. The White Star Line, owned by American financier J.P. Morgan, introduced the most luxurious passenger ships ever seen in the Olympic (complete with swimming pool and tennis court) and Titanic. Space and passenger comfort now took precedence over speed in the design of these ships-resulting in larger, more stable liners. The sinking of the Titanic on its maiden voyage in 1912 devastated the White Star Line. In 1934, Cunard bought out White Star; the resulting company name, Cunard White Star, is seen in the advertisements in this project.

World War I interrupted the building of new cruise ships, and many older liners were used as troop transports. German superliners were given to both Great Britain and the United States as reparations at the end of the war. The years between 1920 and 1940 were considered the most glamorous years for transatlantic passenger ships. These ships catered to the rich and famous who were seen enjoying luxurious settings on numerous newsreels viewed by the general public. American tourists interested in visiting Europe replaced immigrant passengers. Advertisements promoted the fashion of ocean travel, featuring the elegant food and on-board activities.

Cruise liners again were converted into troop carriers in World War II, and all transatlantic cruising ceased until after the war. European lines then reaped the benefits of transporting refugees to America and Canada, and business travelers and tourists to Europe.

The lack of American ocean liners at this time, and thus the loss of profits, spurred the U.S. government to subsidize the building of cruise liners. In addition to the luxurious amenities, ships were designed according to specifications for possible conversion into troop carriers. Increasing air travel and the first non-stop flight to Europe in 1958, however, marked the ending of transatlantic business for ocean liners. Passenger ships were sold and lines went bankrupt from the lack of business.

The 1960s witnessed the beginnings of the modern cruise industry. Cruise ship companies concentrated on vacation trips in the Caribbean, and created a "fun ship" image which attracted many passengers who would have never had the opportunity to travel on the superliners of the 1930s and 1940s. Cruise ships concentrated on creating a casual environment and providing extensive on-board entertainment. There was a decrease in the role of ships for transporting people to a particular destination; rather, the emphasis was on the voyage itself. The new cruise line image was solidified with the popularity of the TV series "The Love Boat" which ran from 1977 until 1986.

A HISTORY OF FINE CRUISING

Celebrity Cruises, the award-winning cruise line marked by the iconic "X", is designed for discerning cruisers, with modern, sophisticated environments, impeccable service, enriching and inspiring onboard programmes, and world-class cuisine. Founded in 1989 with the objective of fulfilling the travel industry's need for a high-quality, premium cruise product at an intelligent price, Celebrity

Cruises succeeded in setting a new, worldwide standard for cruising, and in creating a distinctive expression of superior quality, grand style, attentive service, spacious accommodations, and exceptional dining.

1995: A SPA WITHIN A SHIP

Along with the launch of the Century-class fleet in 1995, Celebrity Cruises created another industry first: a luxurious spa experience within the environment of a cruise ship, with the introduction of the AquaSpa® by Elemis.

1997: THE MERGER

In 1997, Celebrity Cruises merged with Royal Caribbean International, bringing together two extraordinary cruise brands within one corporation, Royal Caribbean Cruises, Ltd (RCL). The RCL family now includes Azamara Club Cruises, Crosiere de France, Pullmantur, SkySea Cruise Line, and TUI Cruises (the last two via joint ventures).

2000: WELCOMING THE NEW MILLENNIUM

In the year 2000, Celebrity Cruises launched Celebrity Millennium, which featured the cruise industry's first application of gas turbine engines that reduced exhaust emissions by up to 95 percent over traditional propulsion systems. Celebrity Millennium and her sister Millennium-class ships – Celebrity Infinity, Celebrity Summit, and Celebrity Constellation – nearly doubled the line's capacity in just two years (2000-2002).

2003: SERVING "NEW TASTES OF LUXURY"

More than 100 brand enhancements and new "tastes of luxury" were introduced across the fleet in 2003, including welcome champagne and mimosas; cold towels and fresh sorbet poolside; expanded options in dining, including Sushi Cafés and pasta/pizza bars, sunset yoga, Pilates classes, and more. Celebrity Cruises also introduced "Concierge Class," an enhanced level of accommodations featuring new amenities and priority services, and introduced "Acupuncture at Sea," another undisputed industry first.

2004: EXCITING XPEDITIONS

In 2004, the luxurious mega yacht Celebrity Xpedition was introduced to bring guests to unique itineraries, including cruises to the enchanting Galapagos Islands, in a very unique and exclusive setting.

2008-2012: BRIGHT LIKE THE SUMMER SOLSTICE

The stylishly-decorated Celebrity Solstice, the first of five stunning Solstice-class vessels was launched in 2008. With a guest capacity of 2,850 and an award- winning design, Celebrity Solstice continued the brand's rich tradition of style and innovation with even more industry firsts, among them the magnificent Lawn Club. After the launch of Celebrity Reflection, the fifth Solstice-class ship, the rest of the Celebrity Cruises fleet was "solsticized," and received major upgrades that gave them modern features that were found in the Solstice class.

SAILING TOWARDS THE FUTURE

Today, the iconic "X" remains passionately dedicated to providing guests with a cruise experience that embodies modern luxury. Celebrity Cruises is ever-evolving, and at the heart of every innovation is our greatest focus: the best vacation experience for the discerning cruiser. As such, partnerships with Apple, Diageo, MGM Resorts, Project Runway, Top Chef, and other exciting brands serve to further enrich the guest experience at sea and while on land.

Two new ships measuring 984 feet long, 123 feet wide, and 190 feet high will join the Celebrity Cruises fleet in 2018 and 2020. Developed under the project name EDGE, the two ships each have a capacity of 2,900 guests and will combine the very best aspects of the cruise line's Solstice-class and Millennium-class vessels to deliver small-ship itineraries with large-ship amenities.

THE AUSTRALIAN CRUISE MARKET

Australia has become an increasingly important market for New Zealand and it is now the world's leading cruise market in terms of growth and market penetration. This growth has been driven by increased local capacity and product improvements. The Australian industry has a 2020 target of one million passengers, with analysts predicting that this target will now be reached by 2016.

- In 2014 Australian cruise passenger numbers hit a record high of 1,003,256.
- Australia is New Zealand's largest source market, with 104,500 Australian passengers cruising here in 2014.
- Three cruise brands are dominant in Australia - Princess, Royal Caribbean and Holland America.

THE NORTH AMERICAN CRUISE MARKET

Traditionally when most people think about cruise, they think of Americans. They are indeed the world's largest source of cruise passengers and they are one of New Zealand's largest source markets for this type of tourism.

With more turnarounds on the cruise calendar, more North Americans are expected to fly in and cruise out, or cruise in and fly out, utilising the Shed 10 cruise terminal on Auckland's Queen's Wharf. Cruise constitutes a significant proportion of North American travellers to New Zealand.

North Americans who cruise to New Zealand:

- Are experienced cruise travellers who have already cruised to the Caribbean, Alaska and Europe;
- Do not know what to expect in New Zealand beyond stunning scenery;
- Are internet savvy;
- Are not exclusively cruisers, they are frequent travellers who cruise as part of their vacation mix; and
- Use travel agents as a vital part of their cruise booking process (up to 80 per cent use an agent to book their cruise).

While New Zealand is still seen as an exotic destination to both the industry and potential passengers, knowledge about New Zealand as a cruise destination is low.

THE EUROPEAN CRUISE MARKET

The UK is currently the leading market in Europe. However, in the past five years Germany, Italy, Spain and France have grown at a faster rate (Italy and Spain grew 26 per cent and 20 per cent respectively between 2009-2014). Globally, the UK is the second largest single country source market (after North America).

- UK consumers research cruise holidays online, but 80-90 per cent still book through a travel agent.
- It is predicted that the German market could grow up to four times its current size.
- Europeans tend to buy longer cruises than US passengers and are not averse to travelling long-haul for cruises.

CRUISE INDUSTRY TRENDS

- Globally, the average age of cruise passengers continues to decrease, with the average age of first time guests being well under 40. Their age depends on a number of factors, including the cruise line, destination and length of itinerary.
- The cruise industry invests more in agents than any other part of the travel industry with estimates that 80-90 per cent of cruise bookings are made through travel agents.
- Cruise consumers have a high level of commitment to brand.
- According to Cruise Lines International Association (CLIA), 80 per cent of cruise passengers agree that cruise is a good way to sample destinations that they may wish to visit again on a land-based holiday.

Nearly 40 per cent of cruise passengers state that they had returned to holiday at a destination first visited on a cruise.

DEPLOYMENT DECISIONS

Deployment decisions are based on a number of factors including customer interest, as well as logistical issues such as distance, fuel requirements, government policy and weather. Cruise New Zealand actively works with cruise lines regarding deployment decisions and this is a major focus of their efforts. The cruise industry is a customer-driven business with deployment strategies based on the premise 'we go where people think they want to go'. Cruise executives advise that the most valuable support a destination can offer is to create demand through marketing to consumers and creating awareness for trade. It is acknowledged that at the heart of a successful cruise industry is the destination and there needs to be commitment from destinations to offer good value for money to consumers.

THE MAJOR PLAYERS

The global industry is dominated by three major players who operate over 80 per cent of global capacity.

1. Carnival Corporation includes Carnival Cruise Lines, Costa Cruises, Cunard Line, Holland America Line, P and O Cruises Australia, Princess Cruises, Seabourn Cruise Line (also AIDA and Ibero Cruceros, who do not currently visit New Zealand).
2. Royal Caribbean Cruises includes Celebrity Cruises, Royal Caribbean International (also Azamara, Croisieres de France, Pullmanter and TUI Cruises, who do not currently visit New Zealand).
3. Genting Hong Kong includes Norwegian Cruise Line (50 per cent ownership shared with Apollo Management) and Star Cruises (Asia).

FUTURE TRENDS

Other trends include the building of much bigger cruise ships, which will bring greater numbers of visitors to New Zealand at any one time and increase the pressure on our infrastructure catering to cruise visitors. This has prompted a renewed focus on work to upgrade New Zealand's infrastructure - with Cruise New Zealand, regional tourism organisations and relevant government bodies working together on this issue.

3

Selling Cruises and Cruise Products

THE MARKET

A market can be described as a "system comprising two sides" (Evans et al., 2003, p. 120), with the "sides" being demand and supply. The cruise market can be further defined, according to common interpretations, in three ways: focused on the product, on satisfying a need, or on passenger identity (Evans et al., 2003). "Product focused" companies have advantages in terms of developing economies of scale, although they may fail to take account of changes that occur within their target market incrementally over time. "Need satisfaction" companies are good at understanding their customers but can have problems in making a strategic decision to identify specific focus. "Passenger identity" companies can target specific groups of passengers. Evans et al. (2003) note that most companies combinedefinitions in order to derive strengths from each of the three approaches.

Knowles, Diamantis, and Bey El-Mourhabi (2004a) describe world events such as the terrorist attack on New York in 2001, the subsequent Gulf War, and the prevailing economic conditions in the United States and other major countries at that time as vital in shaping the fortunes of tourism and leisure providers. Add continuing international unease in the face of potential acts of terrorism, the apparent switch to cruising undertaken by customers as a reaction to risk assessment, cruise companies' strategic decisions to facilitate easy travel to port, and the construction of safe itineraries (International Council of Cruise Lines, 2004a), and a picture emerges of an industry acting to take advantage of market opportunities.

Cruise companies target specific markets and tailor their products and services accordingly (Knowles et al., 2004a). Getting the marketing mix right is, for marketers in the cruise business, a case of building on the traditional 4 Ps of price, product, place, and promotion to include the three additional service-oriented components: people, physical evidence, and process (Aaker, 2001).

Throughout this book, evidence is provided to enable the reader to deconstruct these components so the traditional or extended marketing mix can be thoroughly examined. This chapter describes the type of input that is considered by the stakeholders (cruise operators and travel agents) in the selling of cruises and then considers cruise products and the overall cruise market.

THE CRUISE OPERATORS

The cruise operators or brands dominate the cruise market (Berger, 2004). They either own or lease cruise ships and produce the planned itinerary and cruise product so as to target specific market segments. Cruise operators can be seen as wholesalers and travel agents as retailers or brokers (Dickinson and Vladimir, 1997).

However, in common with many wholesale operations, better profit margins or more attractive selling prices may be achieved if the product can be sold directly to the consumer. Therefore, the majority of cruise operators also sell their products directly to the public, acting as both cruise wholesalers and retailers. Products are developed and packaged using market research, negotiation, and sales and marketing.

All cruise companies exert considerable effort to establish brand values and in constructing cruise products that are designed to meet and, ideally, to exceed passenger expectations. Market research collects data from existing and potential passengers using a variety of research techniques.

This data can be used to interpret customer behaviour and predict buyer responses to new products. Increasingly, anthropologists are employed to study target groups or individuals so that companies better understand why people act as they do.

The products developed are an amalgam of services and facilities, some of which generate revenue while others are included at no additional cost. This means that most cruises have fixed costs relating to elements such as transportation (fuel), food, labour, port administration, and customs and have variable costs relating to other elements such as beverages or shore excursions. The cruise operator aims to reduce costs as much as possible without negatively affecting quality. Negotiation is done to achieve the best ratio of price to quality and to take advantage of economies of scale and negotiating power. Negotiation is therefore undertaken for a range of consumables, from engine or deck department stores through to hotel department stores. In terms of buying power, considerable advantage is accrued by the largest corporations through such negotiations.

Traditionally, cruise companies have used travel agents as a primary distribution channel while concomitantly selling directly. Irrespective of the mode of distribution and despite the growing importance of the Internet as both a distribution and marketing tool, cruise companies rely on the cruise brochure to sell cruises. Vellas and Becherel (1995) describe how tourism operators design brochures with colour images, a carefully planned layout and promotions designed to attract early booking. They note that the ratio of brochures to sales can be between 10 and 30 brochures for one sale. Pricing strategies are carefully considered to encourage early action by promising discounts for early booking. Low season pricing is adjusted to appear less costly than high season pricing. Lead-in prices relate to basic cabin accommodation, and supplements are payable for attractive alternatives such as outside cabins or sea view cabins with balconies.

Premium products, such as suites with butler service, come with premium pricing. Brochures are produced well in advance of the cruise date and planning has to take into account fluctuating prices, rates of exchange for items purchased outside the country of the operator, and changing market conditions (Dickinson and Vladimir, 1997). It is reasonably common for cruise operators to update brochures so as to react to changing conditions. Changes can include offering different prices in later editions and, in some cases, making amendments to the product if the change has come about for reasons outside the cruise operator's control.

The Internet is used predominantly as a complementary marketing tool. A web site can be a point where information is presented to potential and actual customers to help them to find out more about the cruise package in a way that brochures never can (Berger, 2004). For example, customers can visit the passenger feedback pages to see what passengers are saying about their vacations and customers can follow links to other important information—for example, finding out about immigration or health matters overseas. The Internet can also be used to enable clients to book online. In this mode, the customer assists the cruise operator by providing data in a format that can be easily manipulated and also helps cut out the costs associated with booking through a travel agent or sales assistant. The Internet can also be used to capture data for immigration purposes and for financial control, thus potentially saving on administration costs.

THE TRAVEL AGENT

The travel agent's core purpose is selling tourism products for commission. Most travel agents belong to professional associations that guarantee clients protection if the travel agent has serious financial problems. The American Society of Travel Agents (ASTA) and the Association of British Travel Agents (ABTA) are typical of such associations. Travel agents sell travel products such as airline tickets and tourist packages. They can also arrange insurance, car hire, and hotel accommodation.

However, the traditional travel agent is changing (Hatton, 2004). Faced with ever increasing competition from Internet intermediaries or online agencies, travel agents are finding themselves operating in a volatile marketplace. Airlines have cut commission rates. Travel firms have been aggressive in selling directly to clients, thereby cutting the travel agent out of the distribution system. Hatton notes that the travel agent's strength, providing a highly personal and personalized service, also undermined their status and led travel companies to try to nurture brand loyalty by developing relationships with the client directly. In response, Hatton (2004) highlights the need for agents to accept the changing realities and to work closely with travel companies to develop in-depth product knowledge and retain customer loyalty by being efficient in what they do.

Examples can be seen in the context of cruise vacations. Some travel agents specialize in the cruise industry, forming alliances with cruise brands to focus on selling their product.

In these circumstances, travel agents receive high levels of support from the cruise operators, who provide specialist sales events, training for the sales agents (including orientation cruises), and customized marketing materials. The Passenger Shipping Association (PSA) has established the PSA Retail Agents (PSARA) scheme in the UK with the primary objective of increasing sales through customized product training and dissemination of information to accredited retail travel agents (PSARA, 2005).

MARKETING ACTIONS AND ALLIANCES

A market is the place where sellers and buyers meet to do business (Evans et al., 2003). Marketing as a sophisticated process and discipline has emerged from this basic premise.

Accordingly, cruise operators develop their product to meet customer expectations and then design a plan for marketing the product. The plan can include advertising, promotion, merchandising, and public relations (PR). Advertising uses a number of communications media including: commercials on radio, television, the cinema, the Internet, newspaper and magazines, posters, and billboards. PR can be channelled through editorial or features in travel publications, newspapers, and magazines.

Merchandising reinforces the brand by using items such as pens, desk pads, or other mementos to remind users about their vacation. Promotion can be associated with advertising or it can be incorporated into events for visiting groups on board cruise ships. Cruise operators may form strategic marketing alliances with other service providers to create synergies or provide customers with incentives for remaining loyal. Crystal Cruises is a member of the Luxury Alliance, which includes Silverseas Cruises, Orient-Express Trains and Cruises, Leading Hotels of the World, and Relais and Châteaux (Luxury Alliance, 2005). The "World's Leading Cruise Lines" alliance includes Carnival Cruises, Holland America, Cunard Line, Seabourne, Costa Cruises, Princess Cruises, and Windstar and provides incentives for loyalty within these brands (World's Leading Cruise Lines, 2005).

LOYALTY

Loyalty is important both for the client who enjoys acting as an ambassador for the brand and for the company that values retaining such a customer. In effect, this type of client works for the brand by spreading positive comments about the cruise to friends and acquaintances and, as a result, is an important part of the marketing equation. Companies such as Princess Cruises operate an incentive group called the "Captain's Circle." This club has three levels: Gold (2 to 5 cruises), Platinum (6 to 15 cruises) and Elite (16 cruises and more). The benefits include priority discounts, special events on board, preferential services, and other benefits depending on the level of membership (Princess Cruises, 2003).

THE CRUISE PRODUCT

Like some other tourism products (Vellas and Becherel, 1995), the cruise has three economic features: heterogeneity (the product possesses a broad mix of variable components that render the experience unique for the individual tourist), inelasticity (a cruise product is "perishable" because it cannot be stored if it is not sold) and complementarity (the cruise product is not one single service but a series of complementary services that when taken together form the cruise experience).

The cruise is a defined package that may include travel to the port of embarkation, an itinerary spanning a defined period of time, an element of inclusive services and facilities (such as meals, entertainment, and leisure areas), accommodation to a specified standard, and various other services that are available at an extra charge. The inclusive nature of the package will depend on the pricing strategy of the cruise operator. Some operators offer cruise-and-stay or cruise-and-tour packages that include an additional element at the beginning or end of the cruise in the form of a tour of an area or a defined number of nights in a resort hotel. The following elements portray the products of cruising.

THE BUFFET

The buffet is a flexible option on a cruise ship. Often it is located on an upper deck and frequently it is designed to extend from one side of the ship to the other with each side being a mirror image of the other. This setup enables large numbers of passengers to move through without creating bottlenecks. At quiet times and when service changes from one meal to another, one side of the operation can be closed for cleaning and changing or replenishing the food items. This practice creates a 24-hour facility that is both flexible and economical.

A small team of chefs under the supervision of a sous chef services the buffet. The galley team is supported by buffet assistants and supervisors who help customers, clear tables, and serve drinks as required. The buffet employs equipment that is designed to present food items at the correct temperature and in the best way to make that food attractive to passengers. Main food items such as soups, meat and fish entrees, cold dishes, and desserts are changed daily according to the duration of the cruise itinerary, although some standard items such as breads, salad items, dressings, and condiments are available daily. Food items are designed with a culinary nod to each approaching port on the itinerary.

The buffet requires fewer staff than the traditional restaurant, and because of the way it can be operated with simple table layouts, standardized areas, for beverages, fewer carpeted areas, and large picture windows overlooking either the sea or the port, the servicing routines are more easily carried out. The buffet takes the strain off the restaurant at breakfast and lunch, thus allowing staff to be deployed more effectively and for the galley to plan production more accurately. Very little waste is created because food can be carefully produced in reaction to prior patterns of demand and prevailing consumption.

Buffets are frequently organized with the galley and servery in the middle of the room and tables and chairs around the outside beside the windows. Buffets tend to be designed with a wash-up area beside the galley. Tables are cleared to a collection point (sometimes referred to as a DJ's box). Dirty plates and food residue is then taken by cart to the dish washer. Food and supplies are transported in the specially allocated lifts from the main galley to the buffet galley.

Fig. Buffet Servery.

THE MAIN RESTAURANT

Passengers can eat as much or as little as they wish, and nowhere is that more evident than in the main restaurants. While passengers may stack their plates full in the buffet, in the main restaurant, food is conveyed to the diner as frequently as the diner requests. Diners who may be concerned about what others might think as they are seen carrying a pile of food from the buffet seem to believe that becomes obscured if quantity is disguised within the routine of ordering courses from a menu. In the main restaurant or restaurants, a menu is produced to reflect and to differentiate the brand.

The way the menu is configured might lean towards acknowledging passengers used to eating out in the United States or in Italy or in the United Kingdom.

This can involve the provision of distinct courses, the names of the types of courses, the food items included within the courses, and the language adopted in describing the food items and courses.

The main restaurants tend to reflect a style and standard that is redolent of a more formal dining experience, with the use of uniforms to identify the maître d' (the abbreviated version of maitre d'hotel, meaning the overall restaurant manager), head waiters, waiters, and assistant waiters or commis waiters, and the presence of professionals such as sommeliers or wine waiters. The combination of white tablecloths, sparkling cutlery and glassware, careful selection of colours and hues, materials and furniture, and subdued lighting add to the effect, as do the provision of music (sometimes live) and the theatricality of the environment.

The setting is important in getting passengers to interact with each other and with staff. The food and wine are the reason for being in the restaurant, but the experience is enhanced by the social factors.

Service styles vary depending on the brand and passenger expectation. Full silver service may be adopted by the luxury brands, semi-silver or plated service by the contemporary and premium brands, and budget brands may have a combination of buffet and plated service. Each style of service is correlated to the skills of the server and the ratio of staff to passengers. Full silver service requires the greatest degree of skill in serving and presenting food, and as a result there is a need for a lower ratio of staff to customers. Whichever service style is used, the common denominator for service staff is the need to develop the appropriate level of interpersonal skills. Table sizes vary, with tables available for between two and eight people. Larger tables are more common on two-sitting dining plans. Many cruise brands are introducing free dining situations where customers can prebook tables for certain times and ask to dine privately or join a group.

The formality of the dining area is not without reason. Formality and dress codes are features on many cruises. While new brands place an emphasis on informality, the norm for most cruise brands is still towards creating opportunities for passengers to dress to impress. On these cruises, passengers have the opportunity to dress formally once every 4 or 5 days.

OTHER DINING OPTIONS

While most meals are regarded as a composite part of the cruise experience and inclusive with the cost of the vacation, increasingly, cruise brands opt to generate revenue by providing more choices that add value to the overall dining experience. For example, on the 'Star Princess', passengers can reserve a table in a variety of alternative restaurants, such as Sabatini's, an upscale Italian restaurant, or the Tex-Mex grill, both of which cost extra. On 'Ocean Village' the Bistro is a restaurant that has food produced to the specification of a leading UK-based chef, and this option is also charged at a supplement. Al fresco dining is offered by some cruise brands, creating an opportunity for passengers to eat under the stars (Princess Cruises, 2003).

Other restaurants such as pizzerias and burger and hot dog grills create alternative options that might be seen by certain of passengers, such as children, as more appealing than the formal setting of the restaurants. Ice cream stands may also be located on decks close to swimming pools and sunbathing or leisure areas. Afternoon tea and, in some cases, high tea (for young families) are served from restaurants and buffets. Finally, passengers make use of room service if the choice of dining options really does not meet their needs.

BARS

Generally, most bars begin to get busy after dinner. The routines of sailing are established relatively quickly as passengers find their way around and work out what they want to do and where they want to go. The busy times are from around 22.00 (10:00 pm) onward, but there are numerous opportunities for passengers to purchase drinks and for bars to generate revenue:

Sailing day: Drinks are available on upper decks as the ship departs from port. Working from bars at key points, bar waiters mingle among the passengers selling cocktails and drinks to celebrate the departure. Live music is played to add to the atmosphere.

Pre-ordering dinner: A wine preordering point is usually made available so that customers can ensure they order the wine that they want for dinner. During dinner, wine and beverages are available from a dispense bar usually located within the galley. Lists for wine, liqueur, Cognac, and fine whiskies, and liqueur trolleys and merchandising displays all support the sales initiative. Sommeliers and wine waiters are on hand to help passengers.

Theater: Table service is available in all the entertainment venues. Cocktails of the day and special promotions are offered to highlight the range of options available.

Bars: Various bars are targeted at particular groups of passengers, such as sports bars with sporting memorabilia and recorded or live sports displayed on television screens or traditional lounge bars that use dark wood and comfortable settees and chairs to give a "club" feel. Champagne and caviar bars appeal to a certain clientele and exude quality and exclusivity. Piano bars combine relaxed intimacy and friendly ambience.

Nightclub: These venues generally have table service and a cocktail menu. Depending on the clientele on board, different products are likely to be available. Cocktails are popular on cruise ships, and many bars use premixed blends that must to be combined with a spirit and ice before being shaken or blended and garnished.

During the day: Drinks can be purchased from at least one bar inside the vessel and from pool bars on the sun decks throughout the day. Drinks are also available from mobile points in the buffet and in the restaurant when meals are being served.

LOUNGES

Passengers congregate in a variety of places for quiet moments or to play cards or read a book. While bar service is an option, tea and coffee are more likely to be consumed. Ships often develop a range of lounges according to the needs of passengers. These areas might include a library, a card or bridge room, a writing room, an observation lounge, or general lounges. These areas can be used for quizzes and competitions, wine tastings, and small group meetings. The various bars can also be used for a range of activities including art auctions, competitions, karaoke, dance classes, fashion shows, and other entertainment. The bar staff work through a rotation that covers the various areas within the ship and creates a fair and equitable pattern of work for everyone.

Fig. Bar on 'Aurora'.

ENTERTAINMENT

The entertainment staff works for the cruise director, who in turn reports to the hotel services or passenger services director. This element of the cruise product does not generally create additional revenue, although sales arising from entertainment activities can be made indirectly. Theaters are the venue for the headline activities such as musical extravaganzas, comedy clubs, cabaret, or magic shows.

The theaters are also the largest gathering areas for passengers, so they can also be used for emergency drills and as a meeting point for shore excursions. There are usually two or three shows each evening. Shows and performances operate on a rotating schedule, which is designed to ensure that the programme appears fresh, interesting, and new.

The daytime activity programme is produced by the entertainment staff. Events during the day are published in the ship's newspaper. These events can be very diverse to suit the types of passengers on board. The team also includes port lecturers, dance instructors, and lecturers for cyber cafes or IT suites.

The entertainment staff can manage fashion shows, arts and crafts demonstrations, culinary demonstrations, and wine tastings, often working with staff from other departments on board. Musicians are employed to provide support for theatrical productions, show bars and bar areas, sailing days, deck parties, and piano bars. A technical team provides cinema support, IT support for computers on board, stage support for lighting, sound, and special effects. They also are available to help the musicians if they require technical support.

The leisure staff provides support for sporting activities such as onboard golf, and various water sports such as jet skis, water skiing, scuba, and windsurfing that may be available from the aft section of some cruise ships. The vessel may rent bicycles to passengers to take ashore. Fitness classes such as aerobics, Pilates, and yoga are operated within fitness suites. A separate team can design activities for children, noting the specific needs that relate to different ages. Princess Cruises operates the "Pelican Club" for 3- to 7-year-olds, the "Pirateers" for children aged 8 to 12, and "Off Limits" for teenagers 13 to 17 (Princess Cruises, 2003).

SHORE EXCURSIONS

Shore excursions are sold before and during the cruise. They generate revenue but are also designed to add value to the cruise experience. Because of the constraints on time, shore excursions or tours ashore are configured to maximize the experience for passengers. The range of transport options can be vast, depending on the port of call, and can include traveling on launches, by coach, by bicycle, by horse-drawn buggy, or taking a helicopter trip. Booking through the cruise company provides certain advantages. For example, if something were to go wrong such as a vehicle breakdown, the cruise company would take full responsibility to sort the problem out and ensure the passenger was not overly inconvenienced.

Shore excursions often use third-party tour operators to provide tours as well as a network of contacts to develop their shore excursion programme (some cruise companies also own tour operations and can take advantage of this fact). The organization of tours for passengers is like a military operation involving planning, crowd control, careful timing, and efficient communication.

ACCOMMODATION

For many passengers, the choice of accommodation seems to be simply a matter of identifying the price that is acceptable relative to the standard of accommodation available. However, a glance at the pricing structures operated by cruise companies quickly reveals that selecting accommodation is more complex than would first appear to be the case.

Some cruise companies refer to the accommodation as cabins, but terms such as staterooms, minisuites, and suites are frequently used to replace or complement this nautical term. Some cruise companies sell penthouse suites on board their vessels, and these tend to be the largest, most luxurious, and most expensive options (Mancini, 2000).

Although cabin sizes can vary from just under 11 square meters (120 square feet) to over 85 square metres (900 square feet), the norm tends to be approximately 18 to 23 square meters (200 to 250 square feet). Even a cabin of approximately 14 square meters (150 square feet) is likely to have four beds configured as lower and upper berths. The upper berths can be folded back to create more space or to cater to two passengers rather than the maximum of four. Cabins may also permit the lower berths to be moved together to form a large queen- or king-size bed. The largest cabins can be configured as suites with a lounge area. All cabins on modern cruise ships tend to be ensuite; that is, they have a shower, room and toilet or a bath, shower and toilet (Dervaes, 2003).

Generally, cabins are compact versions of the equivalent hotel bedroom accommodation. The storage areas are carefully designed to maximize the use of space so as to create an impression of a very efficient, customized facility. Space is typically at a premium on cruise ships, and vessels are constructed to maximize the area that can generate revenue. Because of this design constraint, some cabins will inevitably be preferable to others. They may have a good view or a restricted view, a location that is perceived to be more or less appealing because of proximity to certain facilities.

For example, if a cabin to located close to elevators or other sound-generating elements, some passengers may be unhappy about the resulting background noise. Ships are carefully designed to minimize noise, yet, on most vessels (as in hotels ashore), some cabins are recognized as being potentially problematic.

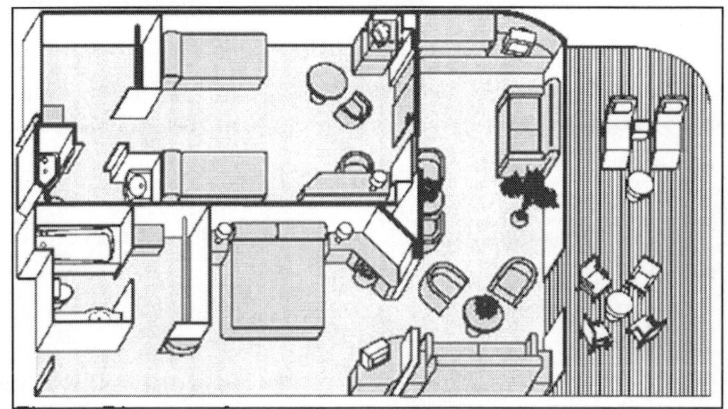

Fig. Diagram of a Stateroom.

Customers learn how to make decisions from the brochure or cruise brand web site. These information sources provide a variety of data that is intended to help the customer make a selection. Floor plans provide a miniaturized cut-away view of the cabin that shows the placement of the furnishings, main features, typical layout, and ensuite facilities. Generally, photographs are used in conjunction with the floor plans or, in the case of the web site, a 360° scanning view can be shown. A description of the cabin contents usually accompanies these images.

The most common way of identifying cabin locations is by using deck plans. These are representational ship's plans that, when viewed in conjunction with a cross-section diagram of the ship, help customers to identify the precise location of a cabin or facility on board.

These plans are unique to each vessel, although similar vessels may well have many common features. The deck plans are produced in colour so that a code can be used to identify cabins by type and, therefore, by cost. On some vessels, cabins that are on lower decks are less expensive while cabins that are on higher decks are more expensive. However, this pattern is not reliable for all ships.

It is possible on a deck plan to identify cabins as follows:

- Inside cabins or staterooms. These cabins lack natural light, although use of ventilation, air conditioning, mirrors, and artificial light frequently disguises this fact. Inside cabins tend to be the least expensive accommodation on offer.
- Outside cabins or staterooms. These cabins will have a porthole or a window. Most modern cabins tend to have larger picture windows.
- Outside cabins or staterooms with a veranda or balcony. As cruising develops, more accommodation is being produced to include private verandas or balconies with more private space.

- Penthouse suites or suites that may be with or without a veranda or balcony. These cabins tend to be the most expensive accommodation on offer.
- Cabins or staterooms with additional beds (berths).
- Cabins or staterooms with interconnecting doors.
- Cabins or staterooms or suites with facilities that are appropriate for people with disabilities.
- Cabins or staterooms with either shower or bath.
- The proximity to facilities, lifts and location compared to other decks and cabins.
- The proximity to safety equipment such as lifeboats, which may obscure the view from a picture window.

It is suggested that passengers expect more from cabin accommodation or staterooms than was previously the case. In many respects a cruise brand, carrying thousands of passengers and crew on large ships that offer a broad spectrum of leisure activities, can provide a balance for those seeking enhanced levels of privacy by offering more spacious cabins that have attractive features such as balconies.

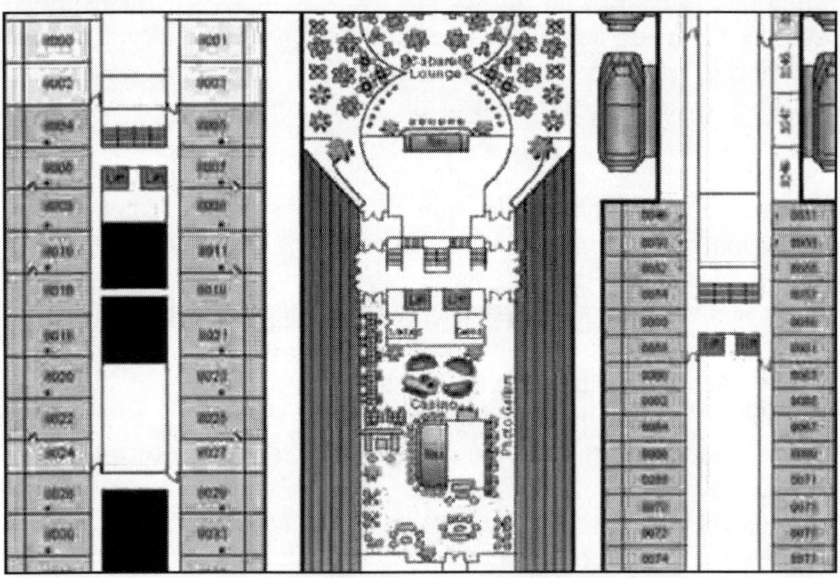

Fig. Deck Plans.

Using a deck plan, customers can select the accommodation to a precise degree. Doing so can benefit repeat passengers who have distinct preferences or satisfy passengers who have exacting requirements. However, a problem can occur because of what appears to be a commonly held misconception about upgrading. Some travel agents are reported to advise passengers that when they get on board the expected procedure is to complain in order to get a higher category of accommodation without paying more. Sales and reservation teams aim for 100 per cent capacity, and the flexibility on board is severely constrained by the occupancies achieved through this approach. Spare cabins are scarce resources that are vital for dealing with problems that may arise, such as plumbing faults or electrical failure, and as a result upgrades are virtually impossible.

By producing deck plans, the cruise company can help prospective clients to identify the cabin location of their choice. Also, in a more practical sense, they also assist the passenger when he or she boards the vessel to be oriented more easily into shipboard life. Deck plans are reproduced in a folddown version to act as an easy reference map for passengers on board.

Cabin facilities vary depending on the cruise brand, but a basic cabin or stateroom is likely to include the following:

- Two single beds that can convert to a queen- or king-size bed.
- Optionally, an extra two upper berths that can recess into the internal wall and are reached by storeaway ladder.
- Bedside tables.
- A vanity unit and writing desk with built-in drawers, storage areas, mirrors, and chair.
- An additional small table and chair.
- Television and radio with remote control. The range of programming can include films and an onboard TV channel.

Tea- and coffee-making facilities.

Safe, hairdryer, refrigerator/minibar.

- Direct-dial telephone.
- Bathroom with shower and toilet.
- Air conditioning.

Some brands may also upgrade the facilities to provide:

- Internet terminals.
- CD/DVD/VCR and stereo.
- Balcony with furniture.
- Separate living area or lounge with suitable furnishings.
- Separate dressing area.
- Hot tub.
- Separate toilet.

The décor in passenger cabins reflects the standards associated with the brand. Soft furnishings are coordinated with carpeting and artwork to create the desired ambiance. Colour schemes are selected to fit the mood and to create an overall harmony with décor and furnishings. Lighting is strategically located to provide the appropriate level of light for the purpose, whether reading, writing, or personal care.

Mirrors are used strategically to accentuate space and light. Passenger cabins and staterooms are attended to by cabin stewards who monitor the general condition of the accommodation and perform routine cleaning and service. The steward's daily tasks include making up beds, changing linen and towels as required, cleaning and vacuuming and ensuring that the cabin is prepared to a prescribed specification (for example, the bathroom is laid out and the complementary items are displayed). The steward also checks the room minibar and works with supervisors to deal with technical problems. Housekeeping supervisors and managers inspect cabins to ensure that standards are maintained.

Room service may be provided by the room steward or separate personnel. Many large cruise ships have what is called a bell box, where a small team of chefs and room service stewards address requests for food and drink to passenger cabins as required. Some suites and penthouse suites are allocated a butler to provide more personal service. The butler can facilitate the catering and service of parties and can arrange for other services and products that may be requested by the passenger.

DINING ON BOARD

The archetypal view of a cruise ship as a place to indulge in good food, good wine, and good company is as true today as it was in the heyday of the traditional liners. Food is perceived to be a significant element of the cruise product. For most passengers, the cost of eating on board is included in the price of the voyage. There are exceptions such as restaurants, which carry a supplementary charge, but in the main the inclusive nature and the high customer expectation of the dining experience are a fundamental issues. Most cruise brands aim to differentiate what they do through the provision of food and dining options.

They can create opportunities to define the product and to differentiate the brand by constructing menus with a focus on a particular style of cuisine and by designing restaurant and dining areas with a particular décor and atmosphere in mind.

Therefore, on certain ships the restaurant may have an Asian theme with Japanese cuisine and on others there may be an Italian theme. Cruise dining can be a densely calorific affair, yet corporate chefs take great care to meet specific dietary needs when they design menus.

Some brands have introduced greater options for personal choice in dining. By moving away from traditional dining arrangements that offered two sittings at dinner supplemented by open sitting at breakfast and lunch in large dining rooms, these companies were able to change the formula and attract clients who wanted more flexibility.

Most large cruise ships operate at least two large 500-plusseat restaurants that sit to either side of a galley with a double-ended servery or hotplate. (The servery or hotplate is the area in the galley where waiters collect food for service.) This arrangement facilitates the service of large numbers of people at dinner without the creation of lines at the door. Linking dinner service sittings with entertainment schedules ensures that passengers are not left disgruntled at having to go to one sitting or another. Coordinating breakfast and lunch is usually less of an issue because passengers have alternatives such as buffet or room service breakfast and buffet lunch. Because the ship tends to visit ports during the day that also has a secondary effect for producing and serving breakfast and lunch.

BEAUTY, THERAPY, AND HAIR CARE

This area is also generates revenue. Some cruise brands contract the service as a concession (an arrangement where the operator comes to a financial agreement with the cruise company to operate on board) and others employ their own staff directly. A number of well know beauty or hair stylist brands such as Steiners operate on cruise ships and there are some brands, such as Lotus Spa, that are created to uniquely identify the style of operation that is run on board specific cruise ships. Increasingly, cruise ships recognize the growth in “well-being” or “spas” as contemporary lifestyle choices.

Treatments available include chakra stone therapy, thalassotherapy, foot massage, manicures and pedicures, hair styling, oxygenating facials, body wraps, and health and nutrition lectures.

SHOPS

Shops on board provide a welcome indulgence for passengers seeking to enhance their usual routine of retail therapy. Just because they are at sea does not mean they cannot browse and pick up items of interest, or in some cases, necessity. Indeed, an added benefit that attracts shoppers is that the goods are sold as duty free. Ships traveling in international waters do not generally pay duty. As with beauty therapy, shops on board can be either concessionary or operated directly. If they are operated directly they tend to be line managed by the staff purser administration or someone of similar rank. The range of shops can include a jeweler, fashion stores for women and men, a gift shop, and a more general store that may also sell alcohol and cigarettes.

Shops on board usually occupy a central area within the ship that mimics the shopping mall of a large city. The trend to construct a large impressive atrium on megacruisers suits this tendency and creates an additional advantage in allowing shops to develop temporary market stall areas by moving into the spaces opposite and adjacent to the shops’ main locations. This practice increases the overall trading area and helps to create a bustling market feel. Shops operating under concession are managed by companies such as Miami Cruiseline Holdings, Harding Brothers Duty Free, Nuance Global Ships, and Flagship Retail Services Incorporated.

PHOTOGRAPHY

The ship's photographers are kept busy in the endless cycle of capturing magic moments. The opportunities to record important events occur from the point of embarkation right through to departure from the last port of call. This ensures that passengers can purchase posed, professional pictures in special presentation packs and have something special to remember. Contemporary cruise companies have invested heavily in digital technology so as to customize photographs with digitally composed and mastered backdrops that are relevant to the port of call or event.

In this way, passengers photographed disembarking in Venice will have their photograph framed within a montage of Venetian images as appropriate. Photographers appear at the gangway when passengers arrive onboard and are present during cocktail parties, gala dinners, and formal events. They accompany tours and attend passenger meetings. Their job is to get the picture and then to sell the picture to the passenger.

Pictures are presented in corridor display areas so as to be easily viewed by passengers who may be on their way from a restaurant to a show bar. It is difficult for passengers not to stop and look, and the sale can be confirmed with the application of carefully considered sales techniques. Some photographers are employed directly by cruise brands, and others are contracted by concessionary operators such as the Cruise Ship Picture Company, Image Photo Services, Inc., Ocean Images, Ltd., and Digital Seas Internet Cafes.

CASINO

Casinos on board seem to meet the expectations of some passengers for that James Bond moment. Casinos are described as a venue for "action and excitement" (NCL); "you'll have the time of your life" in a Carnival Cruises casino and Royal Caribbean says, "There's nothing like the excitement of a winning hand at poker or a slot machine paying off." The glitz and glamor that are portrayed in Las Vegas–style casinos are emulated on board cruise ships. Gambling is perceived as a pastime for winners, and correspondingly the cruise, as a type of vacation, is synonymous with success. Cashless ships are becoming commonplace in the cruise industry.

Passengers receive a card that allows them to purchase goods on-board and credit that to their account. Casinos also use this mode of purchase and sell tokens for slot machines or chips for gambling. Casinos are allowed to open upon sailing, although some ports permit the casino to trade even when the ship is in port. In certain jurisdictions cruise ships cannot open the casino until they are 3 miles from shore. Casinos are generally operated to strict codes. For example, the International Council of Cruise Lines (ICCL), a nonprofit trade association consisting of the 17 largest passenger cruise lines that call on major ports in the United States and abroad, publishes guidelines as seen in Table

2.1. Casinos are open to players over the age of 18 (21 in Alaska and some other ports). Most casinos have a dress code and are operated with minimum and maximum bets posted clearly at tables. Typical games on offer can include blackjack, craps, roulette, Caribbean stud poker, three-card poker, baccarat, and video poker.

SELLING CRUISES AND CRUISE PRODUCTS

The ICCL is dedicated to helping the cruise industry provide a safe, secure, fun, and entertaining ship environment for its passengers. Among the services that illustrate this commitment to fun entertainment are the gambling casinos found on most of the ICCL member vessels. Industry guidelines address the equipment, conduct of games, internal controls, and customer service for casinos on cruise ships.

The guidelines generally foster the following goals:

- To provide reasonable rules by which all gambling onboard member vessels is conducted to ensure fair and professional gaming at the highest level of integrity to the player.
- To provide internal controls upon which passengers can rely to assure them that the gambling is operated with the utmost integrity.
- To provide a form of entertainment for passengers that is responsive to the customers' requests.

WEDDINGS, RENEWAL OF VOWS, AND OTHER CELEBRATIONS

While on board, passengers can elect to celebrate special occasions, and on some vessels couples can get married. The ability to perform weddings does not exist on all ships because of national laws that apply to the various ships and their flags or registration. However, where the law allows, the ship's captain can perform a marriage ceremony.

This creates a unique opportunity for passengers, and in response cruise companies have developed a selection of inclusive packages to cater to these market, including coordination of the entire event. The package can include champagne, photographs, the wedding reception, flowers, the ceremony, the wedding cake, and souvenir items. Other passengers can purchase a package to renew their vows. Again, the captain presides over the event and the package can be customized to include spa treatments, champagne, and a formal ceremony. Honeymoons, anniversaries, birthdays, and other special celebrations can all be catered to as part of a package.

BRAND VALUES AND VESSEL CLASSIFICATION

The size of the ship will have a major impact on the kind of cruise experience passengers enjoy. Large megaliners typically feature multiple swimming pools, casinos, spas, many dining options, and lots of activities. Small ships forgo some amenities in favour of focusing on a destination and a different kind of cruise experience. Cruise observers classify ships in a variety of ways, such as the number of passengers the ship holds; the quality of food, drink, and accommodation; and an overall measurement of the cruise experience. While no single standard exists, there is value in analyzing what is done to establish classifications and standards of quality. Many cruise lines operate ships in different classes so as to attract a targeted clientele. In this way a company can design specific itineraries that are commensurate with the size, the product range, the target market, and the selling price.

Classification of Scale

While Spartan Travel (2005) also identifies three expense category ratings—budget, midrange, and luxury—other industry observers take a broader view in their analysis. For example, CLIA lists five categories: Luxury, Premium, Resort or Contemporary, Niche or Speciality, and Value or Traditional (CLIA, 2005c). This classification is also adopted by Bjornsen (2003).

Table. Defining Vessel Types.

Definition	Description
Megaliner	over 2,000 passengers
Superliner	between 1,000 and 2,000 passengers
Midsize	between 400 and 1,000 passengers
Small	less than 400 passengers
Boutique	special purpose, usually less than 300 passengers
Sailing Vessel	a ship primarily powered by wind
River Barge	a ship that primarily cruises on inland rivers

An analysis of this classification suggests that ships that offer the ultimate in comfort, cuisine, and attentive service are called luxury brands. This product tends to be the most expensive, and while ships in this category are usually small, there are exceptions. The accommodation and public areas are always finely appointed and carry relatively few passengers in spacious staterooms, suites, or duplexes, which tend to have balconies. Service options may include butler service.

These ships are usually the equivalent of what used to be called "five star" quality. Some brands, such as Crystal Cruises, have adopted the rubric of "six stars" to identify their unique level of quality. Next in rank are premium brands, which offer above-average food, service, and amenities, including a high number of outside cabins with balconies.

These lines aim to appeal to broad age groups by providing a diversity of attractions for children, young adults, and older adults together with wide range of entertainment. Premium brands, like luxury lines, have a high ratio of space to each passenger. Contemporary brands are the equivalent of floating resorts with capacity spanning from the midsize vessel to the most recent megaliner or megacruise ship. These vessels provide choice and value with a contemporary twist. On board amenities, such as an ice rink, golf range, or climbing wall, are often impressive. Style may well be casual, although opportunities still exist for passengers to dress up on optional formal evenings.

Niche or speciality cruises focus on a specific aspect of the cruise, such as the destinations, in order to develop a unique product. These types of cruise companies are specialists in their fields. They pride themselves on having expertise in aspects such as cultural interpretation, soft adventure, or enrichment activities.

These cruise companies target the more experienced traveler. Budget or value brands usually use medium-size, refurbished, older ships with fewer facilities than the new megaships. This product will often take advantage of lower staffing ratios by using, for example, self-service options for main dining events. The ships are generally classically designed, and while the products are economically priced, the options of choice and travel make this form of vacation attractive to those who are relatively new to cruising.

A ROYAL SAILING WITH STAR CLIPPERS

For me, the word "sailing" conjures up images of conquistadors supervising deckhands under sprawling canvas sails as they cross the ocean to a new world, or the navies of the Roman Empire as they glide into battle on the sparkling Mediterranean Sea. Though the imagery is archaic, the spirit of those grand voyages is alive and well on the largest five-masted, fully rigged ship on the sea today, the Royal Clipper.

From its complex network of ropes and rigging to richly embellished, nautical themed interiors and understated amenities, the Royal Clipper introduced my fiance, Michael, and me to the world of niche cruising on a 10-day late-summer trip down Croatia's Dalmatian Coast and to lively Greek and Italian ports.

At just more than 439 feet long, the Royal Clipper is the largest of three cruise vessels owned and operated by Star Clippers cruise line and the only five-masted sailing ship launched since the beginning of the last century. During the end of the 19th century and beginning of the 20th century, sailing ships were built for speed to quickly deliver goods on expanding trade routes. To celebrate this grand age of sailing, Star Clippers' owner, Mikael Krafft, designed the Royal Clipper in the likeness of the Preussen, a German ship that was launched in 1902.

The Royal Clipper debuted in 2000. Meticulously crafted as the ultimate sailing ocean vessel, it can travel at 20 knots at full sail.

The Royal Clipper has twin 2,500-horsepower diesel engines that the captain can use when wind conditions are not suitable for itinerary requirements, which is quite often. But, sailing is Star Clippers' passion and, when possible, the motors are turned off. We rode the wind for nearly a full day while we cruised from Corfu in Greece to Sicily. With the sound of a gentle August breeze floating between the sails, and the warm Mediterranean sun bathing me in my lounge chair near one of the three saltwater pools on deck, I felt like part of an elite club.

There were only about 200 members of my so-called club on board for this trip, which is near passenger capacity for the Royal Clipper. A 109-member crew is on hand for a maximum guest count of 227, making for attentive, personal service. Quality time with the charming Capt. Sergiy Paschenko and his first officer, Sergiy Tonikov, was easy to come by (the Royal Clipper's bridge is always open). Our ever-present cruise director, Monica Matos Nogueira, patiently answered our endless questions every morning.

Dining on the Royal Clipper is more like a gathering at a country club. There is a multilevel dining room highlighted by a central, sun-filled atrium that's flanked by two ornate spiral staircases. If the Royal Clipper is a castle, the dining room is the throne room where all meals are served. Breakfast and lunch are casual buffets loaded with international cuisine. Dinner is a more formal affair, although there is no official dress code and no need to bring an evening gown or tuxedo.

The captain's dinner, set aside for one special night, does lend itself to casually elegant attire. There are no seating assignments, and many return passengers note that the dining atmosphere is one of the selling points of any Star Clippers cruise.

Our first night on board, we sidestepped the maitre d'hotel, Mateo Martinic, and found a table on our own. We quickly discovered that we had insulted him, as he thought we didn't trust that he could find suitable dinner companions for us. We explained we meant no offence, and by the next night the three of us were like old friends. For the remainder of our trip, we looked forward to Mateo's usual questions: "Just the two lovebirds for dinner tonight? How about a table of friendly English-speaking guests?"

English, French and German are the official languages on the Royal Clipper. Announcements are made in all three languages, and every crew member speaks English. On our cruise, there were more than 25 nationalities represented by the crew and 18 nationalities among the passengers. Germans, Americans, French, Australians, South Africans, Britons and many others gathered every night in the Tropical Bar on the main deck for after-dinner activities.

You won't hear the incessant clang of slot machines, attend a Broadway-style show or see a first-run movie aboard the Royal Clipper. Nightly entertainment includes passenger-participation events such as games and fashion and talent shows, followed by lively music and mingling.

If you aren't up for dancing or socializing, you can check your e-mail in the Observation Lounge, shop for souvenirs in the Sloop Shop, play cards in the Piano Lounge or curl up with a good book in the library. Then, of course, there is always the refreshing night air and sparkling stars overhead as you stroll on deck.

For a rejuvenating retreat, head for the Captain Nemo Lounge, a beauty and wellness spa on the bottom level of the ship. A variety of exercise equipment is available, and the range of treatments and services includes manicures, pedicures, facials, mineral baths and massages. I had heard that the traditional Thai massage was a treat, so I scheduled a 60-minute appointment. I was surprised at the strength of my tiny masseuse. As I was lying on my stomach, she stretched my arms behind my back and nearly lifted my entire body off the floor mat. I left the session with a feeling somewhere between relaxation and invigoration.

A water sports crew is on hand to encourage passengers to enjoy the sea. At ports where the Royal Clipper is anchored offshore, the marina platform at the aft of the ship is lowered so that you can windsurf, kayak, water-ski, take a banana boat ride, swim or just put on a life vest and float. The sports team is also active in on-board activities like morning aerobics and mast climbing, which is sure to get your heart pumping, as it did for me. And though there are no facilities or activities designed specifically for children, the several kids on our cruise loved partaking in the water sports.

Every evening, we returned to our spacious and comfortable cabin. Each stateroom is decorated in rich hues of gold and blue with mahogany trim, polished brass fittings and prints of famous sailing ships. Amenities common to all Royal Clipper cabins are televisions with in-house video and satellite news in port, DVD players, private safes, direct-dial telephones and hair dryers. All cabins, except those in Category Six, feature bathrooms outfitted in marble.

The 14 popular deluxe suites offer a whirlpool tub, sitting area, 24-hour room service and private veranda. The largest and most elegant staterooms are the two 355-square-foot owner's suites. Complete with two double beds in separate rooms, a large sitting area, minibar, powder room, whirlpool tub and room service, the owner's suites offer small-ship luxury at its best. The magnificence of Royal Clipper's nautical tradition and elegance was matched by the beauty, history and culture we experienced in each port. Michael and I arrived in Venice — our port of departure — with only five hours to spend wandering the magically confusing maze of streets along the city's famous canals.

We marveled at Venetian craftsmanship in shops full of flamboyant carnival masks and intricately designed Murano glass jewelry, vases and sculptures. Somehow, in our exhaustion from traveling from the United States, we missed St. Mark's Square and its majestic basilica — all the more reason to return to the city of canals and stay a few days.

As the Royal Clipper embarked from Venice under a bright, shining moon, more than 16,000 square feet of canvas sails were unfurled from long, yellow cylinders as Vangelis' epic song "Conquest of Paradise" played through speakers surrounding the passengers on deck. The ceremony would start anew as we left each port on our voyage, and though fewer guests were present on deck each time for the spectacle as the trip progressed, I never tired of hearing the song and watching the choreography of the crew. We awoke the next morning as the ship passed tiny islands popping out of the Adriatic on its approach to Rovinj, Croatia. With the campanile of St. Euphemia's church rising above the town ahead of us, we could sense the excitement on board as everyone prepared to explore the first port.

Rovinj is characterized by winding and narrow cobblestone streets that reminded me of an Old World San Francisco. The church named for Rovinj's patron saint stands tall atop a large hill as a symbol of the city's Catholic heritage. St. Euphemia was a religious martyr killed in A.D. 304 under the rule of Roman Emperor Diocletian. As the local story goes, St. Euphemia's sarcophagus, which rested in Calcedon and later Constantinople, somehow went astray around A.D. 800 and was spotted near Rovinj's shore, where it was pulled from the sea by a young boy and his two calves. The markets of Rovinj are full of life. We meandered amid souvenir stands and tables that displayed an enticing assortment of cheeses, herbs and liquors — including a fig brandy that our family back home thoroughly enjoyed.

After a day of tasting local wines and meats near freshly picked lavender fields on the Croatian island of Hvar, we arrived in Dubrovnik. Long known as a vacation destination for Europeans and a center of Croatian culture, Dubrovnik is more recently recognized as the site of a heavy artillery attack in 1991 during the Yugoslav Wars. Though much of the city's historic buildings were severely damaged, hardly any physical evidence of the conflict can be seen today. With the help of UNESCO (Dubrovnik's old town, Stari Grad, has been designated a World Heritage Site), Croatians have restored this city's Gothic, Renaissance and Baroque monasteries, palaces, churches and fountains.

We joined the walking tour of Stari Grad, entering the walled city and strolling the polished limestone main street called Stradun, past lively restaurants and shops. Our guide, Dinka, led us through the Franciscan monastery that is home to the oldest operating pharmacy in Europe, open since 1317. The monastery's museum and landscaped cloister served as a backdrop for Dinka as she told us stories of her days as a teenager in Dubrovnik during the war. Dinka was candid about her feelings regarding the 1991 shellings and the restoration process, and her anecdotes helped us understand the modern human condition among Dubrovnik's medieval architecture. Ambling along Dubrovnik's broad wall, we gazed at hundreds of red clay tile roofs that spread across the city, interrupted only by the occasional bell tower or church dome. We took advantage of the time left after our tour to peruse the city's open-air markets and shop for handmade crafts along the seaside promenade.

The following three days were filled with the charm of the Italian influence in Corfu, Greece, where we witnessed an opulent baptism; refreshing sea breezes as we sailed from Greece to Italy; and the distinctive shops and sophisticated atmosphere of Taormina, Sicily. When we arrived at the Italian island of Lipari, just north of Sicily, the morning haze was rising to unveil the stunning seascape before us. Lipari is the largest of the seven Aeolian Islands. This volcanic archipelago spans the gap between two famous volcanoes, Mount Etna and Mount Vesuvius, and is home to spectacular beaches, bays and grottoes.

In Lipari we visited an archaeological museum, where artifacts date to the sixth century. We shopped for obsidian pendants, formed from polished shards of volcanic rock that is ubiquitous in the region. The highlight of our time in Lipari was a Zodiak safari to the grottoes that surround the island. As our inflatable speedboat entered several quiet caves, we marveled at the towering rock formations and watched thousands of baby jellyfish bob through the clear, warm water. That night we sailed past Stromboli, an active volcano, and witnessed three small volcanic eruptions light up the night sky. Wandering the streets and enjoying the scenery in Capri, followed by a day of water sports and sunbathing, helped ease us into the end of our voyage aboard the Royal Clipper. We arrived refreshed and relaxed in Civitavecchia, the port for Rome and the final destination of the cruise.

BRANDING IS CRUCIAL

"You're always answering the question, 'Why should I do business with you?' Most agents cannot tell you what they do that would inspire a client to tell 10 other people about them," said Koepf. Being able to define your difference is usually the last thing that the starting agent thinks of, but it should be the first, according to Joni Rein, vice president of worldwide sales for Carnival Cruise Lines. Rein suggests that agents distinguish themselves with a specialty. "If I were just starting out, I would focus on multigenerational family vacations," she said.

"That's narrow and deep and you can build other vacations from it. Older clients will move to luxury, girlfriends' getaways and so on." This process of defining your strategy is a distinction in itself, according to Andy Stuart, Norwegian Cruise Line executive of global sales and passenger services. "Agents who can sum up their marketing strategies in one sentence produce far better than agents with a vague plan," he said. "They create a unique experience so they can't be comparison shopped and they figure out how to make price the second question, not the first."

Vickie Freed, Royal Caribbean International's senior vice president of sales and trade support and services, suggests a technique. "If clients ask you to book something they saw based on price, tell them you can certainly do that and much more. Put that issue aside while you ask them qualifying questions," she said. "You have to diagnose like a doctor before you prescribe." Bob Dickinson, former president and CEO of Carnival Cruise Lines and now consultant to Carnival Corp., urges agents to treat all customers as prospects, no matter how many times they have done business with you. His view is supported by Tom Baker, co-owner of CruiseCenter in Houston, and recognized by Conde Nast Traveler as a top Cruise Specialist, who says the cardinal sin of agents is making assumptions.

IN-DEPTH KNOWLEDGE

Mark Kammerer, senior vice president of marketing and North America sales for Holland America Line, believes agents who move to the next level know it's a privilege to help people get the most from their precious discretionary time. Baker embraces this philosophy to ensure his clients exceptional value. For shore trips, he uses ShoreExcursionsGroup.com, led by former cruise line executives, and develops his own relationships on the ground.

"In Italian ports where clients are charged [exorbitant prices] for a private tour driver, I can get them a good one for [about $120] a day, and my clients are riding in a Mercedes," Kammerer said. Sue Ratliff, owner of Sea World Cruises and Tours in Athens, Texas, also feels strongly that intimate knowledge of the product is key to her success. Ratliff has received Avoya's Best of the Best and President's Circle honours, and she certainly goes the extra mile: She once made a booking in a hospital on the verge of surgery.

Much in-depth knowledge is available to agents from the suppliers. "Cruise lines invest a huge amount of money in tools," Stuart said. "If you look at the data, those who complete their training are much more profitable." Sunni Drisgill, cruise specialist for BTS Cruise Center in Baltimore, Md., certainly has found this to be true.

Drisgill, who has served on CLIA's advisory board, has more than 100 certificates of completion for educational resources. American Express Pacesetter Diane Bower, owner of the The Diane Bower Agency in Charlotte, N.C., is legendary among Avoya agents for closing a Seabourn sale on horseback; she is also meticulous in researching.

"A lot of people have dealt with agents who didn't have in-depth knowledge. I can tell them which taxi driver will pick them up. I tell them what I have experienced in ports — they want to do what you do," said Bower. Recently, she surprised her customers at a recommended restaurant in Europe, meeting them face-to-face for the first time. "It's all part of relationship-building," she added. "Without relationships, we have nothing." Baker noted that relationship-building is not just with the client.

"Strengthen your relationships with your district sales manager and with cruise line executives so you can go to bat for your clients when they need it," he said. Baker cites a Celebrity cruise where his clients were sailing with friends who hadn't realized their Aqua-class dining room was different from the main dining room. Baker contacted Dondra Ritzenthaler, Celebrity Cruises senior vice president of sales, trade support and services, who made arrangements for them to be together.

SELLING TO NEW CRUISERS

Bob Dickinson pointed out that there is tremendous potential for income among new cruisers. "There are at least 75 million people who could cruise in terms of time and money, but haven't," he said. "That's the target. The repeat market is already sold. Non-cruisers don't know how good cruising is." Los Angeles-based Jason Coleman, owner of Jason Coleman, Inc., couldn't agree more. "I am not focused on the repeat cruiser — that doesn't do anything for the larger industry," he said. "The repeat cruiser is low-hanging fruit, and I don't really see much in the way of sales involved."

Coleman creates theme group cruises and develops ongoing relationships with participants. He does a lot of online advertising and works with publicists in Los Angeles to promote his theme sailings. On a recent soap opera reunion, Coleman had a publicist recruit the stars. The vast majority of fans who come on board because of their interest in meeting the stars had never cruised, and once they experienced cruising, the myths and obstacles go by the wayside. Coleman's approach is unusual, but Ritzenthaler notes that there are very different models among stellar agents. "You own your own destiny," she said. "If you're willing to work harder and smarter, there's no reason you can't be wildly successful. I see it all the time."

SELLING CRUISES: DOES IT STILL PAY?

For travel agents, the profit margin on sales of non-luxury cruises is smaller today than at any time in the history of the modern cruise industry. That statement may not be verifiable, but it's certainly the feeling among many travel agents who sell cruises.

While the cruise industry now offers more capacity and variety than ever before, that growth and diversification make the sales process more time-intensive for agents. Every extra hour spent on a cruise booking means smaller profits for the agent.

Meanwhile, persistently low cruise fares and the upward creep of non-commissionable fees (NCFs) reduce the dollar amount on which agents are compensated, while making it more difficult for them to reach cruise line sales goals and advance to higher commission levels. Can agents still make money selling non-luxury cruises? At what point does selling mainstream and mid-market cruises stop being worth an agent's time?

PROFITABILITY THRESHOLD

Robert Joselyn, president of TAMS, told Travel Market Report that a recent data review of TAMS member agencies showed that to be profitable, an agent needs to produce, on average, between $60 and $70 an hour in revenue. Obviously, this number will vary from agency to agency. But for agents selling inexpensive cruises to couples or families, hitting this mark on commissions alone is next to impossible.

CASE IN POINT

Let's say an agent has sold a four-night cruise on Royal Caribbean's Enchantment of the Seas to a family of four with two children. The price for a large ocean view stateroom for a Bahamas cruise departing May 5 is $1,145.12 for the four cruisers. Taxes, fees and port expenses account for $296.12 of the fare, according to Royal Caribbean's online booking engine. In other words, nearly 26 per cent of the fare is non-commissionable.

This drops the commissionable fare to $849. Let's further assume an agent is making a 12 per cent commission: He or she will earn $101.88 on the booking, barring any future re-pricing.

This amounts to $25.47 per cruiser. If he or she spent five hours on the sale from start to finish, walking the client through various cruise and vacation options, booking the Royal Caribbean cruise and printing out documentation, he or she will have earned $20.38 per hour.

FAULTY LOGIC

"Basically, the whole commissions structure has some faulty logic," said Joselyn. Not necessarily for the cruise companies though. "The lines look at their P and L [profit and loss statements] and see the cost of distribution going down as a percentage of revenue," Joselyn said. That's due in large part to NCFs, he said. Meanwhile, agents are earning less money on the same sale. In a Travel Market Report reader poll earlier this year, more than eight in 10 respondents said sales of mass market cruises became less profitable for them in 2013.

FEES, TAXES AND PORT CHARGES

For many agents, NCFs are the bad boy in the cruise profitability equation. Agent Bryan Harris of Operation Destinations Travel in Nashville was shocked to see the bite that non-commissionable taxes, fees and port charges took out of a Carnival cruise he sold last fall. He booked five inside staterooms with an average total cost, including taxes and NCFs, of between $920 and $1100 per stateroom. His average commission per stateroom? $35 to $62. "When I saw the commission on the invoice, I literally did a double and triple take," said Harris, an independent contractor for A Way to Go Travel, a Signature member in Greensboro, N.C.

DOUBLE BLOW

As cruise lines have lowered their pricing in order keep their ships filled, it has created a double whammy for agents. Obviously lower cruise fares mean smaller commissions. "They're going to say they're still giving you 11 per cent of the base fare of $600, but that fare used to be $850," said Harris. Lower fares also mean NCFs are a larger portion of the cruise fare. "NCFs are a fixed amount, so the percentage of commissionable cruise fare has shrunk," said Alex Sharpe, president of Signature Travel Network.

NCFS ARE 29 PER CENT

Data from World Travel Holdings for 2012 showed that NCFs represented 29 per cent of the total cruise price for WTH's retail cruise-selling outlets. "It really is a reflection of where the average selling point is," Brad Tolkin toldTravel Market Report shortly after WTH released its 2012 data. The impact on agent commissions can be dramatic. "It's sad when you hear the horror story of a cruise agent having a commission of $4, because NCFs are high and fares are automatically repriced lower by the lines," Sharpe said.

SALES THRESHOLDS

Another factor affecting the profitability of cruise sales, especially for smaller and unaffiliated agencies, are changes to the cruise lines' commission structures. There's been a solid trend for years of cruise lines adjusting compensation thresholds in ways that make it harder for agents to reach the sales goals that would qualify them for higher commission levels. "Lines have shifted their thresholds, and mostly at the small agency level," said Gary Davis, president of Acendas in Mission, Kan., a Vacation.com agency.

"The cruise lines have to make money for their shareholders." Tougher thresholds was a complaint heard from many agents after Carnival Cruise Lines revised its commission structure in 2012, earning the wrath of many. "They're breaking the kneecaps of the agencies that do the majority of their business," one agent said at the time.

CHANGING ECONOMICS

While it's standard for suppliers to tweak their commission models over time, as agents earn less on each booking, the economics of the travel-selling business shift.

"What separates good agencies from the rest is the ability to figure out how to reach that threshold," said Sharpe. Agents who sell non-luxury cruises told Travel Market Report that low commissions have directly affected the kinds of vacations they market. "Am I going to use my marketing avenues to push cruise over other types of vacations if I can't make money on it?" asked Harris of Operation Destinations Travel.

Even former cruise agency exec Dwain Wall, now CLIA's senior vice president of agent and trade relations, has said that the most profitable portion of a non-luxury cruise sale can be commissions on the non-cruise portions of a booking, such as travel insurance, pre- and post-cruise itineraries and custom shore excursions. "When combined with a group booking, these types of vacations can be very profitable, even on a low-cost cruise," Wall said.

SELLING CRUISES CAN MEAN PROFITS

Cruise

As every travel agent knows, it takes time, energy and expertise to turn a strong profit from cruise sales. Prompted by the need to balance those requirements against a transaction's financial return, many agents are focusing their cruise sales on one or more areas of specialization.

In that pursuit, price point alone is not sufficient to identify which cruises are most profitable to sell. In general, transactions based on higher price points — including luxury cruises, long cruises, river cruises and group or charter cruises — yield the best profit levels. But transaction time, an agent's customer base, commission payment structure through a marketing group affiliation and the cash flow requirements of the business are all factors that can shape cruise sale profitability.

Time is the essential determining factor of cruise sale profitability for Jason Olson, president of Cruise Holidays in Redding, Calif. Olson focuses his sales on luxury lines and all-inclusive lines such as Regent Seven Seas Cruises, which pays agents commission on all aspects of the cruise vacation. Another reason he focuses his cruise sales on luxury lines is that most are not prone to price promotions.

"With luxury lines, I don't have clients calling every month about a new offer they saw," Olson says. "There is much less maintenance. If you are giving clients the kind of care and service you should, they are happy. And you aren't updating their cruise every few weeks because of a new offer, as happens with contemporary lines.

That's like reselling the same cruise over and over." Beth Levich, owner of Oregon-based Cruise Holidays of Portland, says she sat down to think about ways to make maximum profit in her business and settled on selling groups, luxury lines and river cruises.

Whenever possible, she combines the three, as she did on a recent sailing on AmaWaterways, where she sold a 65-guest partial group charter following a wedding. Levich says this transaction was ideal as it involved a group leader — a pied piper — who bought space on the sailing then spread the word to fill the cabins. In this case, the group leader was the patriarch of the family, who loves to bring other members along when he travels. He is already working with Levich to book a June 2015 Baltic cruise. Selling group cruises has its own challenges and rewards.

"The leader has to know that when you buy space, you own it," Levich says. "I received a wonderful net price from AmaWaterways and was able to give my client a great deal while retaining a good commission. With Ama, if you guarantee 10 or more staterooms, you have a partial charter and can build on that, although I will not build outside the group." Cruise Holidays coordinates the whole vacation for group cruise sales, including air, hotels, transfers and the cruise itself. Levich says she often gets grateful e-mails from the group leaders acknowledging that they couldn't have done it without her. She does not take the risk of buying blocked space on cruises herself.

"I prefer to use a pied piper who blocks the space without marketing costs for me and has a ready-made group," she says. "And I'm going with them. I hope that when some of these 65 people make their own travel plans, they will think of me." Clients who generate more clients are also central to the successful business run by Anne Halsey-Smith, owner of Halsey-Smith Private Travel in La Jolla, Calif. One of her focuses is on selling world cruises, which intrinsically have higher yields and a strong repeat factor.

"World cruises are the most profitable cruises," she says. "It takes as much work to sell a two-week cruise as a four-month cruise, and there's so much more commission." Halsey-Smith plans special activities and opportunities for her cruise clients, such as an excursion with lunch on a private Chinese junk (a small boat) in Halong Bay, China. "Other guests asked how they got that, and you acquire more clients through these arrangements, as well as pleasing the current ones," she says. "Onboard there are referrals from customers, and you build your clientele."

Halsey-Smith started selling cruises with the now defunct Royal Viking Line, and generations of loyal clients have followed. She sells younger clients two-week cruises, and as they mature and have more time and financial resources, she moves them into longer sailings or world cruises. Today Halsey-Smith places most of her clients on Seabourn. She has one repeat Seabourn client who has sailed more than 1,000 days on the line and spent additional time on Silversea sailings. Besides the high profit margin on world cruise bookings, Halsey-Smith says world cruisers often repeat. A world cruise is not a once-in-a-lifetime experience for most, which further enhances the profitability factor of the segment.

Adrienne Forst, a travel advisor with Protravel International in Beverly Hills, Calif., says 90 percent of her business is upscale travel. She approaches profitability on cruise sales from a broader perspective. "Protravel was big, but now that we are owned by Travel Leaders, we are enormous, and they negotiate for us," Forst says. "My commission is based on overall revenue, not on individual sales." While group cruise sales are bigticket items that can and do yield healthy profits, Brad Anderson, copresident of Avoya Travel in San Diego, says group sales have a number of inherent risks.

"We would all like to go for the big kill and sell top penthouse suites for a full world cruise, or sell a large group or a full-ship charter, but there's a real cash-flow issue there," Anderson says. "There's nothing worse than having lots of business on your books and not getting paid for it for six months. You can starve waiting for the commission for your group unless you have plenty of cash flow. Unless you have excellent cash flow, be leery of groups."

Anderson advises that agents focus on finding a cruise niche where they have a lot of prospects and making it their passion. They should then ask for referrals and build a prospective customer list. "Getting the leads is the No. 1 issue for any agency, and agencies are generally not good at marketing in today's world," he adds. "Sure, the most profitable cruises on paper are high-priced cruises with no NCFs, but that's only true if you are able to sell them. Be realistic about what you are going to sell and how you will connect with the prospect. Some agents make a lot of money selling contemporary seven-night cruises in the Caribbean. You may be able to sell two to four of them in the same amount of time it would take you to sell one luxury cruise."

The bottom line: What constitutes a profitable cruise sale varies from agent to agent and is likely to change several times during a travel agent's career as outside forces reshape product and consumer expectations. Economic conditions influence cruise sales and profitability. The cruise industry itself is constantly evolving — nobody would have guessed 20 years ago that river cruising would be such a hot segment. At the same time, consumer tastes shift and change, and each new generation of travelers brings a new set of desires to the cruise experience.

There is one constant that has a direct link to profitability, according to agents. Superior customer service will always ensure that agents attract and keep whatever segment of the buying public they have identified as their prime cruise buying market.

A LUXURY CRUISE LINE FOR 30-SOMETHINGS

Travel agents say the cruise industry needs a product designed for the 30-something upscale demographic. Contemporary ships are being designed with features for all age groups and tastes, but upscale lines still cater primarily to an older demographic. That's a missed opportunity, according to travel agents: The industry needs a luxury cruise product designed specifically for a younger, upscale client base.

"The young and successful group is here, and they travel," says Anne Halsey-Smith, owner of Halsey-Smith Private Travel in La Jolla, Calif. "I hear from them all the time. They want something for their generation and have the money to pay for it." She says the upscale segment of the 77-million-member millennial generation wants to pay one fee for an all-inclusive cruise product and then forget about money matters and simply enjoy the vacation.

"They would go if the product was there," she adds. "They are so well-traveled. Going long distances, even for a short trip, is nothing to them." Several agents mentioned that Royal Caribbean International's introduction of high-speed onboard Internet service at reasonable rates could change the game for millennial cruisers; it would open up the market to taking longer cruises if luxury lines offer similar connectivity. They contend that younger, working travelers would feel much freer to sail away, even on longer cruises, if they had a reliable way to keep in touch.

"Luxury and river cruise lines are designing their product for the boomers and beyond, but they are missing the market of 30-something people, which would be huge if the product and marketing were aimed at them," says Mary Lynn Klein, cruise and vacation specialist with Ticket to Travel in San Jose, Calif. "In the San Francisco Bay Area, we have all these younger affluent people who work for eBay, Yahoo, LinkedIn and so forth, and there's really nothing designed for them."

RELATIONSHIP BETWEEN TOURIST PRODUCT AND CRUISE TOURISM ESSAY

This chapter seeks to discuss the concept of product life cycle apply to the cruise product selling in Wing On Travel Agent (Hong Kong). First, the relationship between tourist product and cruise product is defined. Then the concept of product life cycle is introduced. Finally, a case study of Wing On Travel Agent (Hong Kong) is presented to illustrate the life cycle of selling the cruise product. Transportation by carrier; accommodations; rental of motor vehicles; or any other service related to travel. Depending on the jurisdiction this may or may not include time shares. Travel services includes transportation by air, sea, or land, or the provision of other goods or services related to recreational, cultural or educational travel, including but not limited to lodging, food, guided tours, or instruction.

The cruise industry is one of the fastest-growing segments of the travel industry - since 1980 the industry has had an average annual passenger growth rate of 8.1 per cent. Almost 45 million people have cruised at least once; of these, nearly 23 million have cruised in the past 3 years. (By: Miller, Richard K.; Washington, Kelli. Travel and Tourism Market Research Handbook, 2009, p88-91, 4p, 5 Charts;)

Between 1999 and 2005, passenger levels for conventional cruises have expanded from about 8.5 million to 13.9 million. During the same period, the Asia Pacific region accounted for between 5 per cent and 8.6 per cent of the worldwide market. Between 1999 and 2005, Hong Kong's typical rate1 of capture of the Asia Pacific conventional cruise market ranged from 16 per cent to 30 per cent. The total cruise passenger throughput in Hong Kong including local residents and international passengers traveling on conventional cruises and cruises-to-nowhere has increased from 1.38 million in 1999 to 2.15 million in 2005. The number of cruise vessel calls has increased from 409 to 1 051 over the same period.

The growth of tourism even exceeded the growth of GDP worldwide by approximately 1.3 times in the last 25 years of the 20th century (WTO, 2003). The cruise industry is a niche market in the tourism industry. The market share of cruises in the tourism market is small and account for only 0.6 per cent of the hotel beds offered worldwide (WTO, 2003). This number seems small, but the cruise market has shown incredible growth figures and is seen as a market with high potential. The cruise industry has grown with an average annual percentage of 7.4 since 1980. An estimated 15 million travelers cruised in 2008. The North American cruise market dominates the industry and it makes a significant contribution to the American economy. The cruise industry generated $38 billion in the total U.S. economic output in 2007(CLIA, 2009). The cruise industry becomes however more and more globalized with a growing number of destinations and calls in Europe and other regions (Cruise Europe, 2009).

Between 1990 and 2004, passenger levels expanded from 4.4 to 13.2 million worldwide (Bermello-Ajamil and Partners, In 2005c). Accorrdint to B and A, passenger carrying levels could expand from the present 13.2 million to between 19.3 and 30.1 million by 2020.

THE PRODUCT LIFE CYCLE

The product life cycle theory says that the development of sales and profits of new developed products shows a clear pattern. The product life cycle theory states that a product goes, after its introduction, through different phases. From the introduction, the product will know a phase of growth, maturity and finally decline or revitalization (Dekker et al, 1995). Butler developed, based on the product life cycle, the life cycle of tourist locations. Instead of the quantity of products sold, the life cycle of tourism development uses the number of visitors as the indicator of the level of destination development (Butler, 1980 from van der Borg et al, 1996).

The development process of any tourist destination may, just as the development process of products, be represented cyclically (van der Borg et al, 1996). The destination life cycle curve with the phases of introduction, growth, maturity and decline/revitalization.

With reference to the cruise industry the introduction of a cruise destination begins of course with the necessary infrastructure. Initial costs are high since the cruise port should 'often' be made accessible for cruise ships and should have the required facilities to accommodate these cruise ships. During the phase of introduction a limited number of cruise ships visit the cruise port. In this phase costs are relatively high in relation to the benefits.

During the phase of growth the number of cruise ships and cruise passengers visiting the city increase and facilities need to be improved. Since the available capacity is used more efficiently, costs will drop in relation to the revenues. The expenses made by cruise passengers in the city will increase and the cruise sector will contribute significantly to the economical development of the destination.

During the phase of maturity the cruise sector can be considered a major contributor to the local community. The cruise port is visited by a large number of the largest cruise ships and facilities are state of the art. The cruise port city has achieved an international reputation. The destination life cycle shows however that there is a possibility of decline. Cruise destination could lose their position and reputation which would result in a decline of the number of cruise ships visiting the destination. A decline can be caused by, for example, negative environmental impact or nuisance due to the large number of cruise passengers visiting the destination (Gibson, 2006).

The life cycle differs of course for each and every product or tourism destination. Marketing strategies that should be adopted in the different stages of development differ as well. In the phase of product development it is necessary to meet the customer needs.

The needs of cruise lines and cruise passengers should be satisfied in order to develop into thriving cruise destination. The destination should build upon its brand based on the needs of its customers. During the introduction phase it is important to create awareness among cruise lines and cruise passengers. In this way the cruise destination will secure its place in the market. With an increase in passenger volumes, costs will decline and profits will rise. In this stage promotion shifts to creating loyalty in order to remain and improve the obtained position (Plog, 2001).

APPLICATION

Cruise ships are not, like ferries, just seen as a mode of transport. These ships are often a destination on itself, and can be typified as floating hotels, or even floating resorts (Dowling, 2006). This has not always been the case. The main purpose of the big Ocean liners of the past, like the Normandy (1932) and the Queen Mary (1934), was primarily to transport passengers and cargo between Europe and America. Transoceanic liners sailed on fixed schedules and routes and the different classes in the society were separated with first class cabins and public spaces in the front, second class in the middle and steerage class in the back of the ship (Maxton-Graham, 1985 from Chin, 2008). The speed of these ocean liners was not only important economically, but also for prestige.

The Ocean liners lost however market share due to the rising popularity of the airplane and finally lost their function as transport mode. Many ships were taken out of business or were used only to make pleasure trips. The cruise industry as we know it emerged in this period. Nowadays, airplanes do no longer compete with the passenger ships operating in the cruise sector and actually have become an important extension of the cruise product. The cruise product is not, as the ocean liners, based on the transportation of passengers but on the experience they are able to give to their passengers.

MARKET ANALYSIS

The cruise sector is an exclusive part of the leisure industry and has developed rapidly in the last four decades. The sector is still expanding, not only in number of passengers, but it becomes also more and more globalized. In the market analysis we will look more closely to the major cruise regions, the growth of passengers in these regions, the characteristics of cruise passengers, the properties of the cruise product and cruise line economics.

CRUISE REGIONS

The major cruise regions in the world are based in North America and Europe. An overview of the total overnights per region in 2008. The Caribbean is the major cruise region, followed by the Mediterranean and Central America. The Caribbean and Central America are not negatively affected by seasonal weather patterns, apart from the hurricane season, and cruise ships are deployed in these regions throughout the year (Gibson, 2006). Between April and September, a large part of the cruise fleet is however relocated to Europe and Alaska. These regions show a clear seasonal pattern with no cruises in the winter period and a peak in the summer months (Dowling, 2006). Climate can be considered as a determining factor in the deployment of cruise ships.

PASSENGER GROWTH

Cruise tourism has, together with the whole leisure industry, shown a phenomenal growth. The cruise sector developed from a small market with cruise lines operating with only a single ship, to a globalized industry with a fleet of numerous unique vessels (cruiseweb.nl). Table 1 shows that especially the European market and transatlantic voyages have shown significant growth figures between 2000 and 2008 of respectively 238 per cent and 279 per cent. The market of North and Central America showed a passenger growth of 141 per cent. The spectacular growth in number of cruise passengers can also been seen based on the number of cruise ships ordered by the different cruise lines. The CLIA Five-Year Capacity Report and Passenger Carrying Report of 2008 shows that 34 new ships were contracted or planned to be added to the fleet from 2008 to the end of 2012 (CLIA, 2008).

CHARACTERISTICS CRUISE PASSENGERS

The general profile of the cruise vacationer is upscale and well educated, with a median household income of $93,000 and 69 percent having a college degree in 2008. The median age of cruisers is now 46 years old, down from 49 in 2006 (CLIA, 2009). This shows that that the cruise sector continues to attract younger travelers. The cruise market is dominated by American cruise passengers, followed on distance by passengers from Great Britain. Other passengers come mainly from other European countries like Germany, Italy,

Spain and France (Gibbons, 2009). The tourist industry experience the trend that people do no longer take one big holiday per year, but make several shorter trips instead (Bargeman et al, 2002). This trend can also been seen in the cruise industry. The length of the cruises has declined over the years. Especially short cruises with a length between 2 and 5 days have become more popular in comparison with 25 years ago.

CRUISE PRODUCT

The cruise industry is characterized by substantial heterogeneity similarly to other tourism products (Papathelodorou, 2001). Each cruise is different in terms of ports of call, or vessel. Besides that, the experience people have, does differ among every individual. Cruise lines have the opportunity to differentiate in terms of quality and in terms of variety and offerings. Differentiation is used as a strategy by some cruise lines in the cruise industry. Cruise lines developed products that meet the preferences of different types of passengers by offering for example thematic cruises and cruises to different regions. An example is Disney Cruise, which offers cruise passengers a unique experience by focusing on the theme of Disney.

The cruise product, offered by cruise lines, has changed from an 'all-inclusive' package to a more customized product. This means that 'amenities' and 'experiences' can be booked together with the cruise itself. Onboard sales have become a significant proportion of the turnover of a cruise ship and the profits derived from on shore excursions are significant. A typical Royal Caribbean cruise ship can, for example, generate close to a half million dollar tour income with a single call to St. Petersburg, Russia (Peisley, 2003). According to Royal Caribbean's Vice President for Commercial Development, John Tercek, US$100 million of the profit of Royal Caribbean's US$ 351 million profit in 2002/3 was derived solely from shore excursions (Klein, 2006 in Ross, 2006 pp. 262). Most people who take a cruise do not live in the area of the port of departure. Therefore, fly-cruise packages are very popular and play, next to the offering of excursions and other services, an important role (Papatheodorou, 2006).

CRUISE LINE ECONOMICS

Economies of scale are important for cruise lines. The average cost per passenger drop as the scale of operation increases. Two main categories of cost savings can be identified, namely: economies of density and economies of fleet size (Papatheodorou, 2006). Economies of density means that cruise lines are able to operate more efficiently with larger cruise vessels since fixed costs are spread over a large number of passengers. Economies of fleet size are derived by spreading fixed costs over a large number of cruise ships. Besides this, a large fleet makes it for cruise lines easier to expand in many different regions and thus establish a network of operations (Papatheodorou, 2006). Cruise lines are able to operate more efficiently with an increase in the number of ships and capacity, since the variable costs rise by a rate which is less than proportional with the increase of passenger capacity (Blauwens et al, 2007). Ships have therefore become bigger and bigger and are in some cases even considered as the main destination, instead of the ports of call (Chin, 2008). Royal Caribbean has recently ordered a new vessel, the 'Ocean of the Seas' with a capacity of 5400 passengers, which will come in operating in the end of 2009 (www.royalcaribbean.com).

In comparison, in the 1970s and early 1980s, the typical cruise ship accommodated between 500 and 800 passengers (Klein, 2006).

Due to the importance of economies of scale the cruise industry is consolidated among three major players. The passenger capacity of the Carnival Corporation, Royal Caribbean Cruises and Star/NCL Cruises cover 80 per cent of the total worldwide cruise capacity. The allocation of the passenger capacity among the major cruise corporations.

Under the three main cruise corporations, several cruise brands operate with a great degree of independency. Each brand looks after their own itinerary planning, marketing, on shore excursions and other operations. Each of the brands has specific core consumer markets that are based on demographics and nationality.

THE TRAVEL AGENT

So, you've decided to go on a cruise — perhaps your first venture on a vacation at sea — and you're a little overwhelmed. You have to consider how much you're willing to pay, whether to book an inexpensive inside cabin or splurge on a suite, and which cruise line and ship are right for you. Add dinner seatings, shore excursions and cabin location to the list, and planning a relaxing getaway suddenly seems like a second job. In the age of the Internet, many people assume that online is the only way to book travel. But, as booking online can often be confusing, a travel agent may be just what you need. In fact, according to the Cruise Lines International Association's (CLIA) 2008 Cruise Market Profile Study, nearly 75 percent of cruise travelers book their cruises through travel agents. One of the most important things to know is that agents — in particular, cruise specialists — have been onboard the ships and can really give you first-hand advice about different cruise options. They have done a great deal of research through familiarization trips and cruise-line seminars, so you don't have to do the work yourself. Even better, agents often have access to special discounts or perks — or know best where to find them — and as the cruise lines pay their commissions, you don't pay more for their services and expertise. Top of Form Still undecided, or unsure where to find an agent to help you? Here are a few tips to get you started.

REASONS TO CONSIDER A TRAVEL AGENT

If you're used to booking travel independently, consider these reasons why you might want to make use of a travel agent to book your next holiday at sea. Choosing a Cruise: For your first cruise, you may need help in matching your lifestyle and budget with a cruise line and destination. Choosing a cruise is not the same as picking a hotel or flight, as there are many more options to consider.

For example, do you want to cruise close to home from ports like New York, Miami, Galveston or Seattle, or are you willing to fly to Europe for Mediterranean and Baltic sailings? Would you be happier on a large ship — such as Royal Caribbean's 154,407-ton, 3,634-passenger Freedom of the Seas — or on a smaller, more intimate ship — like Seabourn's's 10,000-ton, 208-passenger Seabourn Pride? Do you prefer a casual and lively vibe, as is found on Carnival Cruise Lines, or a more formal atmosphere, such as Silversea's?

Remember, you won't just be using the ship as a home base, like you do with a hotel; it will be your home, restaurant and entertainment venue for a week or more. The right ship and itinerary can make your vacation that much more enjoyable — and an agent can help you determine the best selection for your tastes. In addition, an agent can answer any questions or assuage any apprehensions you might have about taking a cruise for the first time.

Shopping for Great Deals: Contrary to what you might expect, travel agents may actually be able to get you better deals than Internet retailers or even the cruise lines themselves. The best travel agents have access to discounted group rates and exclusive cruise pricing that's not found anywhere else. In addition, agents occasionally give you extra value on your booking — such as prepaid gratuities, a free bottle of Champagne or onboard credit — to sweeten the deal. And if the price of your cruise drops after you book, a good agent will notice and refund you the difference in fare. Finally, as cruise lines pay agent commissions, you don't have to worry about paying extra for their planning services.

Booking the Trip: Once you've chosen your cruise and, with the agent's help, matched your style with your vacation goals, you've got to book the trip. Again, it's a bit more complex than you might think, but a good agent will make the process go smoothly — from securing the right cabin type and location to booking the dinner seating that will suit you and your party. Your agent will also be able to sort out travel insurance, if required, and will collect payment for the cruise (usually a deposit at the time of booking and the full amount 60 to 90 days before departure). In addition, the agent can help you with the rest of your travel plans, such as pre- or post-cruise stays, airfare and transfers.

Special Requirements: If you have special needs of any kind — whether it's help in arranging a wedding ceremony onboard, ordering gluten-free or kosher meals, or dealing with accessibility issues — a qualified agent should be able to make the proper arrangements for you or advise you on how to handle the issue yourself.

Establishing Relationships: Booking with a travel agent gives your transaction a personal touch — you have a resource for asking questions and someone to contact if something goes wrong during your travels. But, your relationship with an agent doesn't tend to end after one trip. The agent will keep you in his or her database, alert you to deals or sales and can even suggest future trip ideas.

HOW TO SELECT A TRAVEL AGENT

So how do you find the right travel agent for you? Look for the following:

Training and Credentials: Many agents become accredited cruise counselors through CLIA's Cruise Academy or take courses through the different cruise lines to become more expert at selling their products. Enquire whether the agent has attended any of these training programmes. In addition, you can look for affiliations with the National Association of Cruise Oriented Agencies (NACOA), Better Business Bureau (BBB), American Society of Travel Agents (ASTA) or even the American Automobile Association (AAA).

Cruising Experience and Knowledge: Question the agents on cruising trends or up-and-coming destinations, and ask them to explain the differences between cruise lines. Find out how many cruises they've taken that year and with which lines they've personally cruised. The more knowledgeable an agent is, the better advice you'll get. If the agent has rarely cruised, you might want to take your business elsewhere. In addition, you might want to look for an agent who is a cruise specialist — either at a cruise-dedicated agency or within a larger general agency — to get the best service.

Inventory/Niche: If you're interested in a specific type of cruising (such as river cruising or luxury travel), look for agencies that specialize in the line or type of cruising you prefer. They'll often have more complete knowledge of your choices than a generalist. For example, if you want to cruise one of

Europe's rivers in an intimate barge or riverboat, you may not want to book with an agent who specializes in selling holidays on 3,000-person mega-ships.

Interview: The best cruise agents will do a thorough job of interviewing potential clients to find out which ship, line and itinerary would be the best fit. In that initial interview, they should ask you what kind of vacation you normally take (beach, city, active, for example), who is going (family, couple, singles), your travel style (entertainment and activity preferences, dining habits) and your budget.

Cruise Line Connections: Find out if the travel agent has preferred status with any cruise lines or whether he or she belongs to travel consortiums that would enable him or her to get you better deals, upgrades, etc. But watch out — some agents will push a particular line too aggressively for your tastes. You don't want to get caught in an agent's agenda if the cruise line isn't right for you.

Special Offers: Look for agents offering discounts, free perks and other incentives. If you don't see a sign or advertisement, always ask — the agent may have fabulous offers the cruise lines won't let him or her publicize. In addition, ask if the agent can meet or beat the best price you've seen elsewhere.

Size: You can book a cruise through a huge travel retailer with branches around the country, a local cruise agency or even a home-based agent who will talk cruising with you at your local coffee shop. You'll find pros and cons of working with the different types of agencies; for example, you might get more personal service from an independent agent but better deals from a large company with a high volume of bookings. Shop around and see what size fits your needs best.

HOW TO LOCATE AN AGENT

If you'd like to book a cruise through a travel agent, you can pop into a downtown storefront or search for cruise sellers online. If you want to look for agents registered with travel organizations, here are some resources for finding agencies near you.

Cruise Lines International Association: You can search for a CLIA-certified travel agent on the organization's Web site. Use the search tool to locate agents in your area with a variety of levels of CLIA training.

American Society of Travel Agents (ASTA): Use ASTA's consumer Web site to locate a travel agent who has agreed to conduct their business activities in accordance with the organization's code of ethics. Select "cruises" or "cruise lines" under Specialties to find agents that focus on selling cruise travel.

WHEN TO GO IT ALONE

Using a travel agent isn't always necessary. Here's how to determine if it's okay to book on your own.

You're Experienced: If you have cruised before and know exactly what you want — the cruise line, destination, duration and cabin — booking on the Internet can be quite easy.

Most online cruise retailers have comprehensive search functions, as well as pages that list their best or newest deals. Many also offer additional resources, such as deck plans, photos and reviews. A step-by-step process will guide you through the booking and payment procedures.

You're Independent: If you're a do-it-yourself type, and you have the time and inclination to thoroughly research your own trip using resources like Cruise Critic, then go right ahead. For many of us, planning is half the fun of taking a trip.

USING A TRAVEL AGENT

The rise of the internet has spurred many travelers to book their vacations independently, but booking a cruise can be a complex operation and here's an important fact to chew on: Most people book their cruises through a travel agent (68 per cent of them in 2011, according to the Cruise Lines International Association). The cruise lines actually prefer this arrangement. They have small reservation staffs, rely on agents for the bulk of their sales and even list preferred agents on their web sites.

A good travel agent can stop you from making a dumb planning error. They can also be of assistance if things go wrong, such as if your cruise is cancelled or you miss your flight to the port.

Fig. Booking through a travel agent can take the hassle out of cruise planning- and may get you an exclusive deal.

Even if you're the most stubborn DIY type, if you're cruising for the first time, seeking the assistance of a travel agent is a smart idea. If you're not a cruise novice, you may still run into questions regarding such things as location of a specific cabin or dining reservations. Using a travel agent, especially a cruise specialist, is not a bad idea then either.

The reality is you're not likely to find greater savings by booking on your own through the cruise line — erasing one particular argument against booking with an agent — and you may even get a better deal through an agency that specializes in cruising. Plus, said agencies may not charge customers for their services (though some now have a consultation fee). The bulk of their pay is via the cruise line in the form of commissions, so it won't cost you anything to make use of their expertise. Finally, those of you who wouldn't dream of picking up a phone or walking into a travel agency office, can, on the larger agency web sites, link up with an agent in a chat room to ask questions — a way to have your cake and eat it too.

Travel agents can help:

- Choose the line that's right for you.
- Make your booking.
- Choose an appropriate cabin.
- Assist with dining times, and submit any special meal requests.
- Arrange airfare and transportation to the ship.
- Help with pre and postcruise arrangements.
- Advise on shore excursions.
- Advise on travel insurance.
- Arrange for a refund, if needed.

Reasons not to work with an agent:

- You like to do everything yourself.
- You have plenty of time on your hands to do research.
- For you, planning is half the fun of the trip.
- You know exactly what you want.
- You don't want to pay the fee some agents charge for consultation, typically under $100 per couple (though occasionally more).

Making the Right Choice

It's important to keep in mind that when booking a cruise you're making the bulk of your vacation decisions in one fell swoop — everything from transportation, to dining, to lodging, to entertainment. All of these factors will have an impact on your cruise experience, making the right choice crucial. A good agent will steer you towards the right selections for your vacation, so getting the right agent is vital.

Conduct an interview with an agent before you commit. You are, in fact, hiring the agent and you'll want someone with cruise experience, preferably on the line(s) you're considering.

Ask the Agent

Have they actually cruised on the line/ship? The more they've sailed, the better. Have they been to your chosen destination before? Firsthand knowledge of a destination or itinerary is always preferable.

Do they have a preferential rela-tionship with specific lines? If they have a close relationship with the line you want to sail on, you might be able to get a better deal or special perks.

The best way to find an agent is a referral through a friend. But if that's not possible, try to find an agency that is cruiseonly, a homebased agent who specializes in cruises, or a fullservice agency that has a cruise desk.

Look for an agency that's a member of either (or both) of the following:

Cruise Lines International Association, the industry's main marketing group, now a worldwide organization. CLIA agents have had training in cruises; those agents accredited as Certified Cruise Counselors by CLIA have particularly extensive training. CLIA's web site has a search tool to find an agent in your area.

American Society of Travel Agents, which monitors agencies for ethical practices. Use the search function on the web site to find ASTA agents who have specialties in "cruises" or "cruise lines."

Note that not all agents represent all cruise lines. They may limit their offerings to one or two mainstream, premium, and luxury lines (this maximizes their sales with the lines, increasing their commissions). Be cautious about being pushed to a line just because the agent wants to earn more. A good agent should ask questions about your specific vacation preferences and book accordingly.

Generally, you'll get more personalized care from a smaller agency rather than the mega online agencies such as Travelocity.com, Expedia.com, or Orbitz.com and big agencies that specialize in cruises (icruise.com, Cruise.com, Cruise411.com, 7blueseas.com). That said, the big agencies do have phone numbers you can call and/or online chat forums where you can ask questions. Get the name and direct number of the agent you deal with, if possible, in case you have follow up questions.

How Agents Save You Money

The cruise lines tend to communicate deals to their top agents first, before they appear in public. Some of these deals will never appear in your local newspaper, on bargain travel web sites, or even on the web sites of the cruise lines themselves.

Some of these promotional offers are confusing, but good agents know how to play the game. For example: A line offers a "guarantee cabin" promotion that allows you to book a category of cabin rather than a specific cabin, and guarantees that your cabin will be in that catego-ry or better. An informed agent can direct you to a category where your chances of an upgrade are better. The cruise lines will also sometimes upgrade passengers as a favour to their topproducing agents.

Depending on the agency you choose, you may run across other incentives for booking through an agent. Some agencies buy blocks of space on a ship in advance and offer it to their clients at a reduced "group" price. Others may throw in perks such as a bottle of champagne.

Remember: Always make sure you understand what's included in any fare you are quoted to determine if you're actually realizing any savings. Is it cruiseonly or does it include port charges, taxes, and fees? How much are airfare and airport transfers? Is insurance extra? One agent/web site might break down the charges in a price quote, while another bundles them all together. Make sure you're comparing apples with apples when making price comparisons.

Beware Scams

The travel business tends to attract its share of scam artists. If you get a solicitation by phone, fax, mail or e-mail that doesn't sound right from an agency (especially if you're told you won a free cruise), call your state consumerprotection agency or the local office of the Better Business Bureau, or call the cruise line and see if they've ever heard of the agency.

Protect yourself by making sure the deposit you pay goes directly to the cruise line rather than into a travel agency account – if that's not the case, be wary. And always use a credit card to pay the bill if that's an option.

CRUISE LINE LOYALTY PROGRAMMES

Cruise lines' loyalty programmes — the equivalent of airlines' frequent flyer programmes — are in a state of upheaval. The idea — which centers on rewarding loyal travelers with extra perks, such as onboard cocktail receptions and exclusive discounts — originated some 160 years ago withCunard and continues in a variety of forms today. However, as more people turn to cruising for their vacations and repeat with the same line, loyalty club membership numbers are swelling into the upper echelons. And that can be expensive for cruise lines.

On one end of the spectrum is Azamara, which upset many of its frequent passengers in 2014, when it tried to remove many of the most valuable perks including free laundry and Internet minutes. Uproar over the change forced the line to roll back some of its changes. Carnival, similarly upset many of its loyal passengers in 2012 when it expanded its loyalty programme to five tiers from two, making it more difficult to get to a higher tier, while also downgrading some members to a lower membership level and taking away perks loyal cruisers had previously enjoyed.

On the other side are cruise lines that have expanded the perks of their programmes or are making it easier for cruise travelers to attain uppertier status. Crystal Cruises, for instance, announced that as of fall 2014, any member of its Crystal Society programme will get 60 minutes of free Internet access every day of his or her cruise.

Princess rewards big spenders (namely suite guests and solo travelers who may have to pay twice the regular rates to get a cabin to themselves) with a faster track up the ranks of its past passenger programme. Celebrity added benefits to its programme a few years ago, including free or discounted laundry service, complimentary Internet packages and new parties for all Captain's Club members. Oceania has also added a wealth of perks, including a free cruise and $1,000 in onboard credit — but these benefits are only available to frequent cruisers who have sailed between 21 and 100 times with the cruise line.

If you don't have the vacation time (let alone the money) to cruise multiple times a year and attain those uppertier perks, is it worth your while to stick with one cruise line over another? Here, we take a look at the tier structures, perks and membersonly discounts offered to repeat passengers, so you can decide based on your travel habits.

Still on the fence? We give seven reasons why you should be loyal to your cruise line.

Azamara Club Cruises	MSC Cruises
Carnival Cruise Lines	Norwegian Cruise Line
Celebrity Cruises	Oceania
Costa Cruises	P&O Cruises
Crystal Cruises	Princess Cruises
Cunard Line	Regent Seven Seas Cruises
Disney Cruise Line	Royal Caribbean International
Fred. Olsen	Seabourn Cruises
Holland America Line	Silversea Cruises
Hurtigruten	Windstar Cruises

AZAMARA CLUB CRUISES

The Programme: Le Club Voyage is a fivetiered programme that has some reciprocal rewards with the Captain's Club on Celebrity Cruises and the Crown and Anchor Society on Royal Caribbean. Points are earned based on the length of your cruise and category of your stateroom.

Adventurer – up to 149 points
Explorer – 150 to 299 points
Discoverer – 300 to 749 points
Discoverer Plus – 750 to 2,999 points
Discoverer Platinum – 3,000 points and up

Perks: Preferential services such as presailing dining reservations, first crack at shore excursion waitlists and priority tender service give past passengers VIP status. (Perks vary by level.) Lower-level members get perks like access to a dedicated host, free Internet, an invitation to Le Club Voyage parties and spa discounts. As you move up the tiers, perks start to include complimentary laundry, more free Internet, greater discounts and, best of all, free nights.

The free nights start immediately upon moving from Adventurer to Explorer level, with two nights awarded. On progressing to Discoverer level, four free nights are awarded. Discoverer Plus members receive a onetime reward of six free nights, plus three more free nights at 1,500 points and three more at 2,250 points. Discoverer Platinum members receive a onetime reward of 10 free nights, plus three more free nights with every 750 points earned, without limit. Free nights can be redeemed on cruises of seven nights or longer; the fare will be prorated based on the pernight price of the cruise.

MembersOnly Deals: Le Club Voyage members are offered several special discounted sailings per year through the newsletter and in the membersonly section of the web site. Based on space available (priority determined by member level), members also may upgrade for $199 per person ($389 for single occupancy passengers). Compare prices to verify the savings.

Drawbacks: Free nights must be booked within 12 months of reaching the new membership tier.

CARNIVAL CRUISE LINES

The Programme: Carnival's fivetier Very Important Fun Person (VIFP) Club is available to all passengers, whether they've sailed yet or not.

Blue – Never sailed through first sailing
Red – Up to 24 cruise days
Gold – 25 to 74 days
Platinum – 75 to 199 days
Diamond – 200 days and up

Perks: Benefits start with a free bottle of water, and progress to include priority checkin, boarding, debarkation, tender boarding, and restaurant and spa reservations. At higher levels, perks also include VIFP parties, member pins, free laundry, casino discounts, complimentary specialty restaurant meals, and a one-time free cabin upgrade or free fares for third and fourth passengers in one cabin.

Members who sail on "milestone" 25th, 50th and 75th Carnival cruises receive shipboard credits of 25, 50 or 75 percent of the cruise fare paid, respectively. On the 100th milestone, a complimentary Caribbean, Mexican Riviera or Alaska voyage of up to eight days is offered.

Members-Only Deals: Occasional specials are offered to all past passengers, but they're not that great of a bargain. Shopping around can sometimes net a lower rate.

Drawbacks: True benefits don't really kick in until a member has sailed at least 75 days.

CELEBRITY CRUISES

The Programme: The sixtiered Captain's Club has some reciprocal rewards with Le Club Voyage on Azamara Club Cruises and the Crown and Anchor Society on Royal Caribbean. Points are earned based on the length of your cruise and category of your stateroom.

Preview – 0 points (must sign up prior to first cruise)
Classic – 2 to 149 points
Select – 150 to 299 points
Elite – 300 to 749 points
Elite Plus – 750 to 2,999 points
Zenith – 3,000 points and up

Perks: Celebrity's points system rewards those people who cruise frequently in a lower-level cabin, as well as those who sail less frequently in higher-category cabins. Passengers who enroll in the programme before their first cruise are considered Preview members, and receive access to the Captain's Club Loyalty Desk and a Captain's Club newsletter. All levels have access to the loyalty desk and host, upgrade opportunities and limited seating set aside for specialty restaurant reservations.

All members also receive an onboard discount booklet, a free scoop of gelato, discounts on Internet packages or free Internet (varies by tier) and an invitation to the Captain's Club Celebration. As members progress through the tiers, perks start to include free pressing, priority embarkation, priority tender service, access to the Captain's Club Lounge, one free port day access to the Persian Garden, free laundry and dry cleaning, private debarkation departure lounge, discounts on specialty dining and beverages, and more parties. At the highest level, members receive access to Michael's Club Lounge, a beverage package, complimentary laundry, upgraded bath amenities, priority seating in the theater, and a 1,600-minute Internet package. Best of all, Zenith members receive a free seven-night Caribbean or Bermuda cruise in a balcony stateroom when they reach that milestone.

Drawback: Some of these benefits are included with a higher-class cabin on Celebrity ships, so they are not completely exclusive to past passengers.

Members-Only Deals: Captain's Club members are offered several special discounted sailings per year, some of which can be a good deal compared to retail rates, especially if they also include an onboard credit or discount certificate. Compare prices to verify the savings.

COSTA CRUISES

The Programme: Costa Club is a four-tiered system. You get points for days sailed (100 points for each day) and money spent onboard (40 points for every 52 euros spent).

Aquamarine – Up to 2,000 points

Coral – 2,001 to 5,000 points

Pearl – 5,001 to 13,000 points

Gold Pearl – 13,001 points (must have been on three cruises in the past three years)

Perks: All members receive souvenir photos, Captain's Cocktail invitations, in-cabin treats, and discounts on branded items, spa and beauty services, Internet and wine packages, minibar items, laundry services and spa products (discount varies by tier). Higher-tier members receive priority boarding and/or embarkation, free bottle of sparkling wine, in-cabin dinner service, free specialty restaurant meal, casino chips and a VIP waiting room in cruise terminals (where available).

Members-Only Deals: Costa Club members are offered 5 percent off select sailings — which they can extend to travel companions staying in the same cabin. Throughout the year, they'll be notified of extra discounts on an additional selection of departures.

CRYSTAL CRUISES

The Programme: Crystal Society members earn credits based on cruises sailed. Credits vary by cruise length: 5- to 15-day sailings earn one credit, while 16-day or longer sailings earn two credits. Basic perks are offered to all members, varying by cabin category, with the most significant perks rewarded for milestone sailings.

Perks: All Crystal Society members receive a Crystal Society tote bag and lapel pin, as well as invitations to exclusive Crystal Society shore excursions and Passport, a quarterly magazine. A Crystal Society host or hostess is available to members on every sailing. Depending on milestone level, members will receive additional perks. For example, you begin with a one-time onboard credit of $150 to $200 (after five cruises), progress to a free upgrade (after 10 cruises), snag a free weeklong cruise (after 30 cruises) and progress to $300 shipboard credit (after 55 cruises). The ultimate prize for the 100-cruise mark: A free cruise up to 12 days long in the Crystal penthouse, with a private dinner in the Vintage Room. Crystal's Society Sailings (there are usually one to two each year) offer special programming, onboard parties and events.

Members-Only Deals: All Crystal Society members are eligible for the Crystal Society savings, available on every cruise.

CUNARD LINE

The Programme: The multitiered Cunard World Club bases its levels on cruises taken.

Silver – One cruise completed
Gold – Two cruises or minimum 20 nights sailed
Platinum – Seven cruises or minimum 70 nights
Diamond – 15 cruises or minimum 150 nights

Perks: All members enjoy notification of special offers, a dedicated Cunard World Club Desk shoreside for telephone assistance, onboard representatives and a dedicated Cunard World Club web site. As members progress through the tiers, they receive tier pins, free Internet, cocktail party invitations, preferred reservations in specialty restaurants, savings on laundry, priority check-in, embarkation and disembarkation in select ports, free wine tastings, priority luggage delivery and a free meal at a specialty restaurant.

Members-Only Deals: Special rates are offered to World Club members on select sailings, which might include upgrades and/or onboard credits.

Drawback: You will only get the benefits of the membership level you have reached prior to embarkation. If you reach enough days sailed for a new level while you are on a cruise, you will have to wait until your next cruise to receive any of those benefits. Also, doublecheck the special fares to see if they really are better than the rates you can get on your own.

DISNEY CRUISE LINE

The Programme: The multitiered Castaway Club has only three levels, based on number of cruises sailed.

Silver – One to four cruises
Gold – Five to nine cruises
Platinum – Ten or more cruises

Perks: Once you have sailed, you are automatically a member. All members receive special booking offers, in-room amenities not offered for purchase and a lanyard upon check-in at the port. Gold and Platinum members also receive an onboard reception, an earlier booking window, merchandise discounts and, for Platinum members, priority check-in and boarding and a free dinner at Palo.

Members-Only Deals: Disney ships sail full all the time; very few dates are offered at a discount. However, members do receive exclusive discounts on select merchandise.

Drawbacks: Compared to the past-passenger perks of other cruise lines, this programme offers very little.

FRED. OLSEN CRUISE LINES

The Programme: In the multitiered Oceans programme, passengers earn one cruise point for every night sailed.

Blue – Up to 30 points
Silver – 31 to 100 points
Gold – 101-plus points

Perks: Perks include discounts on onboard spending and shore tours booked prior to departure, advance notice of next season's cruises, and an invitation to the Oceans Cocktail Party onboard. Top-tier customers (Silver and Gold) receive 5 percent off their onboard account, while Gold passengers also receive 5 percent off prebooked tours, in addition to priority boarding in U.K. ports, personalized luggage labels, free shuttle bus passes and a welcome gift.

Members-Only Deals: The top tier receive a 5 percent discount when booking at least six months in advance of departure date, while the second tier gets the same discount for booking at least nine months in advance of departure. The third tier must book at least 12 months in advance of departure to get the 5 percent discount.

HOLLAND AMERICA LINE

The Programme: As members of the multitiered Mariner Society, passengers earn credits based on days sailed, with double points for suite guests and one bonus credit for every $300 spent onboard (limit one credit per day).

One Star – At least one cruise sailed
Two Star – 30-plus credits
Three Star – 75-plus credits
Four Star – 200-plus credits
Five Star – 500-plus credits

Perks: All members receive invites to an exclusive Mariner embarkation lunch and complimentary Champagne brunch during the cruise, a collectible gift and a subscription to Mariner magazine. Among the additional perks members earn as they progress through the tiers are lapel pins; varied discounts on logo clothing, specialty dining charges, Internet packages, Explorations Cafe purchases, wine packages, minibar purchases, and spa treatments; free wine tastings, laundry and pressing; priority disembarkation, tendering and check-in; complimentary day pass to the Greenhouse Spa thermal suite; free dinners at the Pinnacle Grill; and a free cooking class at the onboard Culinary Arts Center.

Members-Only Deals: All Mariner Society members receive special offers on select sailings (typically 5 to 20 percent off), but — as always — check the savings against the regular discount rates available. In addition, One-Star, Two-Star and Three-Star members receive a 50 percent discount on third and fourth passengers in a stateroom on select sailings, while Four- and Five-Star members get free third and fourth passengers on select cruises.

HURTIGRUTEN

The Programme: The 1893 Ambassador Programme is one size fits all.

Perks: Past-passenger perks include fruit baskets delivered to your cabin, free bicycle rentals and a quarterly newsletter.

Members-Only Deals: Loyalty programme members receive cruise discounts, including 5 percent off Norwegian Coastal Voyages and Explorer Voyage sailings. Discounts can be combined with early-booking rates and group discounts. Members are also eligible for a 5 percent discount on select shore excursions during Norwegian Coastal Voyages.

Drawbacks: The 1893 Ambassador programme does not have tiers like other lines' programmes, so cruising more does not get you additional perks.

MSC CRUISES

The Programme: MSC Cruises revamped and renamed its MSC Club in July 2015, adding a fifth tier of membership — Welcome — removing the age restriction (previously 14-years-old) to join and renaming it the MSC Voyagers Club. Levels (Welcome, Classic, Silver, Gold and Black) are no longer based on cruise nights, but on what cruise 'experience' (i.e. what type of cruise) you book, and the number of onboard extras such as spa treatments and shore excursions that you pre-book. 100 points are awarded for every €/$150 spent.

Welcome – 0 to 99 points
Classic – 1 to 2199 points
Silver – 2200 to 4299 points
Gold – 4300 to 9999 points
Black – 10000 points and up

Perks: Classic and above are invited to an exclusive MSC Club welcome cocktail reception, have a dedicated help desk onboard and are have various special offers onboard. Discounts (varying by membership level) are given via a members discount booklet onboard on minibar items, spa treatments, MSC logo items, specialty restaurant charges and Internet packages. Freebies (varying by membership level) include fruit baskets, bottles of Champagne, dinner with the captain and a pass to the onboard thermal suite.

Members-Only Deals: All members get a five per cent discount on early-booking rates, without seasonal restrictions. Members also qualify for discounts of an additional 5 per cent or 15 per cent off a selection of cruises known as the Voyages Selection (an extra discount is dependent of sailing selected). Silver, Gold and Black card members will also receive €/$50 of onboard credit per person when booking a cruise from the Voyages Selection.

NORWEGIAN CRUISE LINE

The Programme: As part of Norwegian's Latitudes rewards programme, members earn one point for each cruise night traveled with extra points earned for booking a suite or Haven accommodations, booking nine months or more in advance, or taking advantage of monthly insider offers.

Bronze – One to 19 points
Silver – 20 to 47 points

Gold – 48 to 75 points

Platinum – 76 points and up

Perks: All members receive monthly offers for onboard credits of up to $250 on select sailings; priority check-in; a complimentary subscription to the Latitudes Rewards online magazine; access to an onboard customer service representative; a ship-specific lapel pin; and onboard discounts (varying by tier level).

Most ships also offer members-only cocktail receptions. Additional perks, varying by tier, include in-cabin chocolates, priority disembarkation and tender tickets, concierge service, a free dinner and wine in Le Bistro, an exclusive behind-the-scenes tour and a bottle of sparkling wine.

Members-Only Deals: All members have access to insider offer sailings with onboard credit, as well as exclusive rates offering discounts on select sailings. Members also receive a 10 percent discount on all Norwegian logo merchandise at the duty-free shop and discounts on Internet packages. Silver members and above also receive 15 to 25 percent off photos and spa treatments on port days.

OCEANIA CRUISES

The Programme: Once you've taken your first cruise, you are automatically enrolled in the multitiered Oceania Club. Passengers earn cruise credits based on the length of each sailing they take, and qualify for tiers based on the total number of credits earned.

Blue – Two to four credits

Bronze – Five to nine credits

Silver – Ten to 14 credits

Gold – 15 to 19 credits

Platinum – 20 to 39 credits

Diamond – 40 or more credits

Perks: All members receive membership pins, invitations to an exclusive cocktail reception, varying discounts on Oceania Cruises logo merchandise and members-only offers. Additional perks, which accumulate as members move through the tiers include discounts on Internet and beverage packages, as well as shore excursions, prepaid tips, free spa treatments, and air deviation fee waivers and a free cruise. Members also get shipboard credit on every cruise they book: $200 for bronze level members, $400 for silver, $500 for gold, $600 for platinum and $1,000 for platinum.

Members-Only Deals: Members receive periodic special offers on select sailings and advance notice of new itineraries. Other offers include onboard savings on future cruises and savings on new bookings made 45 days or less after debarking from your last voyage. Plus, members gain access to the Oceania Club Web page for special announcements and to view past sailings.

P AND O CRUISES

The Programme: Passengers are automatically enrolled in the multi-tiered Peninsular Club once they have accrued 150 points, with each night spent onboard a P and O Cruises ship worth 10 points.

Pacific – 150 to 500 points

Atlantic – 501 to 1,000 points

Mediterranean – 1,001 to 2,000 points

Caribbean – 2,001 or more points

Baltic – 2,501 points and 80 to 200 nights spent onboard in the three years preceding the start of the next cruise

Ligurian – 2,501 points and more than 201 nights spent onboard in the three years preceding the start of the next cruise

Perks: There are few real benefits at the lower levels; the best benefits kick in at the Caribbean level — priority specialty dining bookings, an onboard cocktail party, a discount on P and O insurance, and dedicated check-in and priority embarkation on cruises departing from Southampton. Baltic and Ligurian members get even more perks, including early embarkation and priority cabin access with expedited luggage delivery and a 50 percent laundry discount.

Members-Only Deals: Members receive a discount of 5 to 10 percent off drinks, souvenir items, shore excursions and spa and salon treatments, depending on membership tier.

Drawbacks: There are no discounts offered on future cruise purchases. Also, to maintain status in the very highest membership tiers, you have to be cruising with P and O very regularly. Passengers who have the points but drop below the 80-nights-within-three-years' period needed for the two highest levels get kicked back down to the previous level.

PRINCESS CRUISES

The Programme: Princess Cruises passengers qualify for the four tiers of the Captain's Circle based on either cruise credits or days cruised (whichever is higher). All passengers receive one credit for each cruise taken, and receive extra credits for each cruise booked in a suite or as a solo traveler occupying a cabin alone.

Gold – After first cruise completed

Ruby – After fourth cruise, or 31 to 50 days

Platinum – After sixth cruise, or 51 to 150 days

Elite – After 16th cruise, or 151-plus days

Perks: Other than a membership pin, monthly newsletter and onboard cocktail party, the program's genuine perks lie with folks who achieve Platinum or Elite status.

Princess members in these tiers receive a free Internet credit of 150 to 500 minutes depending on length of sailing. Other hightier perks include expedited embarkation, an exclusive lounge for disembarkation, free dry cleaning and laundry while onboard, priority tender embarkation, priority disembarkation, complimentary shoe shines, afternoon tea served in-cabin, daily canapes, a free wine tasting event on request and complimentary minibar setup (refills are not included). Elite members also get a 10 percent discount on boutique purchases.

Members-Only Deals: Members get access to special pricing on certain cruises, but check against the regular quoted price to see what kind of "deal" you are getting. Plus, all members of the Captain's Circle may benefit from up to $100 in early-booking discounts.

Regent Seven Seas Cruises

The Programme: The multitiered Seven Seas Society is based on nights sailed.

Bronze – Seven to 20 nights

Silver – 21 to 74 nights

Gold – 75 to 199 nights

Platinum – 200 to 399 nights

Titanium – 400-plus nights

Perks: Benefits include Inspirations, a quarterly magazine; special events including a private cocktail reception; and priority booking of online shore excursions and dining reservations. Complimentary garment pressing comes at Silver level and higher; free WiFi and priority disembarkation at select ports for Gold level and higher; Platinum members receive all these perks plus up to nine hours of in-room phone time, unlimited laundry services and free air deviation services; Titanium members receive private transfers to and from the airport (within a 50-mile radius) and free dry cleaning.

Members-Only Deals: Members get special offers on select cruises including early-booking bonuses with up to $5,000 off per person.

ROYAL CARIBBEAN INTERNATIONAL

The Programme: Members of the multitiered Crown and Anchor programme receive one cruise point for every cruise night sailed. Suite bookings earn double the points.

Gold – Three to 29 points
Platinum – 30 to 54 points
Emerald – 55 to 70 points
Diamond – 8 to 174 points
Diamond Plus – 175 to 699 points
Pinnacle – 700 or more points

Perks: All members receive quarterly eletters, invitations to onboard welcome back cocktail receptions hosted by the ship's officers and discount booklets. Real benefits do kick in at the lowest level with priority check-in, access to a private departure lounge with breakfast, an invite to a welcome back party, coupons to use onboard and matching status on Celebrity and Azamara.

Platinum members and up get invites to toptier events and lapel pins; Emerald members get welcome gifts. Diamond, Diamond Plus and Pinnacle Club members get priority waitlists for sold-out excursions and spa appointments, priority departure, special breakfasts and entertainment tours (where applicable). Diamond members also get access to a dedicated Diamond Lounge (where available — not all ships have them) or a nightly event in a designated lounge with some free wine (and discounted drinks).

Diamond Plus and Pinnacle Club members also get access to a Concierge Lounge (with free nightly happy hours), a personalized amenity and behind-the-scenes tours.

Members-Only Deals: Royal Caribbean offers special pricing on member sailings, but check to see if the benefits are really there. Platinum members and higher also get balcony and suite discounts on select sailings. Discount certificates worth $100 to $500 are sometimes offered for select cruises. Past passengers get notified first of any special sale fares (called Going, Going, Gone sales) and get a bonus when booking their next cruise while onboard.

Drawback: Points are not applied until after a sailing is completed so if you are graduating from one level to the next on your sailing, you will not receive the benefits of the next level until your next sailing.

SEABOURN CRUISE LINE

The Programme: Seabourn Club has five levels with points accrued through days spent cruising, and extra points for sailing in a penthouse or premium suite or on an escorted "Seabourn Journey," as well as for spending over $500 in eligible onboard or pre-cruise online purchases. Extra awards are given during milestone cruises (seven intervals between 100 and 2,500 sailed days).

Entry – One to 19 points
Silver – 20 to 69 points
Gold – 70 to 139 points
Platinum – 140 to 249 points
Diamond – 250-plus points

Perks: Tiffany pins are awarded on milestone number cruises. Members get a free seven-night cruise after 140 days and a 14-night cruise after 250 days. Club perks for all members include Seabourn Club Herald, a magazine published three times a year, and a captain's cocktail party. Plus, they can choose one to three onboard perks based on membership level: discounts on shore excursions or on premium wines and spirits; complimentary Internet packages; complimentary telephone use; a massage; day pass to the Spa Serene Area; or one free bag of laundry. Diamond members get all of the above, plus free laundry and pressing and daily delivery of a preferred newspaper. Frequent cruisers may also receive discounts on luggage shipping, travel magazine subscriptions and special luggage tags, depending on membership level.

Members-Only Deals: Past passengers receive a 5 percent discount for onboard future bookings.

SILVERSEA CRUISES

The Programme: Venetian Society, multitiered.
Entry – One to 99 days
Sapphire – 100 to 249 days
Emerald – 250 to 349 days

Ruby – 350 to 499 days
Diamond – 500+ days

Perks: The program's main perk is the ability to earn free cruises. You'll get a free seven-night cruise after you reach the 350-day milestone, a free 14-night cruise after you reach the 500-day milestone and then another free seven-day trip for each additional 150 days.

Other perks include ship visitation privileges for up to two visitors per Venetian Society member (must be requested 21 days in advance); an onboard Venetian Society party; and complimentary laundry (after 100 sailed days). Invite friends or family on certain sailings and receive double cruise credits and $250 in onboard credit on Venetian Society sailing dates, and 5 percent Venetian Society savings for friends and family.

Members-Only Deals: Members can sign up for the Venetian Value Club and receive offers for exclusive savings on sailings departing within 30 days. Plus, members receive a 5 to 10 percent discount, depending on tier level, on cruise bookings; this can be combined with other discounts once a member has passed the 100-day milestone.

Drawbacks: Silversea requires more days spent cruising to reach minimal programme levels that offer the "real benefits" than other upper-end lines.

WINDSTAR CRUISES

The Programme: The Windstar Yacht Club is one size fits all. Passengers are automatically enrolled after their first sailing.

Perks: Members of the Yacht Club, which replaced the previous Foremast Club, receive complimentary one-category cabin upgrades (dependent on availability), a welcome aboard gift, private member cocktail party and dinner with the captain or ship's officers.

Members-Only Deals: Yacht Club members receive a 5 percent savings on standard cruise fares. Plus, for every new friend or family member referred, Yacht Club members and their guests will each receive $100 in onboard credit.

CRUISELINES LOYALTY PROGRAMMES: IS IT WORTH IT?

Cruise lines often reward their loyal customers. This is a way to encourage repeat businesses.

There is little chance loyalty programmes to influence your first choice, but on most cruise lines, after the first cruise, you are automatically enrolled in cruiselines loyalty programmes.

It means a bunch of e-mails which advertise future cruises. Be-fore you dismiss the new status, remember thatrepeat cruisers are offered between 5 per cent and 10 per cent discount (sometimes even higher) on future sailings. You have a reason now for reading the next lines. Most of the cruiselines loyalty programmes have common features they start right after your first cruise and offer "repeat cruisers club only" free drinks' onboard reception. Each member gets subscription to the line's magazine and can receive special offers and inside news by mail or e-mail.

WHAT DO CRUISELINES LOYALTY PROGRAMMES OFFER?

Some loyalty programmes are generally far more rewarding. However, all cruiselines loyalty programmes worth joining. The special offers and onboard amenities will save your time and money. Take advantage of the loyalty programmes representatives onboard they'll help you manage your benefits.

Loyalty Programmes Discounts and Upgrades

More and more cruise lines reward their loyal passengers with discounts on voyages and cabin upgrades (Carnival), but some even provide free sailings (Silversea). Cruisers can also look for reduced prices on specialty dining (MSC), wine packages and shore excursions (Seabourn), fares for third/fourth passenger (Holland America). Discounts through cruiselines loyalty programmes will increase the more and more you cruise. Cruising25 times with Carnival, will get you 25 per cent off the cruise fare; sailing 50 times - 50 per cent off; 75 times - 75 per cent off; cruise 100 times - your week-long voyage is free (which is the ultimate prize for passengers' loyalty). Membership perksvary by lines. For example, "Princess Captain's Circle" loyalty programme enrolls you as Gold Circle member after the first cruise. If you book early on select voyages, you receive $100 discount per person. Another advantage is that you're eligible for half off standard deposit. Read more about Princess Captain's Circle and the various members' benefits. When assessing loyalty deals, better be aware of some catch. The offered discounts may not be combinable with the pricing deals you have found through a travel agent or online. Compare prices check elsewhere to be sure you are getting the best deal. And before booking, read the fine print first.

MULTITIERED LOYALTY PROGRAMMES

Cruiselines loyalty programmes vary according to the lines, especially the advanced levels. Only two tiers are offered by Carnival and 10 cruises are required to get to the top. NCL will get you to the second level after five cruises; the top tier is reached after 15, but the benefits include everything provided by Carnival and much more. Similar is Royal Caribbean loyalty programme, but with more levels and cruises required for getting to the top. The bottom tier of Carnival "Very Important Fun Person" includes Redmember benefits, reached after one cruise. All past guests are offered complimentary beverage at breakfast, lunch, or at George Lopez' Punchliner Comedy Brunch; and enewsletter, as well. On top are the Diamond members (with 200-plus days at sea). They are guaranteed specialty restaurant reservations and dining times; invitation to the captain's special cocktail party; complimentary dinner for two of their choice in the specialty restaurant; complimentary passport holder and luggage tag; onetime upgrade or a third/fourth guest sailing free; $100 contribution to St. Jude Children's Research Hospital; all the benefits of Red, Gold, and Platinum membership. Each line's version of perks is quite different. If you reach Princess Platinum status (after completing at least 51-day period at sea) your Captain Circle perks will include free Internet package. Elite status (150 cruise days) will also get you upgraded bathroom amenities, free dry cleaning, shoe polishing, canapés and afternoon tea in your cabin, and 10 per cent discount in shops onboard.

Faster Embarkation and Disembarkation

Cruise lines don't keep their most precious guests waiting. Several companies, including Princess and Carnival, offer embarkation and disembarkation priority privileges. Certain passengers are allowed to board the ship before the others, access their cabins first and avoid the long lines during debarkation. All Carnival passengers have an option to purchase the package "Faster to the Fun", which allows early boarding and other perks, no loyalty status is needed. While loyal Carnival members might not have rights to priority boarding, however benefit by not paying $50 like general public.

Do you want to feel like VIP? Many cruise lines allow guests access to members-only special lounges, such as Royal Caribbean Diamond Lounge and Celebrity Captain's Club Lounge; give invitations to some exclusive events (Carnival Gold, Platinum, Diamond Parties, P and O Portunus Club Party). Amenities in the restricted areas include free breakfast, appetizers, alcohol, or captain's recognition. Reaching the level of exclusive access can take time and money. Think in advance if the free glass of Champagne you'll take is worth the price of eight cruises.

LUXURY CRUISELINES LOYALTY PROGRAMMES

When the word comes about luxury lines, you'll be more likely to get free cruises if you sail frequently.Seabourn, for example, rewards the members of Seabourn Club with a free 7-days cruise after you've sailed 140 days at sea. After 30 sailings with Crystal, you can qualify for a free cruise. Each Silversea Venetian Society member gets a free 7-days cruise after completing 350 days at sea.

Regent Seven Seas offers one of the best loyalty programmes. Considering spirits and gratuities are included in cruise fare, after you add up to four hours phone time, free Internet access and a daily newspaper, their loyalty programme represents the most inclusive experience in cruising business. Oceania, often put in "deluxe" category, is simple yet substantial it offers true value benefits. You'll get progressively shipboard higher credits with each of the tiers, plus free spa treatments and free gratuities. Oceania gives $200 shipboard credit after five cruises on every next voyage you take. After ten cruises you can get $400 credit and prepaid gratuities - this equals total savings of $700 and even more per cabin.

MULTILINE LOYALTY PROGRAMMES BENEFITS

Repeat passengers may be able to use their loyalty programmes status for discounts on another line in some cases. Two are the parent companies which own lots of cruise brands and provide interchangable benefits. Sail on Princess, Carnival, Costa, Cunard or Seabourn and you qualify as Holland America Mariner program's member. All the listed companies share same owner - Carnival Corporation. For that reason, some of the loyalty programmes benefits are reciprocal.

These six cruise lines will occa-sional-ly offer loyalty discounts under the"World's Leading Cruise Lines" joint banner. However, the details about these interchangable benefits are too vague. For example, Seabourn Cruises promises free 14-days cruise after completing 140 days Seabourn cruising, but nowhere is indicated that it is exempted from WLCL VIP programme. Royal Caribbean Internationalowns Celebrity, Azamara Cruises, and Royal Caribbean Cruise Lines. The Royal Caribbean method to transfer benefits is more clearly defined and the benefits for Azamara and Celebrity are fully transferable.

The guests of Celebrity can join Royal Caribbean programme at any time at the same level. Royal Caribbean passengers can transfer rewards to Azamara or Celebrity. However, neither Royal Caribbean International, nor World's leading Cruise Lines lets combine points from all cruises into a single master acount. With Royal Caribbean you must pick whichever line has given the most points and claim for equal status at some of the other lines. WLCL rules are vague and not documented anywhere publicly available. Reciprocity is reserved for select cruises only. Don't rely on anything interchangable unless you check specifically with the line first and better get everything in writing. Other cruise lines are independent businesses, like NCL, Crystal, Oceania, Silversea and Regent. Each of these has no loyalty status transferability to any other line.

Free Services and Amenities

Those cruisers who are loyal to the line can benefit from a number of complimentary offerings, which includingphotos and casino play onboard Costa, Internet access onboard Seabourn and Princess, laundry serviceonboard Carnival and Norwegian, Holland America Champagne breakfast and alternative dining at NCL Le Bistro restaurant. After you start buying photos, win at the casino or surf the Web, you'll find that you cannot stop, even after you have used all freebies. Before you know it, quite a hefty bill will be accumulated. In addition to the stellar service on most ships, some cruise lines provide the most loyal members with concierge services(NCL), which can help in case you're trying to book spa treatments or shore excursions.

Gifts and Swag

Get cabin upgrades, priority checkin, print and e-mail promotions, depending on the times you've sailed. What you may also benefit from are shipboard perks as casino vouchers, invitations to cocktail parties, logo souvenirs, splendid treats (chocolatecovered strawberries), or free laundry. World Club members on Cunard, for example, only need to com-plete 20 days or two voy-ages and on subsequent sailings get two hours free Inter-net time. People who like to show their cruise love on the lapel, can get a pin which indicates the loyalty level status.

The more you cruise, that sta-tus increas-es. Lines often thank their guests by exclusive linebranded trinkets and tokens. For example, Holland America is famous for the specific line's commemorative tiles, RSSC doles out logowear, NCL offers branded pins, and Disney lanyards. Branded items, though not quite as elite, can also be snagged - try the onboard competitions like bingo and trivia. These items are meant to display, and it's free advertising for the cruise line. Hit top loyalty programmes reward on any line, even though not guaranteed, is aninvitation to sit at captain's table.

CRUISELINES LOYALTY PROGRAMMES RATINGS

- NCL gives the most exciting benefits among mainstream lines as they start with the sixth cruise; just 15 cruises are required for reaching the highest level and receiving a complimentary dinner, laundry services, "behind the scenes tours".
- Royal Caribbean benefits are also good, but may be not so much as NCL. RCCL requires 25 cruises for the highest level; the Diamond

level is reached just after 10 cruises. On Oasis and Freedomclass ships guests get a "Concierge Lounge" and a nightly happy hour with complimentary champagne or wine. Other RCCL ships offer nightly happy hours and concierge breakfast.

- Carnival requires just ten cruises to get to the top level. However, that level doesn't include a number of the better amenities you can get at NCL and RCCL top levels.
- Princess programme is number one in premium category with benefits like free Internet access and laundry services, wine tasting, "behind the scenes tours", and more.

Loyalty programmes are a personal choice about your vacation and the benefits go beyond monetary value measuring them must be more than value equation. Having the laundry done has small money value, but when the steward surprises you with clean clothes, it brightens the entire cruise experience. Better don't ruin your trip by tracking the value benefit of loyalty programmes little things. Consider not only the benefits offered, but how they integrate with the cruise you have chosen. Getting the benefits should be pleasure. Cruiselines loyalty programmes provide a variety of rewards. Every cruise is different. Even though rewards behind the different loyalty programmes can be substantial, they're just a part of the decision about cruise purchase. You still have to weigh the cost of your cruise, the value of benefits and your efforts required to obtain them.

HOW TO CHOOSE A CRUISE SHIP CABIN: WHAT YOU NEED TO KNOW

Your room on a cruise ship is called a cabin (or stateroom) and is akin to a hotel room, but typically much smaller. Choosing a cruise ship cabin can be fun and challenging at the same time, and not just a little bit frustrating on occasion. Cabins fall into different types or "categories," and some cruise lines will present as many as 20 or more categories per ship.

Before you get overwhelmed, it's helpful to remember that there are essentially only four types of cabins on any cruise vessel:

- *Inside:* The smallestsized room, with no window to the outside
- *Outside:* A room with a window or porthole (a round window) with a view to the outside, often similarly sized to an inside cabin or a bit larger; also known as oceanview
- *Balcony:* A room featuring a verandah that allows you to step outside without going up to a public deck
- *Suite:* A larger cabin, often with separate living and sleeping areas, and a wide variety of extra amenities and perks

It's the permutations (size, view, location, amenities and price, for example) of the four basic cabin types that can make choosing difficult. In addition to knowing your cabin options, you need to know yourself: Do you tend to get seasick? Do you prefer to nest peaceably on your balcony rather than hanging with the crowd around the pool area? Conversely, is your idea of a stateroom simply a place to flop into bed at 1 a.m. — no fancy notions necessary? Are there certain amenities you are willing to splurge on, or can you simply not justify paying for unnecessary perks? The answers will help guide you towards selecting the best stateroom for your money.

If you're feeling overwhelmed by choice, we'll help you get started with this guide to choosing the best cruise cabins for you and your travel party.

CABIN LOCATION ON THE SHIP

The "real estate" that your stateroom occupies, no matter the type, can make you seasick or keep you up all night with noise — or it can lull you like a baby and provide exquisite views of your surroundings. That's why doing your homework is important. Here are some factors to consider when picking your cabin's location on the ship.

Stability

If you tend to get seasick, cabin location is really important. It's a question of engineering, really. The lower and more central you are in a ship, the less roll and sway you will feel. Even if you choose a balconied stateroom, choose the lowest level and the most midship one you can find. The higher decks and cabins at the very front (forward) or back (aft) of the ship will rock and roll the most.

Distance

Some cruise travelers prefer their cabins to be near to (or far away from) specific areas of the ship. Sunworshippers might prefer an upperdeck location close to the pools and sun decks, while partiers might want easy access to midship entertainment hubs. Travelers with mobility concerns may prefer a stateroom close to a bank of elevators.

Noise

For some reason, most cruise lines assign their nicest and most expensive cabins to the highest decks, usually just below the pool deck (most likely because if you have a window or balcony, you have a more sweeping vista). Still, it's the pool deck that often causes the most noise problems, so if you don't want to hear scraping chairs at the crack of dawn or yeehawing pool parties until the wee hours, go down a level.

In fact, when it comes to noise, the best bet is to select a cabin that is both above and below other cabins. Other pitfalls include service areas adjacent to or above your stateroom; show lounges or bars adjacent to, above or below your stateroom; and selfservice launderettes across from your cabin. Other cabins that can be problematic are those that are situated low and at the back (because of their proximity to engine noise, vibration and anchor) or low and forward (because of bow thrusters).

CABIN SIZE

In this age of megaships, cabins now come in all shapes and sizes. In addition to the typical boxy inside and outside cabins, you can find expansive suites, duplexes and lofts. Balconies also range in size from small affairs barely able to squeeze in two chairs and a drinks table to huge wraparound decks with outdoor dining tables and hot tubs.

On many ships, basic inside and outside cabins are usually the same size, the difference being that one has a porthole or picture window to let in natural light. Balcony cabins can also be the same size as standard insides and outsides, with the addition of the outdoor space on the verandah; sometimes the interior space is larger.

A basic cabin, regardless of category, is referred to as a "standard" unless there is something about it that makes it different (such as physical layout, being handicapped accessible or a designated family cabin). With minisuites on up, you get bigger and bigger indoor and outdoor spaces.

For many travelers, the decision on what size cabin to get is directly related to price. Who wouldn't go for the huge suite if price were no obstacle? Yet it can be tricky to decide whether a balcony is worth the upgrade from a standard outside, or which suite to choose. Here are a few sizerelated considerations to take into account.

Outdoor Space

Do you need a balcony? Cruise travelers who spend all their time in the public areas — sun decks, lounges, restaurants — or on shore may be perfectly happy with standardsize cabins and no private outdoor space. Those who love to avoid the crowds and lounge quietly on their own verandahs or have private roomservice meals outdoors will surely want balconies. Don't forget to take your itinerary into account; on a chillyweather cruise, you might not be spending too much time outside, so depending on how much space and light you need, a balcony might not be worth the splurge.

Unique Layouts

Pay attention to the unique cabin setups on your ship, as they're not all created equal. Disney's four cruise ships, for example, have large standard staterooms designed to accommodate families. Even inside cabins may have a sleeping section that can be curtained off from the living area along with a split bath system. (One bathroom has the shower/tub and sink, another a toilet and sink.)Carnival is also known for having largerthanaverage standard cabins, while Silversea, Regent Seven Seas Cruises and Seabourn ships feature allsuite accommodations. Norwegian Epic cabins sport the "new wave" design, with curvy walls and separate rooms for showers and toilets; sinks are located in the main cabins. As mentioned earlier, cabins at the very front and back of a ship often have different layouts than the cookiecutter cabins that run the length of the ship.

Family

Since cruising has become a popular family vacation, more new ships have built "family accommodations" into the actual design. These are often suites, each with a separate room for the kids — sometimes a small alcove with bunk beds, sometimes an entire adjoining cabin. Families and groups can also take advantage of regular staterooms with third or fourth berths found in pullout sofas or pulldown bunk beds (called Pullmans). If you're going to squeeze your whole troupe into one cabin, make sure the space is big enough to accommodate the lot of you ... and all your belongings.

Solo Cabins

Very few ships actually have cabins dedicated to solo travelers. These will have sleeping space for one and can be quite small. The studio cabins on select Norwegian ships are the most famous example of this: The 100squarefoot staterooms each contain a fullsize bed, nifty lighting effects and a large round window that looks out into the corridor. If you're a solo traveler, you'll want to price out the cost of a solo cabin (usually somewhat higher than the doubleoccupancy rate of a similarly sized stateroom) compared to the cost of paying the single supplement (an extra fee tacked on if there aren't two people in a cabin; the price can come out to as much as double the regular rate) for a standard cabin. And book early, as solo cabins sell out quickly.

Suites

When it comes to choosing suite accommodations, it's best to figure out how much space you really need, what amenities are important to you and what you can afford to spend. Suites on most ships are often the first category to sell out, partly because there are fewer of them, and partly because they often offer extremely good value. For this reason, it's important to decide early what kind of suite you'd like.

Suites come in all shapes and sizes. For example, among the most over-the-top are Norwegian Cruise Line's 5,000-plus-square-foot, three bedroom Garden Villa suites on its Jewelclass ships. These each feature a private terrace with a hot tub, spacious living and dining areas, and butler service, plus access to an exclusiveaccess deck area. Other suites may come with dining areas, wet bars, deluxe bathrooms, walk-in closets, multiple levels and even pianos. On the other end, a minisuite (found on nearly all ships) is often just a bigger version of a standard balcony cabin, sometimes with more delineation between the living and sleeping areas.

CABIN AMENITIES

All cabins come with basic amenities, such as the services of a cabin steward to clean your room and turn down the beds, soap and shampoo in the bathroom, individual climate control, etc. But certain categories of stateroom come with added perks. Suites come with a variety of extras and privileges, everything from priority boarding to in-cabin bar setups. Spa cabins will offer sparelated perks, such as yoga mats in the cabin or a fancy showerhead; conciergelevel cabins will give you access to a concierge and niceties like afternoon canapes; and even solo cabins might offer extras, such as the use of an exclusive lounge. How do you want to be pampered on your vacation? Here are some extras you may want to sign up (and pay a premium) for.

Concierge Service

A concierge can take care of all those annoying practical matters you need to tend to on a cruise: making dinner and spa reservations, booking shore excursions, making requests of the front desk. Their services are included in the price of many suites, and on some ships the concierge has a desk in an exclusive concierge lounge where suite guests and highlevel past passengers can snack, drink and relax in private. Conciergelevel cabins may also come with incabins amenities including welcome drinks, fruit baskets or afternoon canapes.

Butlers

Having a personal butler can be a wonderfully pampering experience, and some cruise lines include the butler service as part of your fare when you select a suite or "concierge level" cabin. Look carefully at the difference in the cruise fare, and decide if it's really worth it.

Beyond that, look at the services that are offered; some cruise line butlers really do provide extra value. For instance, some can bring you room service from hardtogetinto alternative restaurants, refill your minibar to personal specifications, and serve incabin meals coursebycourse. Butlers can also unpack and repack your bags, draw rosepetal baths and assist you in preparing insuite cocktail parties.

Spa Cabins

Costa started the spa cabin trend, but many mainstream lines quickly followed suit. The concept is simple: Spa aficionados pay more for cabins decked out in Asianinspired Zen decor that come with extra amenities, ranging from fancy showerheads and specialty bath products to fluffy bathrobes, yoga mats and healthier room service menus.

Spa cabin residents are granted free access to spa restaurants (such as Celebrity's Blu or Costa's Ristorante Samsara), complimentary passes to spa pools and sauna/steam room areas, and may get free, discounted or priority spa treatments and fitness classes. And you don't always have to book a huge suite; on Holland America, several inside cabins have been designated as spa cabins with all the associated perks.

Exclusive Spaces

Some lines offer gatedaccess suite complexes where some of the most expensive accommodations are arranged around exclusive deck areas, including private pools, whirlpools, fitness centers, sun decks, restaurants and lounges; MSC Cruises' Yacht Club and Norwegian's Haven are two examples. Norwegian's studio cabins — although tiny inside affairs — also gain you access to a special lounge reserved just for solo travelers.

Other Amenities

Do you have to have a whirlpool bathtub or a walkin closet? Will you be entertaining and thus in need of a dining table that can seat six or eight? Do you want benefits like priority dinner reservations and being first in line to get on or off the ship? Do you want to be pampered with extraplush linens and bathrobes, fancy bath products and insuite coffee and booze? You can find those amenities and more in most of the upperlevel suites.

VIEW FROM YOUR CABIN

If what you see from your cabin is important to you, you might want to think about how cabin location impacts your scenic vistas. Consider both the direction in which your room faces, as well as how the ship's structure might get in the way of your view out to sea.

Forward and AftFacing Balconies

Aft balconied cabins (the ones at very back of the ship) can be the most prized standard balconied cabins afloat. Why? Because they can make you feel as though you are at the end of the world, offering 180° views over the stern's wake. (Read about the multitude of aftlovers.)

And the balconies are almost always at least 50 percent bigger than standard balconies located along the sides of the ship.

They do have a downside, though; they are at the very back of the ship and far away from a lot of activities. Plus, they are almost always "stepped out," allowing passengers in cabins above yours and those looking over the rail from the pool and other public decks to see down into your balcony. Some standard rooms and many suites are located at the aft "corners" of a ship, with balconies that curve around the sides. Take one of those, and you can see where you're going and where you've been at the same time! Frontfacing balconied cabins are almost always suites.

Promenade Cabins

Some older ships have cabins with windows looking out onto the openair walking track (called the promenade) that encircles the ship. These promenade cabins offer the advantage of easy access to fresh air without paying for a balcony. Holland America's Statendam-class ships, for example, have some outside cabins like this, but the line has transformed many of these originally outside cabins into "lanai" cabins with back doors that lead directly from the cabin onto the promenade. The two biggest drawbacks of promenadedeck staterooms are that they tend to be dark because of the wide overhang above the deck, and anyone can see into them when the lights are on. Don't forget to close those drapes!

Obstructed Views

Some supposedly "oceanview" staterooms actually have obstructed, or blocked, views due to the ship's structural design. These include balconied cabins under the pool deck overhang, which limits visibility; cabins above or adjacent to the lifeboats; and forward balconied cabins located close to the bridge wing.

But there is an upside to a blocked vista — they can be a good deal. If the amount of view you get relative to the amount of money you spend is important to you, look for "secret porthole" insides or "obstructed view" outsides. The secret porthole cabins are those sold as inside cabins that actually have windows with blocked views and the partially or fully obstructed cabins are sold as outsides but often at the price of an inside.

Interior Facing Cabins

Windowed and balconied cabins don't always look out to sea. For example, some Royal Caribbeanships have insideview cabins, with windows looking out onto interior public areas. Oasis-class Royal Caribbean ships, for instance, have inwardfacing cabins with views of Central Park (the ship's garden area with live greenery) and the Boardwalk (an amusement parkthemed stretch of ship with a carousel and food stands).

These are typically sold at a price that falls somewhere between the insides and outsides. Virtual views are the latest trend for inside cabins that wouldn't otherwise have a window. Disney and Royal Caribbean have created "magical portholes" and "virtual balconies" by using shipmounted cameras to play realtime images of the sea and port onto high-definition display screens, meant to simulate real cabin windows and add views and light to interior staterooms.

Scenic Views

If scenery is important to you, take a good look at your cruise itinerary before selecting your cabin, specifically if you are choosing an outside or balcony. On a roundtrip Caribbean cruise or a transatlantic crossing, for example, the side of the ship you are on doesn't really matter.

If, on the other hand, you are doing a oneway sailing (such as a southbound Alaska cruise or a trip from Barcelona to Rome), you might want to consider choosing a cabin on the side of the ship that faces the land. Sometimes the views can be breathtaking, and you won't get those views from the cabins that face out to the open sea.

No Views

Inside cabins with no views at all are typically the smallest, cheapest cabins onboard. They are great options for budget-minded travelers who don't intend to spend a lot of time in their stateroom, or who want to sleep all day in absolute pitch dark. They are less ideal for cruisers prone to seasickness, those who need natural light and groups who require a lot of incabin space. Not everyone will be happy in an inside cabin; it's worth upgrading if the lack of light will put a damper on your vacation.

CABIN PRICING

Only you know your vacation budget, but figuring out the best way to spend it can be tricky. Here's our primer on the most important things to know about cruise pricing as related to choosing a cabin.

Price Drops

Cruise fares fluctuate like airfares; they can change daily. Generally speaking, you'll find the lowest fares by booking early (eight months or more prior to sailing) or booking late (two to six weeks before departure). Often, fares drop just after final payment is due (about two months before sailing). But waiting for a higher-category cabin to come down in price to fit into your travel budget is risky; if the cabin category is selling well, fares will just go up.

Value Adds

When trying to determine how much cabin you can afford, don't forget to factor in the cost of the rest of your trip. If you have to spend a lot on airfare, precruise hotels and activities in port, you might not be able to afford the fanciest suite; if you're using frequentflyer miles or don't need to book a hotel, you'll have more money for cruise fare; the money you save on airfare can be used to spring for a nice stateroom. Or, look for valueadded perks from cruiseline and travelagent promotions. Offers for complimentary onboard cash, prepaid tips or included airfare can free up some money to pay for other vacation expenses.

Upgrades

While you can't count on the "upgrade fairy" to pay you a visit after you've booked that lowtier cabin, you can look out for upgrade deals before you book. One common cruise-line promotion is to offer outside cabins for the price of insides, or balconies for the price of outsides. Just be wary of any offer promising a two-category upgrade (or similar); the fine print usually indicates that the line will give you a "better" (whatever that means according to the line) cabin within the same category (inside to better inside, etc.). You will then be stuck with whichever cabin they give you — whether you agree it's better or not.

Guarantee Cabins

A "guarantee" cabin selection is one in which you pay a low rate for the cabin type (inside, outside, etc.) you are willing to take, but you allow the cruise line to select the actual cabin for you. If you luck out, you could get assigned to a higher-category cabin (e.g., book an outside guarantee and end up in a balcony cabin). On the flip side, you might get the worst cabin in the category you chose — the one that's slightly smaller or has a blocked view or is in a noisy corner of the ship. Letting the cruise line choose your cabin is risky, so be sure you'll be happy no matter which cabin you get assigned.

LUXURY ACCOMMODATION ON YOUR P AND O CRUISES SHIP

Throw open the curtains one morning and you might be greeted by the glistening Norwegian Fjords. Open them another and it could be Hong Kong harbour, the walled city of Dubrovnik or the sun rising over Venice. Imagine taking breakfast on your balcony with these iconic sights as your backdrop. Could there be any better way to start your day?

Your balcony is your own private hideaway; a breath of fresh air – literally! Leave the ship's activity behind as the pure ocean air washes over you and the warmth of the sun caresses your skin. This private space is somewhere to share special moments with loved ones too, whether it's watching a dramatic sunset fill the sky or catching dolphins dancing in the waves below. And to help you relax into your surroundings, on all cabin balconies you'll find comfortable chairs and a table, with the majority of suites enjoying the addition of steamer loungers.

ALL INCLUDED IN THE PRICE OF YOUR HOLIDAY

All our cabins are air-conditioned and well designed, to give you as much space as possible and to help you relax into your surroundings. Many feature balconies to give you additional outside space. All feature Egyptian cotton sheets, free tea and coffee making facilities, refrigerator, hairdryer, safe, in-cabin television and good sized ensuite bathrooms with toiletries pack. You will also enjoy the services of a personal cabin steward who will look after your every need, and can enjoy room service from early morning until late evening at no extra cost.

Inside Cabins

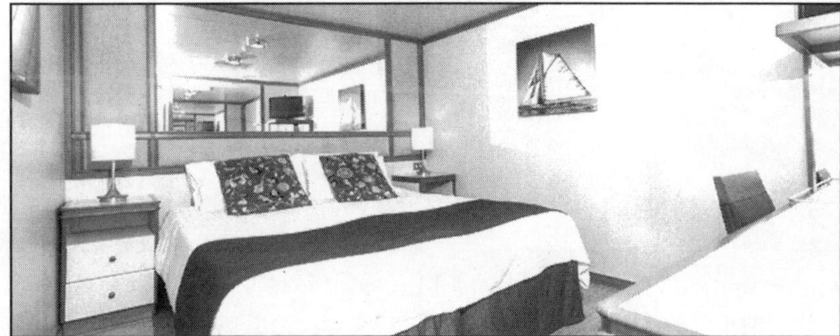

- Two lower beds convertible to a king-size bed**
- Bathroom with shower over bath or shower only and WC
- Outside cabins have a window or portholes, inside cabins have a mirror
- Some exceptions apply.
- When three/four passengers share a cabin with upper berths, for safety reasons the two lower berths cannot be pushed together.

Outside Cabins

- Two lower beds convertible to a king-size bed**
- Bathroom with shower over bath or shower only and WC
- Outside cabins have a window or portholes, inside cabins have a mirror
- Some exceptions apply.
- When three/four passengers share a cabin with upper berths, for safety reasons the two lower berths cannot be pushed together.

Balcony Cabins

Two lower beds convertible to a king-size bed**

- Bathroom with shower over bath or shower only and WC
- Chair and table
- Floor to ceiling sliding glass doors leading to balcony with table and reclining chairs
- On Arcadia the deluxe balcony doors do not slide, they open outwards
- Some exceptions apply.
- When three/four passengers share a cabin with upper berths, for safety reasons the two lower berths cannot be pushed together.

Suites

- Two lower beds convertible to a king-size bed**
- Bathroom with full-size whirlpool bath , separate shower , dual sink vanity unit and WC (The vanity mirror is fixed, but can rotate forward and backwards)
- Dressing area
- Iron and ironing board
- Lounge area with sofa, chairs and table
- Floor to ceiling glass doors leading to balcony with table and chairs and steamers
- Atlas and binoculars for use during your cruise
- Bathrobe and slippers for use during your cruise
- Magazine and newspaper selection (newspapers not available in minisuites)
- Senseo coffee machine (pods replaced daily)

Special touches

- Butler service (inclusive but optional)
- Mineral water on arrival
- Luxurious premier toiletries pack
- Daily canapes
- Fruit basket
- Flowers, Champagne and chocolates on arrival
- some exceptions apply
- when 3/4 passengers share a cabin with upper berths, for safety reasons the two lower berths cannot be pushed together.

Family Suites and Cabins

- Majority of twin cabins, beds fold down from the ceiling or out from the wall.
- In other cabins, minisuites and suites, the extra beds are sofa beds.

Single Cabins

- Choice of either inside (Arcadia, Azura, Britannia, Oriana and Ventura), outside (Aurora, Azura and Ventura) or balcony cabin (Arcadia and Britannia)
- One lower single bed
- Bathroom with shower and WC
- Outside cabins have a window or portholes, inside cabins have a mirror

BEST CRUISE LINES FOR ONBOARD ENTERTAINMENT

"Mamma Mia!." "Rock of Ages." The Second City comedy shows. Dinner theater with hightech twists. These diverse entertainment options used to be hallmarks of land vacations — until enterprising cruise lines brought them to the high seas.

While some cruise lines stick to the old entertainment standards, such as musical revues and poolside bands, others have taken entertainment to another level by offering unique and creative shows and spaces. They provide multiple entertainment options for every kind of cruise traveler, whether that's rock concerts, aerial shows, bigname lecturers, Minnie Mouse meet 'n' greets or Julliard performances.

Who are these trendsetters? They run the gamut from lines with megaships (especially the newer additions to Norwegian and Royal Caribbean's fleets) that can fit multiple performance venues onboard to more upscale lines like Cunard that aim for high-end enrichment and sophisticated evening pastimes. And while we tip our hat to a few small-ship lines, in general, extra onboard space paves the way for entertainment innovation.

Our top lines for onboard entertainment combine longstanding entertainment favourites with some impressive trendsetting.

CARNIVAL CRUISE LINE

Best Ships: Fleetwide, with Carnival Breeze, Carnival Freedom and Carnival Vista leading the way

Why: Carnival's "Fun Ships" are your best bet if you're looking for a variety of live music performances, elabourate and splashy production shows, and top-rated comedy acts. The line is constantly tweaking or adding to its entertainment options, and its ongoing fleetwide "Fun Ship 2.0" initiative has brought enhanced comedy shows, live concerts and superior DJs onboard.

Production Shows: Carnival has long used the latest technology to pull off lavish shows onboard, but its music-driven Playlist Productions, found aboard Carnival Freedom, Carnival Breeze and more than half of the line's 24-ship fleet, takes Carnival's entertainment offerings to the next level.

Using LED screens on stage and assorted special effects, four different hourlong stage shows are performed aboard each Playlist Productions-equipped ship, with a dozen stage shows total offered fleetwide, including "Getaway Island," with wow-factor 3D effects; "80s to the Max," channeling the era of questionable style and big hair; "Motor City," paying tribute to Motown and R and B; and "88 Keys: The Rock and Roll Piano Show," showcasing the music of Jerry Lee Lewis, Elton John and Billy Joel, along with other rock-inspired piano tunes. Carnival Vista will also host brand-new Playlist shows, though details have yet to be released.

Dinner and a Show: Carnival is well known for its singing and dancing waiters in the main dining rooms. They perform everything from old standards to Bollywood hits while parading by the dining tables and grooving on top of serving stations.

Mealtime serenades are taken to even greater heights at Cucina del Capitano, an Italian eatery found on select ships, where dining room staff sing alongside a giant Chianti bottle on wheels.

Live Music: Daytime chillin' includes solo guitarists in the RedFrog Pubs on several ships and on lido decks throughout the fleet. (You'll feel like you're at a beachside watering hole.).

At night, passengers can groove to themed bands ('80s, Woodstock, etc.) at the RedFrog Pub or elsewhere on the ship. If cover bands won't cut it, consider booking one of the line's 2014-debuted Carnival Live Concert Series cruises (spanning numerous itineraries and ships), which host ticketed shipboard concerts while vessels are docked in port (in Cozumel, Mexico; Nassau, Bahamas; and St. Thomas, USVI). They feature acts like Boston, Lionel Richie and Heart. While not technically live music, it's also worth noting that in partnership with DJ Irie (the official DJ of the Miami Heat), all Carnival DJs graduate from a first-of-its-kind DJ Academy at Sea, dubbed Spin'iversity, so you can be sure the nightclubs and deck parties are pumpin'.

Comedy: At night, check out the Punchliner Comedy Club fleetwide, putting on early-evening family-friendly shows and later adults-only comedy sets.

George Lopez is Carnival's "curator of comedy" and helps hand-select comedic onboard talent, with acts that have included Happy Cole, Nery Saenz and Billy D. Washington.

Top of Form

NORWEGIAN CRUISE LINE

Best Ships: Fleetwide, but especially Norwegian Breakaway, Norwegian Getaway, Norwegian Epicand Norwegian Escape

Why: Starting with the introduction of Norwegian Epic in 2010, Norwegian Cruise Line has shown an increased interest in entertainment, bringing on familiar names like Second City and Broadway shows "Rock of Ages" and "Legally Blonde." It has also introduced innovative concepts like the "Cirque Dreams and Dinner" show and the Illusionarium.

Production Shows: Passengers can rock out to tunes from their favourite '80s hair bands during Broadway's "Rock of Ages," playing on Norwegian Breakaway, or catch the comedic tale of a sorority girl with spunk via "Legally Blonde," on Norwegian Getaway. New for fall 2015, Norwegian Epic will put on Broadway show "Priscilla, Queen of the Desert," following the laughfilled adventure of three divas who set out in search of love and friendship. Norwegian Getaway, Breakaway and Epic also feature the sizzling Latin and ballroom dance team behind Burn the Floor.

Norwegian Escape presents two headlining, Tony Awardwinning Broadway musicals, including Harlem's Cotton Clubinspired "After Midnight "and "Million Dollar Quartet," featuring the music of Johnny Cash, Jerry Lee Lewis, Carl Perkins and Elvis Presley.

Dinner and a Show: "Cirque Dreams and Dinner" onboard Norwegian Epic and "Cirque Dreams and Dinner Jungle Fantasy" aboard Norwegian Breakaway are performed in the Spiegel Tent, the only "big top" at sea. The interactive entertainmentand-dining experience intersperses dinner courses with music, aerial performances and acrobatic feats. On Norwegian Getaway, the Illusionarium brings together dining, magic and illusion, featuring a series of magicians who perform special effects under a planetarium-style video projection dome. On Norwegian Escape, look for an exclusive supper club concept, "For the Record," combining motion picture soundtracks from John Hughes' 1980s teen films ("Sixteen Candles," "The Breakfast Club," etc.) with a postmodern cabaret.

Live Music: In the intimate Fat Cats Jazz and Blues Club on Norwegian Breakaway, passengers enjoy soul and blues from the work of B.B. King, Otis Redding and others — along with original music by the renowned house band, Slam Allen. Norwegian Getaway has the GRAMMY Experience, with live jazz and R and B performances by past GRAMMY Award winners and nominees. Or catch rock 'n' roll dueling piano show Howl at the Moon aboard Norwegian Getaway, Breakaway, Epic and Escape. The Jimmy Buffett-themed 5 O'Clock Somewhere Bar offers live nightly tropicsinspired music aboard Norwegian Star and Norwegian Escape. Epic currently has Legends in Concert, with performances and impersonations from Lady Gaga, Tina Turner, Michael Jackson and other celebrity lookalikes. New for fall 2015, Epic gets The Cavern Club, based on the Liverpool venue where the Beatles performed. It will present live British pop music, including — naturally — hits from the Fab Four.

Comedy: Famed Chicago-based improv comedy troupe The Second City puts on sets on several ships, including Norwegian Breakaway, Norwegian Dawn and Norwegian Gem, with early-evening family shows and late-night sets for the 21-and-older crowd.

Top of Form

DISNEY CRUISE LINE

Why: Disney Cruise Line knows how to entertain kids of all ages. After all, it benefits from the collected wisdom of the entire Disney corporation. From big production shows to Disney character interactions with starstruck kids at breakfast and tea time, the line does its utmost to keep everyone happy on vacation.

Production Shows: Disney film favourites are brought to life on shipboard stages with kid-friendly 45- to 60-minute Broadway-style performances that include highlights like Disney's Aladdin — A Musical Spectacular (on Disney Fantasy) and Toy Story — The Musical (on Disney Wonder). New for fall 2015 is Rapunzel-inspired Tangled: The Musical (Disney Magic). Other notable productions include Villains Tonight (Disney Magic, Disney Dream), a cheeky revue-style show featuring "the best of the worst Disney villains"; and Disney's Believe (Disney Dream, Disney Fantasy), with more than 20 Disney characters coming together for a moving father-and-daughter adventure musical.

Fig. *Best Ships:* Disney Magic, Wonder, Dream and Fantasy

Disney Dreams — An Enchanted Classic (Disney Magic, Disney Wonder), which tells the tale of a young girl who realizes the power of her dreams (with a little help from Disney characters, naturally), has been revamped to include a segment featuring the gang from Frozen (Anna, Elsa and Olaf). Finally, don't miss The Golden Mickeys (Disney Wonder, Disney Dream), an awards ceremony-style musical in which Disney characters walk the red carpet and compete for their prizes.

More informal but no less fun: On one night each cruise, Disney launches an all-out deck party (either themed on pirates or the film "Frozen"), complete with an interactive musical show, dance parties and atsea fireworks.

Dinner and a Show: Kids can start the day off right with character breakfasts — or, later, afternoon teas — where they can share a laugh with Goofy or a hug with Snow White. The Royal Court Tea on Disney Fantasy is especially notable, complete with visits from Disney princesses, storytelling, singing and dancing. Come dinnertime, the fleetwide Animator's Palate dinner show combines Pacific Rim cuisine with a high-tech space where animated Disney character sketches seemingly come to life.

Live Music: Adult cruisers will enjoy adult-focused entertainment in the nightlife districts aboard all four ships. The best bet for live music is the Cadillac

Lounge piano bar on Disney Wonder, touting a classic Cadillac them and live pianists tickling the ivories.

ROYAL CARIBBEAN INTERNATIONAL

Best Ships: Fleetwide, leading with Quantum of the Seas, Anthem of the Seas, Oasis of the Seasand Allure of the Seas

Why: Royal Caribbean has long been at the forefront of innovative onboard entertainment, introducing unique offerings never before seen at sea on its new ships over the years. It's the first (and only) line to offer ice skating shows in an onboard rink and water-based acrobatic shows in a pool-based stage area. Plus, it's brought Broadway to the high seas with shows like "Mamma Mia!," "CATS" and "We Will Rock You."

Production Shows: Catch lighthearted ABBA-scored musical "Mamma Mia!" (on Quantum of the Seas and Allure of the Seas — one of the best shows we've seen at sea); Broadway classic "CATS" (Oasis of the Seas); the music-of-Queen-inspired "We Will Rock You" (Anthem of the Seas); or "Saturday Night Fever" (Liberty of the Seas). The shows continue to receive rave reviews, and booking seats in advance of a sailing is highly recommended.

Royal Caribbean's ice shows have been fan favourites since they debuted on Voyager-class vessels in 1999. (They've since expanded to Voyager- and Oasis-class ships.) Watching professional figure skaters complete double axels and tricky spins while the ship rocks and rolls never gets old. The line keeps the shows fresh with updated offerings like Freedom-Ice.com onFreedom of the Seas, a 60-minute show featuring a dozen pro skaters.

Oasis and Allure, meanwhile, feature the AquaTheater, where divers and acrobats dazzle in the deepest pool at sea, complete with 30-foot-high diving platforms.

On Quantum-class ships, the expansive Two70 entertainment venue — a multimedia theater that combines virtual concerts, robotics, aerial shows and video projection — provides technology-enhanced spectacles like "Spectra's Cabaret" (Anthem of the Seas) and "Starwater" (Quantum of the Seas).

Royal Caribbean has also expanded vertically with the transformation of the popular Centrum areas aboard Vision-class ships into chic bars and performance spaces, which feature dazzling acrobatic displays that take place in the air above the audience.

Dinner and a Show: Catch the interactive Mystery Dinner Theater, where passengers play detective and the joke-cracking cast mixes in with diners at Portofino or Giovanni's Table, gourmet Italian specialty restaurants aboard 11 Royal Caribbean ships. (Shows are only available on sailings of seven nights or longer; advance booking is recommended.)

Live Music: Quantum-class ships tout rock 'n' roll temple Music Hall, where cruisers can rock out to cover bands of The Beatles, Bon Jovi and more, and dance to music spun by late-night DJs. Royal Caribbean entertainment also thrives in even smaller venues, including Oasis-class options like Jazz on 4 or the bustling Central Park areas that often feature small acts, including strolling musicians, duos and trios. You might even stumble upon the "stowaway pianist" on Anthem of the Seas, who sporadically appears around the ship with his piano, surprising passengers with impromptu sing-alongs.

Comedy: Sail aboard Oasis or Allure for the Comedy LIVE venue, hosting two headliner comedians with sets inspired by NYC's stand-up clubs.

SHORE EXCURSIONS

Snorkeling through coral reefs, exploring ancient Roman ruins, hiking on glaciers, shopping at local outdoor markets — all of these shoreside activities are as much a part of the cruise experience as enjoying the onboard amenities of your ship. Indeed, half the fun of taking a cruise is exploring exciting new places — tropical islands, bustling metropolises, exotic countries.

So to enhance each port visit (as well as to increase their profits), cruise lines offer organized shore excursions on all ships for additional fees. These land-based trips run the gamut from sightseeing city tours to cultural events and active pursuits. You can take a sunset pleasure cruise in St. Lucia, visit penguin colonies in the Falkland Islands, go wine tasting in Provence or rollerblade through Copenhagen. The tours can be booked onboard at your ship's excursions desk or online before you depart on your trip.

The benefits of booking ship-sponsored tours are many. You can skip the hassle of arranging your own onshore activities, you'll know the tour provider is licensed and reputable, and the ship won't depart until all of its tour buses have returned — even the tardy ones. You may also meet other shipmates whose company you'll enjoy back on the ship.

But ship tours are not always the way to go. The pleasurability and efficiency of tour operators varies from ship to ship, and some tour offerings are simply duds. All too often, shore excursions translate into time-consuming bus rides with drop-offs at shopping centers proffering souvenirs you can live without. For example, following a long, hot (but worthwhile) tour of the Acropolis outside of Athens, passengers who thought they were being driven back to their ship were squirreled into a tacky little shop, belonging to the tour guide's brother-in-law. Finally, you will often pay more for the privilege of letting the cruise line arrange your day than you would if you booked directly with a provider. To give you the skills to make the best decisions about your days in port, here is our best advice on what to expect from a shore excursion and how to make the most of your time ashore.

WHAT TO EXPECT: SHORE EXCURSIONS

Cruise lines offer a mind-boggling array of tours — everything from basic snorkeling trips to more involved, overnight tours to see the Great Pyramids in Egypt. Here's a primer on what you can expect to see on offer.

Active vs. Sightseeing Tours: Shore excursions cover all levels of activity and interest and vary greatly, depending on what's available in each destination. Active tours could be anything from water sports to ziplining, hiking, biking and dog-sledding.

Activity-based trips might feature a day at the spa or beach, a pleasure cruise on a sailboat, wine or food tasting, a cultural performance or a visit to a museum. Sightseeing excursions are typically bus tours that take passengers to the highlights and shopping areas of the port city or nearby destinations. Remember that excursions look different in different parts of the word. In the Caribbean, you'll find options like snorkeling with sting rays or transportation to private beaches; European tours focus more on sightseeing — for example, full-day tours from the port of Livorno to the museums and cathedrals of Florence or multi-hour lunches, featuring local produce, meats and wine at a farmhouse in Tuscany.

Full vs. Half-Day Tours: Shore excursions vary in length. Some take up all your time in port, while others are just a few hours of an all-day visit. Choose a full-day tour to see the most you can in one trip or for journeys to destinations outside the port city. A half-day tour might only focus on one specific itinerary — a three-hour kayak trip or a highlights tour of a city — but gives you free time to explore the port on your own before or after.

Guided vs. Free Time: Not all shore excursions involve busloads of tourists, dutifully following flag- or umbrella-waving guides. You will find these types of sightseeing tours, as well as athletic endeavors overseen by dive masters or hike leaders. However, some tours simply bring you to a destination where you're free to explore until it's time to meet the bus to go home, while others feature guided components, followed by an hour or two of free time.

Highlights vs. In-Depth: Some shore excursions — such as daylong trips from Tunis to the marketplace, museum and ancient Carthage – pack many activities into one trip. Others focus on one destination or activity, like a trip to the Mayan ruins from Cozumel. It's up to you whether you'd prefer to see many things for short amounts of time or focus on one place, in-depth.

Concierge or Boutique: Some of the newest trends in shore excursions include intimate tours that are limited to 25 or so guests. Many lines offer these "boutique" excursions, which could be cooking classes at a renowned French cooking school or a behindthescenes tour of the Hermitage in St. Petersburg. Many lines also offer car-and-driver packages (so you can customize your own tour) or have concierges to arrange shoreside activities exclusively for your travel party. You can skip the caravan of four large tour buses and trade up for a more exclusive experience.

SHORE EXCURSIONS VS. INDEPENDENT EXPLORATION

One of the biggest questions cruisers have is whether or not to take a ship-sponsored shore excursion. The answer banks on your budget, as well as your inclinations. Port tours vary in price, depending on the cruise line, and can run you anywhere from $40 per person for a simple beach break to hundreds of dollars each for such higher-priced options as helicopter rides, golf and long-day or overnight tours. Taking a tour in every port can quickly inflate your onboard bill.

Shore excursions are worth it if you want to venture to attractions that are located far from the pier, learn more about an area through a guide or participate in physical activities where gear is required (biking, diving, golf). However, if all you want to do is walk around town, shop or visit the beach, it could be much cheaper and less time-consuming to get a map and go it on your own. For instance, in St. Thomas, the shops are a stone's throw from the ship, but beaches are a cab ride away. (Although it still might be less expensive to hail a taxi to the beach than to participate in a tour.) And, in tiny Monte Carlo, the castle, cathedral and casino are all within walking distance of your ship. Don't forget about arranging your own transportation, too. In Hawaii, many ports offer on-site car rentals or rental agency pickups. In Barcelona, you can easily use a combination of local buses, the subway and hop-on, hop-off tourist buses to get around.

However, in big cities like Athens, Rome and Florence — which are far from the port — it may make more sense to spring for a tour. It is also wiser to take a shore excursion in any third world country or in foreign ports, where language and customs might prove to be barriers. For example, in Brunei, you would definitely want to take the guided tour to sites like the biggest mosque in Asia — Omar Ali Saifuddin Mosque. You'd probably never find it on your own. And, without guidance, you may not realize the necessity to respect local customs by covering your body from head to toe in long pants, long skirts and long sleeves. (Don't laugh — this happened on a recent visit. Luckily, the locals are used to this and have a few robes on-hand to loan visitors.) In Tunis, you might not wish to participate in the aggressive haggling, conducted by the taxi drivers at the pier. Opt, instead, for a ship-arranged tour to the souk or ancient Carthage.

The third option is the hybrid: Book your own tour in advance through a local provider. You can often save money by eliminating the cruise-line middleman, or customize the trip to your interests. However, remember that, while the cruise ship will wait for any late-returning, ship-sponsored tours, you run the risk of getting stranded in port if your independent tour gets stuck in traffic and is late returning to the pier.

ADVANCE PLANNING AND RESOURCES

Cruisers have multiple resources for researching in-port activities.

The secret to a wonderful day ashore is to plan ahead. Learn about the attractions in each port, so you can decide whether to book a tour or go it alone. For example, you'll want to know that Livorno is actually the port for Florence and Pisa, but both destinations are quite far from the port. It's also helpful to note that in the Greek Isles, Santorini does not have great beaches, while Mykonos is internationally renowned for its sandy spots. Planning ahead will let you balance relaxing beach days with days spent shopping, sightseeing or in active pursuits.

- Look up your cruise line's list of shore excursions with tour descriptions and prices. Many cruise lines have this information available online — you will also be sent a booklet of all the tours with your cruise documents. Some lines allow you to reserve tours in advance through their Web sites (see our Online Reservations feature) or through a travel agent.
- Once you know your itinerary, visit Cruise Critic's Ports of Call area for tips on spending your day ashore. You'll find information on the best excursions, as well as suggestions for restaurants, beaches and must-see attractions.
- Browse guidebooks on the destinations you're planning to visit. If you find that it's pricey to buy multiple guidebooks for all the regions your ship will visit, consider borrowing them from your local library and photocopying pertinent pages to take on your vacation. Or, buy a guide aimed at cruisers, such as "Frommer's Cruises and Ports of Call" or "Fodor's The Complete Guide to Caribbean (or European) Ports of Call."
- Contact the tourism bureau for your destination. Tourism Web sites typically offer a wealth of information, and the bureaus will often send you maps or print materials that detail activities, restaurants and tour companies. You may want to find out if there's a tourism office at or near the port, so you can pick up a map and get information.

Don't forget to come up with a Plan B, in case your desired tour gets canceled or is sold out. If you've done your research and have decided to book ship tours, think carefully about whether to book in advance or wait until you get onboard. It's best to book in advance for limited-availability excursions (like flightseeing in Alaska or Hawaii) and must-do tours.

(For example, if you'd be heart-broken if you didn't go snorkeling in Cozumel or to the Hermitage Museum in St. Petersburg, book in advance.) If you're uncertain or are happy with several options, waiting might be a good idea. Some cruise lines charge penalty fees for canceling shore excursions onboard or within 24 to 48 hours of the port call, so you might want to wait to see how the weather is or how you like the line's tours before booking all of your excursions.

HOW TO GET THE MOST FROM YOUR SHORE EXCURSION

Here are a few final tips to keep in mind in order to get the best experience out of your shore excursion.

- Read shore excursion descriptions very carefully to understand exactly how your time will be spent on the tour. Add up how much time is spent on the bus, driving between attractions, and compare that to how much time is spent at each destination. If you are unsure, ask the shore excursion manager to describe the tour in detail. You may have to decide between spending short amounts of time in a variety of places and getting an in-depth tour of one area, while missing out on several others.
- Some tours involve strenuous treks in hot, humid climes or long days with lots of walking. Cruise lines are typically good at pointing out which excursions are strenuous and even which are best for travelers with limited mobility. Be sure to pick tours that you can handle physically.
- Staff members who work aboard ships are great sources of information on the best local beaches, restaurants and shopping (since they often visit the same ports every week). Ask where they go — the purser's office is an especially good resource.
- Your final bill can add up if you buy a shore excursion in every port. However, in some ports — especially in Alaska, Europe or exotic destinations — shore excursions are the only way to go. Budget accordingly.

- If you are a scuba diver, check out local dive clubs in the islands you intend to visit. They are listed in information obtained from tourist offices.
- Hiring a private taxi is often less expensive than the ship's excursion, depending on the number of people you have in your group. When hiring a taxi, be sure to negotiate a flat rate — based on your destination and the approximate amount of time you'll need — before you depart. If you want narration in addition to transportation, choose a driver with a good command of English.
- When renting a car in port, it's always best to reserve it before departure; rates are lower, and you know the agency won't be sold out. Check with your rental company to find out whether you'll need an International Driving Permit (available through AAA and other automobile associations) or if your driver's license will suffice.

SHIP-SPONSORED OR INDEPENDENT SHORE EXCURSIONS: WHICH IS RIGHT FOR YOU?

Should you book your shore excursions independently of your cruise line — and save a few bucks — or is it better to take those tours offered through your ship?

The question we posed above is one of the most commonly asked by cruise travelers, and it doesn't have an easy answer. It all depends — not just on circumstances but also on the ports of call and the travelers' own penchant (or lack thereof) for independent travel.

And no question, for the most part cruise lines do charge more than non-cruise-related operators for just about the same tour. Sure, shore excursions are profit centers for the cruise lines, but you can consider the extra you pay as a kind of insurance. Cruise lines hold tour operators responsible for quality control as well as make sure that all necessities — liability insurance, registration and other areas of compliance — are complete. Plus, they guarantee that the ship will not leave before participants on a ship-sponsored tour are back onboard.

And while many of cruising's shore tours remain way too dependent on motorcoach tours that sweep through an area with little chance of personalization, the cruise lines are putting lots of effort into creating more active, handson and unusual experiences, ranging from cycling trips through European cities to cooking classes in Alaska and private after-hours tours at St. Petersburg's Hermitage. Often, you'd be hard pressed to put together the same tour on your own.

On the flip side, sometimes it's nice to escape the large group tours for more intimate explorations with just your friends and family. Plan a day on your own, and you'll see the sights you want to see and at your pace — rather than some prearranged plan by the ship-arranged tour guides. And saving money is a huge consideration when you're looking at flightseeing tours or other pricey expeditions that cost hundreds of dollars a person. If you trust the company and know you won't miss the ship, it certainly makes sense to pay less by booking independently a tour you could pay more for onboard.

Following is a set of rough rules that will help you decide between touring independently or booking cruise line travel:

GOOD TIMES TO BOOK CRUISE LINE-ORGANIZED TOURS

- You're a first-time cruiser. Visiting a port of call on a one-day visit to a foreign place is a whole lot different than spending a week at a resort or in a hotel. You've got a real deadline — that ship very well may not wait if you get lost and are a few minutes late. (And meeting up with the ship in the next port is on your dime.) Plus, ship terminals are often located outside the main tourist area, and it can be confusing to figure out how to get to the top attractions if you've never been to a port before. It's worth the extra money to book a few ship's tours until you've figured out the port-of-call drill.

- The port is particularly exotic. On my first cruise to the Middle East, a place as foreign in culture and language as anywhere I'd ever been, the comfort of the tours arranged by the cruise line was indisputable, especially in challenging places such as Yemen's Aden and Oman's Salalah. I'd also book cruise line shore excursions in smaller, more offbeat ports on Asian itineraries, in South Africa, South America (particularly in the Amazon) and in Russia's St. Petersburg.
- The port is a long ride from the main attraction. This applies particularly in Europe, where some of the most important destinations — i.e. Paris, Rome, Florence, Berlin and London — are miles and miles (and 1.5 to 3 hours away) from where the ship actually docks. In many cases, ships will arrange two types of outing. One is for independent-minded folks who want the ease of being transported — and then want to venture out on their own. Their only deadline is meeting the bus (or train) for the return journey in this traffic-congested part of the world. Or, you can opt for a variety of city tours. Similarly, in some parts of the world nature experiences can require quite a journey. Cruise Critic's Melissa Paloti, traveling on a round-the-horn cruise of South America, embarked on a Penguin Reserve at Punta Tombo tour while at Puerto Madryn. The trip, which lasted nine hours, featured a 2.5-hour drive — each way — to the penguin reserve.
- You want to experience a broad swath of a region. Paloti, on the same South America cruise, also booked a ship-sponsored excursion for the call at Puerto Montt. The eight-hour trip, including lunch, featured stops at three quite different locales — Osorno Volcano, Petrohue River and Puerto Varas — and would have been hard to replicate on her own.
- The cruise line specializes in a particular area. In some cases, cruise lines really go to a lot of effort to offer special shore excursions and tour opportunities. Want to learn to scuba dive in Costa Rica? Cruise Critic's Steve Faber tells us that "with onboard PADI instructors, Windstar's dive programme is second to none, offering not only ship-conducted dive trips, but also different certifications and specialties, everything from Discover Scuba to Advanced." (In other destinations, Windstar offers dive trips through its shore excursion programme.) Norwegian Cruise Line's Pride of America, which is exclusively devoted to Hawaii, not only offers an onboard golf pro and a rental shop for equipment, but ties them both together with chances to play at top courses on each island.
- It's a high-risk trip. When taking a tour that involves traveling on helicopters, planes, parasails and even boats, the extra protection

provided by the cruise line is really key. A popular tour on some South American cruises, for instance, is a day-long visit to Antarctica via airplane where weather might be a factor in getting you back to the ship on time. It's also even more important that such operators are properly vetted for safety issues. (However, for shorter trips like helicopter rides in Alaska, you could certainly do your own research — or find out which companies the cruise line uses and see if you can book them independently.)

GOOD TIMES TO TOUR INDEPENDENTLY

- The port is located close to downtown. Whether you're visiting San Francisco or Barcelona, these cities are so conveniently situated to cruise terminals that it couldn't be easier to get around via a short walk or taxi ride (one tip, too, is to research "hop on, hop off" bus options for sightseeing — they're a great way to get around and get your bearings). Other easy urban ports are Helsinki, Stockholm, Copenhagen, Nice, Cannes, Venice, Dubrovnik, Buenos Aires, Sydney, Auckland, Quebec City, Montreal, Honolulu, San Francisco, Seattle, Vancouver, Tampa, New Orleans and Philadelphia — to name just a few.

- You want a simple beach break. While cruise lines often offer beach "tours," particularly in the very well-known beach destinations of the Caribbean, it really is more cost effective — and more freeing, frankly – to simply hop into a safari bus for the ride to the beach. I wouldn't hesitate to do so at St. Thomas' Magen's Bay, Virgin Gorda's The Rocks, Grenada's Grande Anse, St. Lucia's Rodney Bay, and Grand Cayman's Seven Mile Beach. They offer major services (including eateries) and cab drivers flock there so you'll be assured a ride back to the ship. Where you need to be a bit more careful is with off-the-track beaches (I love any of the beaches in St. John, particularly the little-known Salt Pond, but would not want to count on taxi pick-up).
- You want personal attention and in-depth information. I've cruised twice to Russia's St. Petersburg. The first time I was one of 100 people on a city tour. The second? Through Red October, a tour agency, we arranged for a private guide and driver. The difference was immeasurable. We saw so much more with the latter, the experience was superb, and we never were rushed. Plus we made a connection with our guide and driver that we'll always remember. So in places that are particularly significant in an historic or cultural sense, a private guide can make the experience. Other places I'd recommend for this approach include Turkey's Ephesus and Italy's Venice. This approach, however, requires you to do serious homework; visit Cruise Critic'sdestination forums for recommendations of which ports are best suited to independent touring, and make sure guides are properly accredited. In some cases (and mostly on luxury lines) cruise lines will provide concierge services onboard that can book a guide for you — Regent Seven Seas Cruises, for instance, has a designated travel concierge — and you can assume these folks are properly trained, licensed and certified.
- You want to shop 'til you drop. Do a little homework before you leave home to map out the types of shops that interest you, and their locales ... and then just go. Note: Cruise ship staffers can be a great source of tips. One of my favourite finds came from a Celebrity Cruises' social hostess: a fabulous formal dress boutique in Antigua (alas, it's now closed); our own contributor Joyce Adamadis, a longtime onboard staffer, steered Paloti to a fabulous custom leather and sweater shop in Buenos Aires.
- Snorkeling, sailing and scuba are the order of the day. As long as you check out operators — start with tourist boards and dive clubs, and go from there — snorkeling, sailing and scuba diving expeditions

in major watersports ports such as St. Thomas or Grand Cayman are good bets for independent booking (the operators are often the same ones that serve cruise lines).

- You're traveling in a pack. If you're cruising with a large group of friends or family, it may be more cost effective for you to hire a tour guide, rent a car or take a taxi tour than to book sightseeing excursions through the cruise line. You'll have more control over where you go and the timing of the day — and you already know that you'll like the other people on your tour! This is also a useful strategy when you're traveling with kids who may need more breaks or play time than a ship's tour would allow. Traveling on your own and want to connect with others to form a tour group? Find the Roll Call forum for your cruise, where you can meet other people on your sailing and arrange to tour together.

WEDDINGS AND RENEWAL OF VOWS AND CELEBRATORY ITEMS IN CRUISE HOSPITALITY

PLANNING A CRUISE WEDDING

Weddings at sea can be the ultimate in romance. Imagine tying the knot under a palm tree on a Caribbean island or being married by a uniformed captain in the middle of the ocean. And cruise-ship weddings are necessarily small, meaning you don't have to worry who is going to drive Great Aunt Hilda to the wedding or how to get out of inviting all those uncouth second cousins.

On the other hand, planning a cruise wedding involves some logistical challenges that a land-based wedding in your hometown does not. You'll need to figure out how to get a wedding license in Jamaica or think through a Plan B if bad weather or mechanical troubles cause your ship to call off a port visit on your intended wedding day. Plus, do you really want your mother-in-law on your honeymoon cruise?

Bottom of Form

If you're thinking about a wedding onboard or in port, here are some key things to consider before you take the plunge.

1. For the most part, it's the big-ship, mass-market cruise lines that have embraced full-service weddings. Some don't allow onboard weddings. Others — mostly in the high-priced luxury category — like Seabourn, don't have a problem with wedding or vowrenewal plans, but they eschew packages, opting to provide customized amenities to these passengers.
2. Weddings have become so popular on some ships that Carnival, Celebrity, Azamara, Holland America and Royal Caribbean levy surcharges for certain times of the year. The lines all have dedicated wedding planning event coordinators, so you'll be dealing with people who plan hundreds of nuptials a year.
3. If you want to get married at sea by the captain, you're limited to only a handful of cruise lines, due to legal limitations that are based on ships' countries of registry. On the "can officiate" list are Celebrity Cruises and Azamara Club Cruises, whose ships are now registered in Malta.Princess Cruises' and Cunard's captains are also able to marry couples at sea; those lines have registered their ships in Bermuda.
4. Several cruises lines have private islands for wedding or vow renewals. Disney Cruise Line captains can lead wedding ceremonies onboard or atCastaway Cay. However, because senior officers can't perform legal ceremonies, the actual "legal" marriage (and paperwork signing) must occur in the cruise terminal before the ship leaves Port Canaveral — not terribly romantic. Holland America conducts weddings and vow renewals at its private island, Half Moon Cay, during its Caribbean and Panama Canal cruises.
5. Weddings in ports of call can be fabulous, but what happens if the ship has to cancel the call? Consider very carefully ports that require ships to tender; Grand Cayman, for instance, can be a highly unpredictable site, as winds often hamper tender operations, causing cruise ships to skip stops at the island. For the same reason, we don't recommend planning a shoreside wedding at a Caribbean locale during hurricane season (June through November).

6. If you want to get married onboard and want to choose the clergy to perform the ceremony or invite people who won't be sailing, consider having your wedding onboard while the ship is still docked at its homeport. Clergy and guests can come aboard for the wedding and after-party, then debark before the ship sails. And you get the cruise as a honeymoon. Note that it might make for a rushed start to your special day. The wedding party will typically board early, after previous passengers have disembarked but before embarkation officially begins, and the ceremony will take place around midday, so guests have enough time to celebrate before leaving in the late afternoon before sailaway.

7. Cruise-ship weddings might not be for everyone. If you've always dreamed of picking out each flower yourself or getting married in your hometown in front of 300 people, you might not be happy with this simple approach. Also think about the realities of getting married on a ship — your cabin could be small, you might have to eat meals with other people, and, if you're inviting friends and family to your at-sea wedding, you might have an entourage for your honeymoon.
8. Getting married legally while at sea is complicated, so understand all the logistics before signing on, and plan well in advance. Legalizing a wedding in a foreign port can also be tricky, so ask your wedding planner to explain all the details and suggest which cruise port on your itinerary is your best bet for a wedding spot.
9. And, while many brides start planning their dream nuptials a year to 18 months in advance, don't jump the gun by planning land-based, post-cruise celebrations too early — or ordering invitations, keepsakes with the wedding date, etc. Couples have been bumped from their wedding cruises — because of full-ship charters after they booked — forcing them to reschedule everything.

CELEBRITY CRUISES HONEYMOONS, DESTINATION WEDDINGS AND VOW RENEWALS

Who Performs the Weddings on Celebrity Cruises?

With the recent reregistration of all of Celebrity's ships in Malta (with the exception of Expedition), government regulations have changed to allow for captains to perform legal marriages while the ships sail the seas of the world. These legal, captainled wedding ceremonies are performed under the Maltese flag and complement our existing shipboard, shoreside and vow renewal offerings.

Where do the Celebrity Cruises weddings take place? They are held in the ship's library, chapel, or one of the ship's lounges. Destinations weddings take place at the venue of your choice.

Where are Celebrity Cruises receptions held? Wedding or Vow Renewal receptions may be held in the specialty restaurants during regular operating hours or as a private function.

How many guests can be accommodated at a Celebrity Cruises wedding? As a complimentary service provided by Celebrity Cruises, wedding parties may have up to ten (10) non-sailing guests in attendance at the wedding ceremony. If there are more than ten (10) non-sailing guests, a reception package must be booked. Additional cake and champagne does not constitute a reception. If a reception is booked on the ship, additional non-sailing guests may attend the ceremony and reception. Please note that in some ports of call, non-sailing guests are not permitted to board the ship due to security restrictions. Wedding parties with a reception may have a maximum of one hundred and fifty (150) non-sailing guests board the ship for their celebration. Wedding parties with 25-50 guests require the services of an additional Wedding Coordinator and will be charged an additional $150.00 US Dollars. For each additional twenty-five (25) guests, Celebrity Cruises requires the services of one additional Wedding Coordinator. Couples who choose to have a destination wedding ceremony may purchase an onboard reception following their ceremony.

There is an additional fee of $150.00 US Dollars as onboard receptions require a Wedding Coordinator.

What time of day are Celebrity Cruises weddings performed? Ceremony times and locations are assigned according to the requirements of each wedding or onboard event. Celebrity Cruises Package information: (Note: all packages and pricing are approximate and subject to change.)

Test the waters pre-wedding consultation and tour – starting from $275.00 us Test the Waters is for engaged couples and their family. This unique programme offers couples a preview to a cruise wedding and vacation as well as familiarizes you with ship procedures and upgrade options.

The Package includes the following:

- Preinspection arrangements.
- Site inspection with wedding coordinator – Total time: 90 minutes onboard.
- 30-minute tour of the wedding and reception locations.
- 30-minutes of which includes consultation of wedding props, site photography, set-up and question and answer session.
- Join other sailing guests for a 30-minute open buffet lunch.

Package Cost:

$275.00 per couple, 90 minutes, Additional Guests: $45.00 per person

Additional Consultation Hours: $100.00 per hour

Welcome reception – starting from $32.00 us per person

A Welcome Reception is a perfect way to start your wedding cruise with your guests. Contact an Event Manager for details on times and availability of locations.

The package includes the following:

- Preplanning arrangements.
- Onboard event coordinator
- Private indoor wedding location
- One (1) hour of hot and cold canapés with open bar

Guidelines

"Celebrity Weddings" also offers many "a la carte" options to customize your Welcome Reception package such as live music, favours, floral enhancements, additional treats and more. Due to the duties of the ship's staff, packages cannot be held on embarkation day/night or formal day/night. Bridesmaid tea party – starting from $18.00 us per person: A Bridesmaid Tea Party is a nice way to say thank you to your special friends. Sit and chat while enjoying your time together. Contact an Event Manager for upgrade options or more information.

The package is a traditional tea party with a variety of teas and the following components:

- Variety of Specialty teas
- Scones – Served with clotted cream, or Devonshire cream, strawberry jam.
- *Sandwiches:* Smoked Salmon, Egg Salad, Cucumber, Roast Beef
- Pastries
- Chocolate cake
- French Napoleon

Menu is subject to change at the Chef's discretion

Guidelines: Due to the duties of the ship's staff, packages cannot be held on embarkation day/night or formal day/night.

Cigar and Cognac Party – Starting from $28.00 us Per Person

The Cigar and Cognac Party is a great way for the gentleman to celebrate. Contact an Event Manager for details on times and availability of locations.

The package includes the following:

- Preplanning arrangements.
- Onboard event coordinator
- One (1) hour of premium open bar
- Choice of premium cigars

Nautical nuptials – at sea package—$2,500.00 us :

- Pre-Sailing wedding coordinator
- Master-performed legal service
- Onboard event coordinator
- Romantic indoor wedding location
- Elegant bouquet
- Matching boutonniere
- Live music
- Special nautical vows
- Photography service – one hour
- Cake for two
- Bottle of champagne
- Two (2) champagne flutes
- Rose petals on bed at turndown
- 2 logo bathrobes

- Chocolate covered strawberries
- Fresh flowers in stateroom

All photographs will be available for your viewing within 48 hours, at which time, you can select the Wedding photography package you wish to purchase. Photographs are not available individually without purchase of one of the packages. Due to the duties of the ship's staff, At Sea ceremonies cannot be held on embarkation day/night. The cancellation policy for the At Sea package is the same as for other wedding packages. *The At Sea Wedding package is limited in number. Book your package early to ensure availability. Flowers may be substituted or enhanced based on availability.

Marriage License Information:

Marriage licenses will be legal Maltese licenses and cost $500 US plus mailing fees.

Shipboard Weddings:

- Pre-Sailing wedding coordinator
- Priority check-in for the couple and their sailing guests*
- Escort for the bridal couple by their Celebrity wedding coordinator from the pier to their state room*
- Wedding ceremony
- Romantic indoor wedding location
- Wedding officiate from the wedding destination
- Special destination vows
- Wedding coordinator
- Recorded traditional ceremony music
- *Sailing Port:* modern bridal bouquet and boutonniere to complement the bouquet
- *Destination Locations:* A local / seasonal flower bridal bouquet created with floral designer's choice of flowers and a matching boutonniere
- Artistic wedding cake for two
- Bottle of Celebrity's signature sparkling champagne
- Keepsake wedding certificate
- Photography service – We offer a photography service to capture each wedding memory. Your wedding package will include one hour of photography coverage. A minimum of 40 exposures will be taken. This photography coverage of one (1) hour will include 15-20 minutes of ceremony, 15-20 minutes of cake cutting toast and 15-20 minutes photography shoot around the ship or wedding site. All photographs will be available for your viewing within 48 hours, at which time, you can select the Wedding photography package you wish to purchase, or visit www.image.com for packages and pricing. Photographs are not available individually without purchase of one of the packages.

Shoreside Weddings:

- Roundtrip taxi transportation for bridal couple from the ship to the ceremony location
- Romantic wedding ceremony
- Exotic wedding location (most ports of call offer a beach or garden setting)
- Wedding officiate from the wedding destination
- Wedding coordinator
- Recorded traditional ceremony music*
- Sailing Day Ports: Modern bridal bouquet and boutonniere to complement the bouquet**
- Island Ports: A tropical or wild flower bridal bouquet with floral designer's choice of flowers and groom's boutonniere with single matching bloom**
- Artistic wedding cake for two
- Bottle of sparkling wine served at ceremony site (nonalcoholic sparkling wine will be substituted in state parks)
- Keepsake wedding certificate
- Photography service*** – Celebrity offers a photography service to capture each wedding memory. Your wedding package will include one hour of photography coverage. A minimum of 40 exposures will be taken. This photography coverage of 1 hour will include 15-20 minutes of ceremony, 15-20 minutes of cake cutting toast and 15-20 minutes photography shoot around the ship or wedding site. All photographs will be available for your viewing within 6 to 8 weeks, at which time, you can select the Wedding photography package you wish to purchase. Photographs are not available individually without the purchase of one of the packages.

VOW RENEWALS

It's also possible to renew your wedding vows at sea. Vow renewal programmes and vow renewal packages are much like weddings and wedding packages, except without the headache of calculating license fees! You are not required to obtain a marriage license or any other legal document before your vow renewal service. All you will need with you is proof that your marriage is valid. A marriage license is sufficient. As with weddings, once you decide you want to renew your vows, you need to select a cruise and book it. Then we will put you in touch with a wedding coordinator or special services agent to design the perfect ceremony. Call us toll free at +1-713-974-2121, and we'll help you plan a cruise to remember!

To learn more about the vow renewal packages offered by each cruise line, click the cruise line name below:

Azamara

Aisle to Isle Renewal ($475.00)

Renew your commitment to each other as you sail off to explore new exotic territories.

- Pre-cruise Event Manager
- Romantic Wedding Location onboard the Ship
- Shipboard Ceremony Officiant
- Recorded Ceremony Music
- Bottle of champagne
- Cake for two
- Commemorative Vow Renewal Certificate
- Single stem rose for Bride*
- Matching boutonniere for Groom
- One hour of photography service - Photos not included, but may be purchased separately
- Floral upgrade available

True Love Knot Renewal ($650.00)

Unique Captain performed ceremony reinforcing the bonds that brought you together from the beginning.

- Pre-cruise Event Manager
- Intimate Wedding Location on board the Ship
- Special Nautical Renewal Ceremony Officiated by Ship's Captain
- Commemorative Vow Renewal Certificate signed by the Captain
- Recorded ceremony music
- Petite Bouquet for Bride*
- Matching Boutonniere for Groom
- One hour Photography Service
- 1–8×10 photograph of the couple with Captain, signed by the Captain
- 1-8×10 photograph of the ship
- Bottle of Champagne
- 2 "Special Memories" engraved champagne flutes
- Cake for Two
- Breakfast for two, delivered to your stateroom

*Floral upgrade available

Carnival

What better way to enhance your anniversary, or just recall that special day, than to renew your wedding vows aboard one of Carnival's fabulous ships with a memorable ceremony performed by the ship's captain.

Services offered - $385.00 Package Price

- Special ceremony location
- Ceremony performed by the Ship's Captain

- Keepsake "Renewal of Marriage Vows" Certificate signed by the Ship's Captain and presented in a leather folio.
- Recorded ceremony music
- Photography Service
- One Long Stemmed Rose for the Wife and matching Rose Boutonniere for the Husband
- 2-Tier Wedding Cake
- Sparkling Wine and 2 Etched ("Love", "Honeymoon" or "Anniversary") Champagne Flutes
- One 8×10 Wedding Photograph (Additional photos available at a reasonable price)

This package accommodates up to a maximum of 8 guests, including the celebrating couple. Additional guests can be included at a rate of $12.00 per person.

Deluxe Package - $735.00 Package Price

- Special ceremony location
- Ceremony performed by the Ship's Captain
- Keepsake "Renewal of Marriage Vows" Certificate signed by the Ship's Captain and presented in a leather folio.
- Recorded ceremony music
- Photography Service
- One Long Stemmed Rose for the Wife and matching Rose Boutonniere for the Husband
- 2-Tier Wedding Cake
- Sparkling Wine and 2 Etched ("Love", "Honeymoon" or "Anniversary") Champagne Flutes
- One 8×10 Wedding Photograph (Additional Photos available at a reasonable price)
- One Hour Open Bar with Hot/Cold Canapés

This package accommodates up to a maximum of 20 guests, including the celebrating couple. Additional guests can be included at a rate of $22.00 per person.

Important Information

The Renewal of Marriage Vows Ceremony is symbolic in nature and has no legal or binding effect. Couples with different last names are required to furnish proof of marriage. Arrangements for the time and location of the ceremony will be made onboard with the Group's Coordinator. We will be unable to grant requests to perform the ceremony on embarkation days or formal nights. Should a circumstance arise whereby the Ship's Captain is unable to perform the ceremony, or the time and location of the ceremony must be changed, Carnival will either reschedule the Ceremony or it shall be conducted by another level of management at the sole discretion of Carnival. Carnival shall have no liability for any compensation or other damages to the wedding couple or any of their guests due to any change.

Celebrity

Aisle to Isle Renewal ($475.00)

Renew your commitment to each other as you sail off to explore new exotic territories.

- Pre-cruise Event Manager
- Romantic Wedding Location onboard the Ship
- Shipboard Ceremony Officiant
- Recorded Ceremony Music
- Bottle of champagne
- Cake for two
- Commemorative Vow Renewal Certificate
- Single stem rose for Bride*
- Matching boutonniere for Groom
- One hour of photography service—Photos not included, but may be purchased separately
- Floral upgrade available
- True Love Knot Renewal ($650.00)

Unique Captain performed ceremony reinforcing the bonds that brought you together from the beginning

- Pre-cruise Event Manager
- Intimate Wedding Location on board the Ship
- Special Nautical Renewal Ceremony Officiated by Ship's Captain
- Commemorative Vow Renewal Certificate signed by the Captain
- Recorded ceremony music
- Petite Bouquet for Bride*
- Matching Boutonniere for Groom
- One hour Photography Service
- 1-8×10 photograph of the couple with Captain, signed by the Captain
- 1-8×10 photograph of the ship
- Bottle of Champagne
- 2 "Special Memories" engraved champagne flutes
- Cake for Two
- Gourmet breakfast for two, delivered to your stateroom
- Floral upgrade available

Costa

Honeymoon/Anniversary Package

- A chilled bottle of sparkling Italian wine in your stateroom
- A spray of fresh flowers just for you

- Keepsake portrait taken by the ship's photographer
- An 8 × 10 silver frame to hold your portrait
- Personalized honeymoon or anniversary certificate
- Cocktail party hosted by the ship's captain
- His and hers Costa robes to take home

Crystal

Repledge your love with a vow renewal ceremony performed by the captain on one of Crystal's beautiful ships. The captain may perform vow renewal ceremonies, provided it is prearranged with On Board Guest Services. Guests are welcome to use the public rooms on board to conduct a ceremony, provided that arrangements are made with OBGS prior to sailing. They will then, in turn, coordinate with the ship.

A standard package is offered for guests who wish to renew their wedding vows onboard. Packages include a certificate and the following:

- Veuve Clicquot Champagne — $98 (inclusive of tips)
- Wedding Bouquet — $40
- Boutonniere Flower — $15

Total Cost — $183.00

Other optional offerings include:

- Cold hors d'oeuvres — $40 (per tray)
- Small cake — Complimentary
- Photographer — Call for quote

Please note: the bar manager is responsible for coordinating all guest arrangements while onboard.

Cunard

Renew your wedding vows on Queen Mary 2, Queen Victoria or Queen Elizabeth for the ultimate celebration. Renewal of Vows is available on voyages of six nights or more and is subject to availability. Renewal of Vows ($400 per couple)

- An attractive ceremony venue on board
- A bouquet and matching buttonhole (or two of either on request)
- A bottle of champagne
- A romantic ceremony conducted by the Captain*
- A celebratory singletier iced cake
- The attendance of a professional photographer at the ceremony
- Your chosen portrait photograph of the ceremony
- A silverplated photo frame
- A commemorative certificate signed by the Captain*
- A gift from Cunard of a pair of contemporary champagne flutes
- If the Captain is unable to conduct the ceremony, his Senior Representative will be asked to perform the role on his behalf.

Disney

The fleet of Disney Cruise Line ships — with their distinctive designs and decorative gold swirls across their bows — inspire awe wherever they pull into port. Mixing grand elegance with an element of fun, the Disney Magic, the Disney Wonder, the Disney Dream, and the Disney Fantasy are the perfect choice for your vow renewal ceremony.

All Disney Cruise Line ceremonies include:

- On–site ceremony coordinator to coordinate your ceremony day events
- Choice of personal fresh floral for the couple (You may also opt to include floral for your bridal party, available at an additional cost)
- Solo musician (pianist) for the Ceremony and Cake and Champagne Celebration
- Officiant to perform the ceremony
- Cake and Champagne Celebration onboard the ship which includes an elegant 2–tier wedding cake with keepsake cake topper, one bottle of champagne and one bottle of sparkling cider (non–alcoholic) for the toast, served by host or hostess
- Dinner for the couple at Palo on night of ceremony
- Disney Cruise Line Commemorative Ceremony Certificate
- Steaming for the couple's ceremony attire
- The special couple will also receive a $100.00 onboard stateroom credit that may be used towards merchandise, spa treatments, port adventures, and other onboard activities . (Any unused portions are non-refundable and non-transferable.)
- Photography packages with Event Photographer, available for an additional cost

Onboard Ceremony Package: $2,500 for up to 8 guests, plus the Couple

Holland America

Renewal of Vows at Half Moon Cay ($89)

- Guests that visit Half Moon Cay, the company's own island paradise, on Holland America Line Caribbean and Panama Canal cruises may renew their wedding vows on the island in a private, traditional Bahamian chapel nestled in a garden overlooking the sea.
- This is a more casual ceremony than on board and participants are encouraged to wear their favourite tropical attire. Champagne and cake are served after the ceremony. Each couple is photographed on the island and the photo is delivered to their stateroom in a souvenir frame. Arrangements for renewal of vows at the chapel may be made through the Guest Relations Manager at the Front Office on board the ship.

Paul Gauguin Cruises

Renewal of Vows Package: $500

- Renewal of Vows ceremony conducted by the Captain and the Cruise Director followed by a special gathering featuring Polynesian blessing ceremony performed by Les Gauguines and hosted by the Cruise Director
- Congratulatory letter from the Captain
- Instateroom celebratory bottle of Champagne
- One 8"×10" photo portrait
- Reception cake
- Box of chocolates
- Hei (crown of flowers) or lei (necklace of flowers)

Princess

Renewal of Vows ($205 per couple)

- A renewal of vows ceremony*.
- Orchid bouquet and boutonniere for ceremony.
- Commemorative certificate for "renewal of vows" signed by the Captain.
- One bottle of champagne in your stateroom.
- Two Princess Cruises engraved souvenir champagne glasses.
- A framed portrait of the ceremony.

Deluxe Renewal of Vows ($485 per couple)

- All the benefits of the above Renewal of Vows Package plus these fabulous extras:
- Champagne breakfast in beda half bottle of French champagne delivered with breakfast in your stateroom the morning of your choice.
- Two Princess Cruises waffle robesa gift for you to take home.
- A visit to the Spa - one 25-minute therapeutic massage or facial per person.
- Choice of canapés or petit fours in your stateroom on selected evenings.
- A personalized invitation from the Captain to visit the bridge while in port.
- Renewal of Vows is a group ceremony at the ship's discretion. All arrangements will be made by the ship's representative onboard.

Pullmantur

Vow renewal with Pullmantur for anyone celebrating 25 or 50 years of marriage includes:

- Up to 10 guests for $275 USD or 225 €
- (Guests 11+ are an additional $10 or 8 € /each)

- Final cost and payment is completed on board.
- Vow renewal ceremony with the captain
- Renewal of vows certificate
- Bride's bouquet
- Cava (house wine) cocktails and canapés
- Personalized wedding cake
- Photo album with 6 photos of the ceremony
- For the day after the ceremony:
  - Complimentary continental breakfast in stateroom with a gift
  - Bottle of cava (house wine) and sweets

Regent

Celebrate the renewal of your vows onboard a Regent ship. We offer a complete package to make this unique celebration cruise even more memorable.

Vow Renewal Package - $500.00

- Congratulations letter from the Captain
- Veuve Clicquot champagne
- One 8"×10" photograph
- Reception cake
- Box of Leonidas chocolates
- Renewal of Vows ceremony conducted by Captain and Cruise Director
- Posy of flowers

Royal Caribbean

Royal Encore Shipboard Vow Renewal ($595.00)

In celebration of your wedding anniversary or for a romantic surprise, Royal Romance can arrange a vow renewal ceremony for your special occasion.

Create your own unique event by adding selections from our "Ceremony Enhancements" listed here:

- Two (2) hours maximum of preplanning with a Royal Romance Wedding Consultant prior to the wedding*
- Ideal ceremony location onboard
- Memorable ceremony performed by your ship's Cruise Programme Administrator
- Romantic, recorded ceremony music
- Simple, elegant bridal bouquet consisting of 3 ivory roses accented with greenery, a crisp neatly tied white ribbon adds the finishing touch**
- Groom's boutonniere with single matching bloom
- Keepsake Royal Romance Vow Renewal certificate
- Four (4) delectable Royal Romance chocolate covered toasting strawberries for bridal couple

- Bottle of Royal Romance sparkling wine
- Strawberries and sparkling wine toast (one hour).
- Professional shipboard photography service for the ceremony. Photos are not included. Photo packages are offered onboard and can be viewed by accessing www.image.com

Labadee Shoreside Vow Renewal ($695.00)

Royal Romance can arrange a shoreside Vow Renewal Ceremony on Labadee, Haiti—Royal Caribbean's own private beach cordoned off from the rest of the island; and the rest of the world. Imagine you and your partner taking the plunge all over again in a shoreside excursion at the romantic and secluded Dragon's Point Beach.

A concealed sanctuary for our passengers to secretly enjoy its tranquil beauty. Learn about the Island's rich history and local culture, or simply do nothing—it's your day.

- Two (2) hours maximum of preplanning with a Royal Romance Wedding Consultant prior to the wedding*
- Ideal ceremony location shoreside at Dragon's Point
- Memorable ceremony performed by your ship's Cruise Programme Administrator
- Simple, elegant bridal bouquet consisting of 3 ivory roses accented with greenery, a crisp neatly tied white ribbon adds the finishing touch**
- Groom's boutonniere with single matching bloom
- Keepsake Royal Romance vow renewal certificate
- Royal Romance chocolate covered strawberries for the bridal couple delivered to your stateroom
- Bottle of sparkling wine delivered to your stateroom
- Professional shipboard photography service for the ceremony and sparkling wine toast (one hour). Photos are not included. Photo packages are offered onboard and can be viewed by accessing www.image.com
- Pre-planning includes, but is not limited to, all phone calls, quotes, bookings, e-mails and finalizations with bridal couples. **Flowers may be substituted based on availability

Vow Renewal Guidelines:

Your Cruise Programme Administrator will coordinate arrangements for the date, time and location of your vow renewal once you are onboard. Unfortunately, requests for ceremonies on the day of sailing or on formal days/nights cannot be accommodated. Please allow a minimum of two (2) weeks prior to sailing for Royal Romance to make arrangements for your vow renewal ceremony. For additional options, please review the "Ceremony Enhancements" section. Please note: unfortunately, floral upgrades are not available. This is not a legal ceremony; bridal couples with different last names will need to bring proof of marriage. Bridal couples must be married at least one (1) year. A copy of the marriage license must be provided for verification.

4

Cruise Onboard Hospitality

ONBOARD EXPERIENCE

Our dedicated staff is there to attend to your every need. And warm smiles will greet you everywhere you go. Click on a topic headline to view detailed information relating to your selection.

ONBOARD ATMOSPHERE

Everyone at Princess is committed to ensuring you have a great time on your cruise. So, to preserve a relaxed and friendly atmosphere onboard, we ask that you observe a few guidelines.

- When formal nights are held, please observe the dress code in the Traditional Dining and Anytime Dining venues for the enjoyment of all our guests. For details regarding this, please see the section on Formal Wear.
- Should you wish to videotape onboard during your cruise, please feel free to do so. However, videotaping the onboard entertainment performances is not allowed for copyright reasons.
- Inappropriate dress such as pool or beach attire, shorts, ball caps and casual jeans (with fraying and/or holes), is not permitted in the dining rooms.

SPECIAL OCCASIONS

Princess makes your birthday, wedding, honeymoon, anniversary or renewal of vows even more memorable. When you're onboard a cruise with Princess, you're surrounded by warm, caring people dedicated to making each day a celebration. And for those times in your life that are special, we've created a collection of memorable celebration experiences to help you savor those moments for years and years to come.

If you or your travel agent advise us of any occasions of particular importance at least 45 days prior to your departure, we'll set our "special occasion" staff in motion to spotlight your special event in the dining room or with our special packages and fabulous "extra mile" service. Choose from a selection of our Celebration offerings, with extra touches like flowers, wine and champagne. To order a gift or to plan a special event, review our selections and complete the order form.

ALCOHOL POLICY

As provided in the Passage Contract, guests agree not to bring alcoholic beverages of any kind onboard for consumption, except one bottle of wine or champagne per adult of drinking age (no larger than 750 ml) per voyage, which will not be subject to a corkage fee if consumed in the stateroom. Additional wine or champagne bottles are welcome, but will incur a $15 corkage fee each, irrespective of where they are intended to be consumed. Liquor, spirits or beers are not permitted. Please remember that luggage will be scanned and alcohol outside of our policy will be removed and discarded.*

Alcoholic beverages that are purchased duty free from the ship's gift shop, or at ports of call, will be collected for safekeeping and delivered to the guest's stateroom on the last day of the cruise. A member of the ship's staff will be at the gangway to assist guests with the storage of their shoreside alcoholic purchases while our Boutiques staff will assist guests with shipboard alcoholic purchases. Princess Cruises is not responsible for any alcoholic beverages removed and discarded by shoreside security staff.

Such items are not eligible for monetary refund or replacement.

ALCOHOL AGE RESTRICTIONS

The legal drinking age of 21 years* is always observed onboard and proof of age may be required. All onboard staff are trained to take their responsibility to not serve alcohol to underage guests seriously. The age restrictions are clearly posted in the bars.

Entry into the disco is limited to guests 18 years and older. However, be sure to check with the child and teen centers for special disco events designed just for kids. Children under the age of 18 are welcome in the gymnasium, spa and jacuzzi; and also in the evening entertainment show lounges when accompanied by a parent or guardian.

*For guests on cruises originating from Australian or Asian ports other than Japan, the minimum age limit for drinking is 18 years or older (20 years or older for guests on cruises originating from Japanese ports). For UK "Homeport" Ship itineraries (which vary each season), the minimum age limit for drinking on board is 18 years old.

SMOKING POLICY CHANGE

Keeping the comfort of our guests a priority, and in consideration of consumer studies which show smokers are a small minority of guests, Princess has implemented the following smoking policy:

Designated Smoking Areas

Clearly marked "Designated Smoking Areas" are available onboard and include a sufficient number of ashtrays that are emptied regularly. Generally, these areas include cigar lounges, a section of the nightclub, as well as a portion of the open decks. The Casino and Casino Bar are non-smoking areas on board, with the exception of designated slot machines where guests are permitted to smoke only while playing at those machines. All table games are non-smoking. The Casino will also have one or more non-smoking nights (6 pm to closing), depending on length of voyage. Show lounges, dining rooms and all food services areas on board all Princess ships are non-smoking. As a safety precaution, guests are reminded to properly dispose of cigarettes, cigars and pipe tobacco, which are never to be thrown overboard as this may be sucked back into the ship and cause fires.

Stateroom Smoking Policy Update

For all voyages departing after January 15th, 2012, Princess Cruises will prohibit smoking in guest staterooms and balconies. This policy change reflects the preferences of a vast majority of our guests who value having their primary living space (both stateroom and balcony) smoke-free. As balconies are a hallmark of Princess Cruises, we believe it is important to keep this peaceful space clear of smoke. Violations to this policy will result in a $250 fine for each occurrence, which will be charged to the guest's stateroom account. Keeping with the global trend towards more restrictive smoking policies and honouring the wishes of our guests, we feel this change will enhance our onboard experience and do more to help our guests escape completely.

Electronic Cigarettes

The use of electronic cigarettes is allowed within the confines of the guest's stateroom (balcony not included) and within designated smoking areas only.

LAUNDRY SERVICES

Take advantage of our onboard laundry, press-only and professional cleaning service for a nominal fee. All laundry is returned within 48 hours, or on the same day with our express service. Full suite guests and Elite Captain's Circle members also enjoy complimentary laundry and professional cleaning service, except for Presto service, which carries a charge.

For your convenience, Princess vessels have self-service launderettes where washers, dryers and laundry products are available for a negligible charge. Please note that irons/ironing boards are available in the self-service laundry rooms. Ironing and using personal clothes steamers are not permitted in any stateroom. Although rare, on certain itineraries environmental regulations relating to the consumption of water may impact the operating hours of the launderettes. These restrictions, when applicable will be posted in the Princess Patter.

ONBOARD CURRENCY

Unless noted, onboard currency is in U.S. dollars. However, on select Australian-based itineraries, the onboard currency is in Australian dollars. One of the best things about cruising with Princess is the convenience of being able to sign for all your expenses and have them charged to your stateroom.

An itemized statement will be delivered to your stateroom prior to disembarkation. By providing your credit card in advance, you are automatically registered for Express Check-Out. There is no need to visit the Guest Services/ Purser's Desk to settle your account. We accept U.S., Canadian, British and Euro currencies, and traveler's checks. American Express/Optima®, Diners Club/Carte Blanche®, Discover® Network, the JCB Card®, MasterCard® and Visa® are also accepted. Those paying by traveler's checks or cash will be required to leave a cash deposit with the Purser's staff at the beginning of the cruise.

For your convenience, Automated Teller Machines for the exchange of foreign currencies are available on vessels sailing out of European ports and on selected exotic itineraries. Use of such machines may involve transaction fees that are subject to change without notice.

SHOPPING ONBOARD

Our boutiques onboard offer more than just accessories and sundries you may have left at home. Shop onboard and benefit from incredible tax-and duty-free savings off suggested U.S. retail prices on fragrances, cosmetics, jewelry and gifts, apparel and liquor. In addition to our everyday savings, we bring you special promotions throughout the cruise. Once onboard, please check the Princess Patter calendar for times and locations of these exciting events. Plus, Elite Captain's Circle members receive a 10 per cent boutiques discount!

THE INTERNET AT SEA

Internet access is available on all Princess vessels through our 24-hour onboard Internet Cafe and wireless network — which is available in staterooms and various public areas including our world famous Piazzas. Use our state-of-the-art computer systems to access your web-based e-mail account, or browse the Internet for world news, sports and stock trading. Or bring your wireless-enabled laptop and access the Internet through our improved onboard wireless service.

Guests who subscribe to e-mail services from an Internet Service Provider (ISP) are advised to verify that their ISP has a web-mail viewing site prior to sailing. Most major ISPs have web sites that allow e-mail access via a web browser using an e-mail address and password. Please contact the Internet Café Manager onboard for information regarding the charges that apply to Internet and wireless services and any other specific requirements. Plus – Platinum and Elite Captain's Circle members benefit from credit towards Internet Café packages.

View Internet Access Packages available to order.

Internet access via satellite is significantly slower than high-speed connections on shore. Princess Cruises reserves the right to filter content accessed via the ship's Internet services. Please note high bandwidth consuming applications such as voice over IP telephony, peertopeer file sharing and streaming media may be restricted onboard Princess vessels.

PRINCESS SEA - COMPLIMENTARY ONBOARD WEB AND MESSAGING SERVICE

Princess Sea is our FREE, mobile friendly onboard service offering quick and convenient access to valuable information about the ship while you're onboard! Plan your day's events and activities, review the ship's itinerary and port guides, browse restaurant menus, even access your stateroom account! Plus, on select ships the Princess Sea Messenger allows you to send text messages to other guests onboard!

Getting started with Princess Sea is easy. Simply connect to the ship's WIFI once onboard, open your browser and Princess Sea will be the default page that appears. It even operates in "Airplane Mode". No cellular or data charges required!

Princess Sea is currently available on select ships.

Learn more about Princess Sea.

SHIP DECK PLANS

We make it easy for you to get to know your ship. With industry-leading interactive deck plans and virtual tours, you'll be able to see your ship before you board.

STAYING HEALTHY

The health and well-being of our guests and crew is our highest priority. And there are several measures that meet or exceed standards set by the US Centers for Disease Control and Prevention which are currently in place to prevent and contain illnesses on our ships. The simplest way for you to stay healthy is to frequently and thoroughly wash your hands with soap and water, especially before eating and after using the toilet. You'll also find hand sanitizers located throughout the ship for your use after washing your hands.

If you feel ill during your voyage, please immediately report to the medical center. All of our onboard medical facilities meet or exceed the standards established by the American College of Emergency Physicians. Our onboard medical facilities are staffed by full-time registered doctors and nurses. In addition to twice-daily office hours, they are available 24 hours a day in the event of an emergency.

Gratuities

During your cruise, regardless of which Princess ship you choose, you will meet staff who provide you with excellent service. Crew members often rotate to different vessels within the Princess fleet which helps to maintain our high standards on every ship. These dedicated workers reflect our philosophy that all crew on all ships are but one family who share in our success.

To simplify the tipping process for our guests, a discretionary gratuity of $12 per person for minisuites and suites, and $11.50 per guest in all other staterooms per day (including children) will be automatically added to your shipboard account on a daily basis. Effective on voyages departing on or after January 1, 2016, the gratuity charge will be $13.95 per guest for minisuites and suites, and $12.95 per guest for interior, oceanview, and balcony staterooms. This gratuity will be shared amongst those staff who help provide and support your cruise experience, including all waitstaff, stateroom stewards, buffet stewards, and housekeeping staff across the fleet.

For your convenience, this gratuity can be prepaid online via Cruise Personalizer. Alternatively, you may call us at 1-855-500-7690 and reference Special Services item number 0591. Pre-payment is available up to 2 days prior to departure.

A 15 per cent gratuity is added to bar charges, dining room wine accounts, and Lotus Spa® services. This is shared amongst the beverage staff, their support staff and Lotus Spa® personnel. Casino dealers and youth staff do not share in these gratuities. We know you will find these services onboard exemplary.

Please note gratuities will be deemed undisputed unless a request to modify is received prior to disembarking the ship.

Stateroom Amenities

The little extras you find in the best hotels — fresh fruit (by request), evening bed turn-down, chocolates on your pillow, complimentary shampoo, conditioner and body lotion — are provided in every stateroom. Waffle weave cloth bathrobes are available upon request from your stateroom steward for your comfort and convenience.

For those of you who wish to enjoy a relaxing drink in the privacy of your stateroom, bottles of liquor and stateroom bar packages are available for purchase at non-duty-free prices through room service. The stateroom directory available onboard lists a complete menu of offerings. Mini-suites include a welcome glass of champagne, two televisions, a sitting area and a spacious closet, while full suites offer all of these premiums plus amenities such as a DVD/CD player and free access to a DVD library. Full suite guests also enjoy complimentary laundry and dry cleaning, use of the Lotus Spa® Thermal Suite (on select ships, excluding Royal Princess), one-time free mini-bar setup and use of our Disembarkation Lounge.

Each stateroom has other luxuries for your convenience, such as a private safe and refrigerator. In addition, each room is equipped with a 110-volt, 60-cycle alternating current (AC) with standard U.S. plug fittings. Please ask your stateroom steward to check your appliances for suitability before use if you have any questions. All ships are equipped with an electric hair dryer in every stateroom.

Television Programming

Getting away from it all doesn't mean being out of touch. Every stateroom on Princess ships has its own TV set featuring our multi-channel Princess Overseas Television programming.*

We offer live satellite reception of MSNBC, CNBC, Fox News and BBC World. In some instances and based on sailing itineraries we offer Sky News and Sky Sports News in lieu of MSNBC and Fox News. Along with a movie channel featuring a wide selection of first-run movies, we also provide the latest sitcoms and dramas, an onboard version of the Discovery Channel, and a wide selection of special programming, including the Academy Awards®. Plus, for sports fans, we offer several major sporting events such as the Super Bowl® , BCS college bowl games, NBA Finals and the NCAA basketball tournament. Closed captioning is available on most Princess ships; please check with the Guest Services Desk for information.

All televisions in cabins onboard Princess ships ^ are equipped with the open captioning feature. All movies are open captioned. However, callers should be advised that this feature does not work with most programmes shown from an international (versus U.S.) satellite (ie: CNN, etc.). When the television receives a U.S. feed, the open captioning feature will work. Most onboard theaters are equipped with assistive listening devices.

*Ship television programming is not guaranteed at all times due to the nature of satellite communications, which are subject to itinerary and possible disruption from weather patterns and various obstructions. Also, Internet access via satellite is significantly slower than high-speed connections on shore.

Medical Assistance

Our medical centers are primarily intended to provide acute care for illness and accidents that may occur while on vacation and are not intended to provide long term care for patients with chronic illnesses or as a substitute for regular health care.

Our intention is to:

- Provide quality maritime medical care for guests and crew members aboard our ships.
- Initiate appropriate stabilization, diagnostic and therapeutic maneuvers for critically ill or medically unstable patients.
- Support, comfort and care for patients onboard.
- Facilitate the timely medical evacuation of patients, if appropriate.

All of our onboard medical facilities meet or exceed the standards established by the American College of Emergency Physicians. Our onboard medical facilities are staffed by full-time registered doctors and nurses. In addition to twice-daily office hours, they are available 24 hours a day in the event of an emergency.

Charges for medical services will be added to your shipboard account, and you will be provided with an itemized account to submit to your insurance company. Important: Princess ships are registered in Bermuda. Verify with your insurer if your coverage applies outside the United States, or purchase appropriate travel insurance.

Religious Services

We respect our guests' religious beliefs and invite them to practice on their own or with their fellow guests. Guests who wish to lead religious services may volunteer by contacting the Guest Services desk or a member of the Cruise Staff. In some cases, our shipboard staff will lead services. However, Princess Cruises does not place clergy on board our vessels.

Clergy traveling as Guests onboard our vessels are welcome to conduct services while sailing. They should leave their name, cabin number, and services offered at the Guest Services Desk and they will be contacted by a member of the Cruise Director's Staff. Approval of services will be made based on schedule suitability, appropriate onboard supplies, etc. Please bring your Letter of Celebret or Letter of Good Standing with you to provide to the onboard staff.

Please note that during Passover, there will be a Seder service (including Passover meal) held onboard. For Hanukkah, services are available and will be guestled with wine, Challah bread, prayers and an electric Menorah (no candles or live flames) provided by Princess. Supplies are present and available for anyone who wants to lead the service at 5:30 PM on Friday evenings. If you would like to bring on your own Menorah, you may. However, since candles are prohibited onboard all Princess ships, it must be electric (no live flame).

Security Guide

Princess Cruises has zero tolerance for crime on board its ships. This guide is designed to offer information to all guests on proper response procedures and available law enforcement processes in the event that an incident occurs.

Guests should immediately report missing persons and criminal activity to ship's personnel so appropriate action may be taken to ensure the safety and security of all persons on board. Timely reporting of an incident is also imperative so that necessary law enforcement notifications can be made as expeditiously as possible.

Incidents may be reported at any time by dialing the Purser's Desk. Missing persons or criminal activity may also be reported to the on board Security Department by dialing the Purser's Desk. Any situations requiring medical assistance can be reported to the Medical Department at any time by dialing 911 or through the Purser's Desk.

Princess Cruises reports all missing persons and serious criminal incidents such as homicide, suspicious death, kidnapping, assault with serious bodily injury, sexual assaults as defined by existing laws, firing or tampering with the vessel, or theft of money or property in excess of $10,000 to appropriate law enforcement authorities.

In addition to our own reporting policies and other legal requirements, on international voyages that embark or disembark in the United States, U.S. federal law requires Princess Cruises to report missing U.S. nationals and the above felonies to the U.S. Federal Bureau of Investigation (FBI) by telephone as soon as possible, to the U.S. Department of Homeland Security electronically, and to the U.S. Coast Guard in writing.

These U.S. requirements apply to all such incidents that occur on board in U.S. territorial waters, or at sea or in another country's territorial waters if the individuals involved are U.S. nationals. The U.S. FBI may assert criminal jurisdiction in all of these circumstances. Each of the countries visited, as well as the ship's country of registry (Bermuda), may also assert jurisdiction and impose additional reporting requirements.

For missing persons or serious criminal incidents that occur within countries visited or their territorial waters, and for incidents within U.S. states, you may independently contact local law enforcement authorities. You may also contact the U.S. FBI or U.S. Coast Guard for incidents that arise at any time during the voyage.

Princess Cruises encourages all guests to learn as much as you can about the local laws and customs of the places you will visit. Good resources are your library, your travel agents, and the embassies, consulates or tourist bureaus of the countries you will visit. In addition, keep track of what is being reported in the media about recent developments in those countries. Contact information for the FBI, U.S. Coast Guard and the National Sexual Assault Hotline is listed below.

Locations of U.S. Embassies or Consulates in the ports visited and contact information for local law enforcement in these ports is listed on the front page of the Princess Patter.

DINING ONBOARD

Dining with Princess is a celebration of the truest sense with dishes created from the freshest ingredients. Opt to fill your nights by catching a production show, dance the night away or visit our Vegas-style casino. Click on a topic headline to view detailed information relating to your selection.

1ST DAY DINING

Shortly after we welcome you onboard your spectacular Princess ship, you're invited to relax and dine at the Horizon Court or in one of the ship's multiple dining rooms. Open from 5 am to 11 pm (12 am on select itineraries), the Horizon Court offers a wide selection of buffet meals or snacks. A primary feature of Princess ships, the top-of-the-ship restaurant features floor-to-ceiling windows with stunning sea views as a backdrop. Or join us in one of our main dining rooms for lunch served up by a staff — from chefs to waiters — dedicated to making your dining experience something special. Together, Princess' unique combination of gracious dining staff, fine continental cuisine and new friends make every meal onboard a memorable occasion.

Anytime Dining

- Anytime Dining offers a flexible dining experience – just like a restaurant would – and gives you the freedom to dine with whomever you wish, at your convenience between 5:30 p.m. and 10 p.m. in elegant, upscale venues. Should you need to change this request, call your travel consultant no later than three weeks before you sail. Requests for preferences and changes are considered on a first-come, first-served basis. It is not always possible to alter dining preferences or seating arrangements once they are reserved. Once onboard and subject to availability, you may attempt to switch preferences with 24 hours notice to the Maitre D'. We will do our best to accommodate your preference.
- Not available on Sun, Dawn, and Sea Princess (while in Australia), Ocean, or Pacific Princess.

Traditional Dining

Traditional Dining is the classic cruise dining experience. Indulge in our freshly-prepared, award-winning cuisine, served at set times in an elegant dining room with the same waitstaff and table mates each evening. Should you need to change this request, call your travel agent no later than three weeks before you sail.

Requests for preferences and changes are considered on a first-come, first-served basis. It is not always possible to alter dining preferences or seating arrangements once they are reserved.

Once onboard and subject to availability, you may attempt to switch preferences with 24 hours notice to the Maitre D'. We will do our best to accommodate your preference. Dining Hours are posted onboard and are subject to change. Actual times may vary based on itinerary per season.

Specialty Restaurants

Variety is the spice of life, especially when it comes to gourmet fare. That's why Princess offers several Specialty Dining options for you to choose from on every ship. These distinctive restaurants provide intimate dining in an upscale atmosphere. Reservations are suggested at these popular venues. And because these restaurants at sea are truly a special treat, a cover charge will apply per person.

Sabatini's: Sabatini's serves up an authentic Italian dining experience in a remarkable eight-course meal. The stellar menu features both local seafood specialties and other regional favourites. Bayou Café and Steakhouse: Experience the first New Orleans-style restaurant at sea, and enjoy fabulous Creole and Cajun traditional cuisine, such as jambalaya, etouffee and crawfish gumbo. Crown Grill: Crown Grill entertains guests with an open, theater-style kitchen where chefs customprepare steamed shellfish - such as lobster, scallops, clams and mussels - and cooked-to-order steaks and chops. Sterling Steakhouse: Experience a more refined approach to the traditional steakhouse. Enjoy the best, most tender cuts of beef, such as New York steak and porterhouse, plus a primerib carving station. Specialty restaurants vary on a ship basis.

Casual Dining Venues

When a casual mood calls, you have plenty of choices – even on formal nights. Whether it be the buffet at the Horizon Court, the pizzeria, burger and hot dog grill, or 24-hour room service, you're able to choose how you dine with us.

Special Dietary Requests

Princess is happy to meet your request for low-sodium, low-fat, low-sugar and vegetarian diets. Visit Cruise Personalizer® to indicate your dietary preferences. In addition, kosher meals and baby food are available upon advance written request. Any other special diet requests must be authorized in advance by the Princess corporate office.

You or your travel consultant must advise Princess in writing of any special diet, allergies or medical needs. Requests must be received no later than 35 days prior to departure for cruises to Alaska, Canada/New England, Caribbean, Hawaii, Mexico, Panama Canal and Coastal Getaways. For all other cruises, requests must be received no later than 65 days prior to departure. Once onboard, please check with the Maitre D' to confirm your request.

Room Service

Guests may call for personal complimentary Room Service at any time of the day or night.

To have continental breakfast delivered to the stateroom, fill out the breakfast card included in the stateroom portfolio (one is also placed on the pillow) and hang it out at night on the stateroom door in order to receive delivery the next morning at the time of your choosing.

For a full stateroom menu, guests may review the stateroom portfolio, call the number listed in the telephone directory or press the "Room Service" button on their phone.

Below are some examples of what's offered on the complimentary Room Service Menu. Please note that Coffee, Iced Tea and Milk are available 24 hours a day. Sandwiches (served with your choice of french fries, potato chips or coleslaw).

- Club House
- Roast Beef
- Roast Turkey Breast
- Tuna Salad
- Peanut Butter and Jelly
- Vegetarian

Soups and Salads

- Soup of the Day with Saltine Crackers
- Assorted Mixed Garden Greens
- Caesar Salad with Grilled Chicken Strips
- Chef's Salad

Hot Dishes

- Beef Chili with Black Beans and Tortilla Chips
- Baked Italian Lasagna
- Moroccan Vegetable Crock Pot with Pita Bread
- Croque Monsieur
- Grilled Hamburger or Cheeseburger
- Hot Dog
- Grilled Chicken Sandwich

From the Pastry Shop

- Caramel Flan
- Chocolate Fudge Cake
- Chocolate Chip Cookie

Formal Nights

We want to make it as easy as possible for you to know what to pack and what to wear when you're dining onboard. An example of formal night schedules based on the length of your cruise.

Length of Cruise	Number of Formal Evenings
1 - 4 Days	0
5 - 6 Days	1
7 - 13 Days	2
14 - 20 Days	3
21 - 28 Days	4
29+ Days	5 Minimum

Princess offers formal wear rental on all cruises – this can be arranged prior to embarkation.

Formal Wear Rentals

Princess offers formal wear rental on all cruises; this can be arranged prior to embarkation. Dress with an elegance and style that is perfect for all the formal activities on your cruise with Princess. Cruiseline Formal Wear delivers beautifully-tailored clothing directly to your stateroom.

Onboard Entertainment

Fill every day with a wide variety of exciting onboard activities from paddle tennis to painting lessons. Take a galley tour; enjoy wine tasting; experience our traditional Champagne Waterfall; or join in games by the pool.

You can even take a backstage tour, or take center stage at our karaoke lounge. Ships filled with amenities, equal in luxury to the finest landbased resorts - that's what makes Princess Cruises the ultimate vacation and a complete escape.

Or opt for an exciting array of stage shows, most of which are written, costumed and choreographed exclusively by Princess. Curtain times vary; check your onboard newsletter, the Princess Patter, for show times. Don't forget to bring along your dancing shoes, because Princess has several dance venues and live entertainment to get you into the swing of things.

We start early and finish late. Just check Princess Patter for the times and places to give your partner a whirl. Every cruise also features a great selection of first-run feature films for your viewing pleasure. On select ships, guests can also experience Movies Under the StarsSM, our 300-square-foot outdoor movie screen and watch the latest films, sporting events and concert videos - all from a comfortable deck chair. Movies Under the Stars lights up your life - day and night.

Guests can also be stars. You can kick up your heels at our Country and Western Party - bring your cowboy boots and hats and join the line dancing. Or bring your tropical wear for our Island Night deck party on all warm weather sailings. There will be limbo contests, games and calypso music for "dancin' in the aisles." And don't be shy - audition for Princess Pop Star and share your vocal talents with the world.

Casino Games

Our casinos offer the most popular table games, including blackjack, roulette, Caribbean stud poker and craps (available on most ships). We also feature a full range of exciting slot and video poker machines, as well as regular Snowball Jackpot Bingo sessions held throughout the cruise.

Complimentary gaming lessons for slots and table games are held on each cruise, along with exciting tournaments. Please check Princess Patter for our daily special promotions and opening hours. Plus, if you want to surprise your friends with a lucky side bet, you can choose a $25, $50, or $100 credit, redeemable in the shipboard casino.

SECRETS THE CRUISE LINES DON'T TELL YOU

Cruise ship life can be a little mysterious. Your choices aren't always spelled out in black and white. The more you cruise, the more you pick up on the unofficial secrets the cruise lines don't tell you — which give you more options, let you save money and generally allow you to have a better time onboard. Maybe it's knowing just what your cabin steward is able to bring you or what the off-the-menu items are at the bar or dining room. Or perhaps it's a tip to getting a good deal on an onboard purchase.

But why wait to figure these things out the hard way — possibly after you've missed your chance? We trawled through all the great advice on Cruise Critic's Message Boards to bring you some of the worstkept cruise secrets… at least among our readers who love to share. But whether you're a first time cruiser or an old seadog, you may find there's something here you didn't already know.

FOOD SECRETS

- You are not limited to one of each appetizer, entree and dessert in the main dining room. You can order two entrees or three desserts if you choose. You can also order appetizer-sized portions of entrees as starters or order a few appetizers for your main meal. It's a great way to try new foods you're not sure you'll like (escargot, anyone?).
- Room service is generally free, except for service charges on certain lines. Royal Caribbean's late-night orders bear a $3.95 fee, while all orders on Norwegian (excluding morning coffee, Continental breakfast and those placed by Haven Suite passengers) cost $7.95. Carnival also is testing a for-fee room service menu. It's recommended you tip your delivery person, but in-room dining is not the splurge it is at a hotel.
- Speaking of breakfast, you may have more options than just the buffet and main dining room. On Norwegian, it's no secret that O'Sheehan's offers tasty made-to-order omelets and corned beef hash, yet many cruisers still don't know about it. Carnival's BlueIguana Cantina and Celebrity's Bistro on Five are other alternative breakfast venues.
- Most people dine in the main dining room or buffet on the first night of the cruise, and many haven't discovered the specialty restaurants yet. If you book an alternative dining venue for the first night of the cruise, you may get a discount on select lines (like Celebrity Cruises) or have an easier time getting a reservation for a popular venue.

Carnival Cruise Line passengers who dine in the steakhouse on the first night get a free bottle of wine.

- Specialty coffee at the designated coffee shops onboard comes with an extra fee, but the pastries, sandwiches and other food at these venues are often free. While some specialty items (like chocolate-covered strawberries) will have a charge, don't assume all the small bites do. Some bars — such as Celebrity's Martini Bar — also offer complimentary snacks; all you have to do is ask.
- Like ice cream? Cruise lines will charge for branded licks like Ben and Jerry's and Celebrity's gelato. However, there's always a free version — whether soft-serve machines on the Lido Deck or hard-serve stations at the buffet. And do your reconnaissance — Cruise Critic members report that soft-serve machines on either side of the deck can have different flavours.
- On embarkation day, most people head straight to the buffet to have lunch and wait for their cabins to open. It's a mob scene. But many cruise ships have alternative venues open — the main dining room or a mini-buffet in the solarium or atrium area. Ask a crew member or check your daily newsletter to find an alternative for a calmer first meal. For example, onPrincess Cruises, the International Cafe, Pizzeria and Grill also are open; on Royal Caribbean ships, Sorrento's, the Solarium and Park Cafes, Giovanni's Table, Cafe Promenade and Starbucks are open on the afternoon of embarkation.
- Don't know which night to make specialty dinner reservations? The main dining room menus are planned for the week, and the purser's desk often has access to those menus. Ask to see them so you can decide which nights are less appealing and which you don't want to miss, and plan your cruise accordingly.

Drink Secrets

- There's no "open beverage" rule onboard. You can bring drinks from a bar or buffet to your cabin or elsewhere on the ship and no one will bat an eye. (Same goes for food.)
- It's often cheaper to buy a bottle of wine than a few glasses — but what do you do if you don't finish the bottle? Cruise ship waiters can mark the bottle with your room number and save it for another night, even for dinner in another onboard venue.
- Groups of beer drinkers can save by ordering buckets of beer. You get four or five beers in a souvenir bucket at a per-beer cost slightly cheaper than ordering individual bottles.
- On most lines, soda is not free — but iced tea in the dining room usually is. Save on soda by buying a soda card, offering a set price for unlimited soft drinks.
- Most cruise lines prohibit passengers from bringing beer and liquor onboard, but do let you bring a bottle or two of wine or Champagne. Some lines (such as Norwegian) also let you bring a reasonable amount of non-alcoholic drinks onboard — which helps save on pricey shipboard sodas and bottled waters. Royal Caribbean passengers are prohibited from bringing any non-alcoholic beverages onboard, while Carnival only allows limited amounts of soda and juice as long as the drinks are in cans or cartons (and not glass containers).
- Enticed by all those special drinks in a souvenir glass? You can refill those glasses at a discount — or ask to have the drink of the day in a regular glass to save money. Also watch your daily programme for drink specials or happy hours with reduced-price beverages.

Cabin Secrets

- Most cabins are made of metal... and therefore they're magnetic. Bring along some magnets (or buy some as souvenirs) and you can keep all your cocktail party invites, alternative dining reservation notices and daily planners hung up on the walls and doors.
- Inside cabins have no natural light. At all. Turn your TV to the bridge cam station, turn off the sound and — voila! — you've got an instant nightlight and a way to see if the sun is up.
- Spa cabins can often be a smart financial decision for avid spagoers. For example, Carnival's Cloud 9 Spa balcony cabins include access to the thalassotherapy pool, steam room and sauna. The extra you'd pay for the cabin (above a regular balcony room) is often less than what you'd pay for a cruise-length spa pass.
- With all of the electronics we tote around with us these days, most people find cruise ship outlets to be insufficient. You can bring your own charging station or power strip, but you may also want to ask your cabin steward. Sometimes there's an extra outlet hidden behind the TV or under the bed.
- Picky about your bedding? Some lines will provide egg crate mattress toppers, top sheets and alternative pillow types by special request. Feel free to ask, before or during your cruise.
- Cabin designers are pretty smart about creating as much storage space as possible. Do a little exploring or ask your cabin steward for a tour. You may be surprised to find extra storage under the bed or couch, inside an ottoman or behind a mirror.

- If you're feeling queasy, don't run out to a pharmacy before making some calls. Room service can bring you green apples and bland crackers (crew members swear by the apple remedy), and often you can get seasickness meds from the purser's desk for free.

Entertainment Secrets

- Casino frequenters can get a hole punched in their room card and a free lanyard from the casino staff for easy play without forgetting your card in the slot machines.
- Many lines offer free minutes if you sign up for an Internet package on the first day of the cruise.
- Cruise ship spas often offer discounts for first-day and port-day treatments. Stop by the spa, or check your daily newsletters to find out about deals.
- If the port talk is at the same time as your massage, don't worry. Presentations and audience-participation shows are often re-broadcast on the ship's channel on your in-room TV. You can still catch the recording if you miss the live show.
- Use of the showers, saunas and stream rooms not located in fancy thermal suites is free. Showering in the spa can often mean access to more clean towels, fancy toiletries and bigger shower stalls — and prevents fights over who gets cabin bathroom access first. Using the free saunas is also a great remedy for that inevitable vacation head cold that stuffs you up.
- If you want to see one of the big-name shows on Royal Caribbean or Norwegian (like "Mamma Mia" or "Rock of Ages"), but tickets are sold out, don't fret. Many people reserve the free tickets but don't show up, so if you get in line prior to showtime, cruise ship staff will let you in if seats are available.

Cruise Line-Specific Secrets

- Celebrity's buffet secrets include delicious ship-made hard-serve ice cream (for free) in the buffet and made-to-order waffles with a choice of toppings. You can also order a cup of candy toppings with no ice cream if that's your treat of choice.
- On Holland America, many cruisers don't know that lunch at Tamarind is free (and discounted to $15 at the Pinnacle Grill), and free chocolate truffles make an appearance in the Explorer's Lounge each evening.
- Royal Caribbean's Promenade Cafe offers high-quality coffee without the price tag. It's no Starbuck's, but it's a step above what you'd find at the buffet.
- The North Star on Royal Caribbean's Quantum-class ships offers amazing views any time you go, but you'll get the best views on sea days. That's because the enclosed, glass capsule —which can rise to 300 feet above sea level — is often restricted from extending out over the side of the ship while in port.

ON BOARD FACILITIES

ACCOMMODATION

Choose from a wide range of well appointed suites and staterooms that include staterooms with balcony on ships like SuperStar Virgo and SuperStar Aquarius. Suite occupants enjoy priority check-in and will be accompanied onboard by Guest Services staff while luggage will be sent directly to the cabin . .

Dining

You can enjoy up to 6 meals a day which are included in the cruise package at the main dining restaurants or dine at our alternative restaurants which includes the Taj, a fully certified 'Halal' outlet on SuperStar Virgo at moderate charges.Please present your Access Card when entering any restaurant for verification purposes.Our restaurants have ample seating to accommodate all guests over the dining periods. However, to avoid any congestion, you may wish to eat earlier or later during the meal period.There is a nominal corkage charge if you bring your own alcoholic beverage to any of the dining outlets.

Gala Dinner

Guests are advised to book early for their gala dinner seating in their choice of restaurant to avoid disappointment.

Medical Facilities

In the event of minor accidents, inconveniences and emergencies while at sea, there is a fully qualified physician and a team of nurses onboard to assist.

The clinic is open daily at posted hours.Emergency medical attention is available around the clock by contacting the Reception. Basic medicine with your doctor's prescription are also available.

Room Service*

Continental breakfast and snacks are available throughout the day at nominal charges.*Cabin Service varies from vessel to vessel.

Shore Excursions

Our friendly crew at the Reception or our Shore Excursion Counter will be happy to explain the different options available at each port of call. You may join one of our pre-arranged tours or opt for free and easy on your own. As seats per tour are limited it is best to pre-book your shore excursion For shore visits, casual wear and comfortable walking shoes or sandals are recommended while suitable beachwear are ideal for island excursions. (Skimpy beachwear is inappropriate in Muslim countries). Bring sports or gym attire if you are planning to play golf, tennis or workout. During shore visits, however, it is wise to avoid consuming tap water or drinks with ice from street vendors.

Swimming Pool

For safety reasons, please do not leave your child unattended and guests are advised to take additional precautions while swimming. As towels are available provided at the poolside, please refrain from bring any from the cabin.The use of the swimming pools and Jacuzzis are for adults and teenagers over the age of 12 years only while there are also children's swimming pools and Jacuzzis on certain vessels.All users of the pools and Jacuzzis must wear proper swimming attire.

CELLULAR PHONE SERVICE AND TEXTING AT SEA

Freestyle Cellular Service

Star Cruises guests can make and receive calls, send and receive text messages, read e-mails and surf the web on their own cell phones and mobile devices just as they do on land when the ship is at sea, thanks to Wireless Maritime Services' Cellular@Sea Service. Just check with your cellular phone carrier that your cell phone will be able to roam internationally. Keeping in touch with your friends and family, while at sea, has never been easier.

5

Maritime Issues and Legislation in Cruise Hospitality

THE SHIPPING INDUSTRY

The cruise industry is a type of passenger travel that arose phoenix-like after the Second World War, when jet planes were introduced as mass transportation vehicles to replace the stately and seemingly invincible transatlantic liners.

Over the last three decades, the renaissance of cruising has been relentless and, for the large cruise corporations, it has also been highly lucrative. A number of issues yet remain that have a broader impact, from a shipping point of view, in terms of operational effectiveness, fair trading, environmentalism, and safety. The shipping industry is, according to Farthing and Brownrigg (1997), the most international of all industries.

This reflects the nature of transporting cargo or goods and people across seas and oceans internationally and the nature of the ships and their crew that are frequently multinational. However, the shipping industry is actually better described as a collection of industries.

According to Lloyd's Register of World Shipping (2004) there were 89,899 ships weighing a combined 605,218,000 GRT in 2003. This puts into stark relief the 255 ships that Ward (2005) identifies as the world cruising fleet in 2004. The Institute of Shipping Economics and Logistics (ISL) comments that, in 2003, around 75 per cent of the world cruise fleet was owned by three major corporations:

Carnival Corporation, 41.7 per cent; Royal Caribbean, 22.9 per cent; and Star Cruises, 8.9 per cent (ISL, 2003). Global ownership may be consolidating, but there is still evidence that a diverse range of ship management and ownership comes from outside this group of owner-managers (Panaydes, 2001), including those who charter, lease, and purchase management services. Some companies, such as Louis Cruises, own a fleet of vessels, some of which are chartered to tour operators (Louis Cruises, 2005). Others, like V Ships, are involved in supplying crew and management services for cruise companies (V Ships, 2005).

The Hanseatic is an example of a small vessel that is currently on long-term lease to German cruise operator Hapag Lloyd (Cruises, 2005). This complex pattern of ownership and management is fundamental for many operators involved in the contemporary cruise industry.

Table. The Components of Shipping.

Wet bulk	Carry wet cargoes such as oil, chemicals, petroleum or anything in liquid form in tanks or specially designed holds (ships may be called tankers)
Dry bulk	Carry dry commodities such as iron ore, coal, grain, fertilizers, and sugar
Cargo liners	Scheduled vessels that carry containers or space onboard to a specific timetable
Coastal and short sea	Sometimes called tramp ships, these vessels offer alternative means of transporting goods rather than using road or rail
Cruise ships or passenger liners	Cruise ships are more common than passenger liners although some services such as Cunard still provide some liner services
Ferries	Tend to provide liner-like scheduled services with facilities to carry people, cars and other transportation
Offshore operations	This sector includes oil and gas rigs and supports exploration for mineral extraction at sea

THE LEGAL ENVIRONMENT

According to Farthing and Brownrigg (1997), the notion of freedom of the seas stems from principles that were set out in the United Nations (UN) Law of the Sea Convention in 1982, which came into force in November 1994. This convention created an umbrella approach for virtually all activities undertaken in, over, or under the sea (including actions on and below the seabed). An important component of the legislation was the recognition that states possess an Exclusive Economic Zone (EEZ) that extends 200 nautical miles seaward. This convention allows freedom of navigation, rights of access or passage to shipping, or both, on the high seas, with certain provisos concerning access to the EEZ.

The regulation is an example of a collective international agreement that is established for the benefit of all signatories to the UN in order to allow for free enterprise, open competition, and economic freedom.

SHIP NATIONALITY, REGISTRATION, AND FLAG

The terms "nationality", "registration", and "flag" are sometimes used as if they were synonymous, but that is not totally accurate. Indeed, a ship may be deemed to have the nationality of a state even if there is no evidence of documentation for that nationality and the ship is unregistered. When a ship is registered, it is recorded officially and indicates that the ship possesses a certain nationality. The registration sets in place the framework for any legal consequences attributed to the ship's owner, the ship's managers, and the ship's crew. In public law, registration allocates the ship to a specific state, together with the jurisdiction that applies from that state, and protection from that state including the right to fly that state's flag.

In private law the registration creates protection for the title of the owner and those who may hold securities in the form of financial interests of the vessel. The flag is symbolic and flown at the ship's stern as a mark of identification but otherwise the term "flag" is shorthand for the nationality of a vessel (Farthing and Brownrigg, 1997).

The implications of nationality for a ship and its owner present serious issues, apart from the aforementioned legal aspects, that can affect operational costs. Some countries require that ships registered in that country be crewed either entirely by nationals or a given percentage of nationals. For example the crewing, ship construction, and ownership requirements to flag a vessel in the United States are said to be among the most restrictive of the maritime nations. Current manning regulations for USflag vessels engaged in coastwise trade mandate that all officers and pilots and 75 per cent of other on board personnel be US citizens or residents. In addition, US-flag vessels engaged in coastwise trade must be owned by US citizens and constructed in US shipyards. This construction requirement applies to the entire hull and superstructure of the ship and the majority of all materials outfitting the vessel. A cruise ship has many options for registration with states or countries that may be other than the owner's nationality.

The reasons and benefits for this are many, including:

- Neutrality in the event of conflict
- Reduced tax liability
- Reduced registration fees
- Reduced crewing costs

Panama, Liberia, Cyprus, the Bahamas, and Malta were stated by Farthing and Brownrigg (1997) to be five of the world's largest fleets, suggesting that these states operated more liberal, economically attractive conditions and that they were seen to be effective and efficient in supporting the needs of ship operators. According to the ISL, nearly half of the world cruise fleet is now attributable to the Bahamas and Panama. The Bahamas, Panama, and Liberia had previously dominated the cruise shipping industry, but in 2003, nineteen vessels switched registration from Liberia to Panama because of the unstable political situation in the west African country (ISL, 2003).

According to the ICCL (2005), the major countries offering flags of registry for cruise vessels are the United Kingdom, Liberia, Panama, Norway, Netherlands, the Bahamas and, despite the stringent regulations, the United

States. All of these countries are member states of the International Maritime Organization (IMO), an organization that is centrally important for maritime developments relating to safety. The ICCL identifies a number of factors that must be met for a valid registry. One is that a flag state must be an IMO member nation, which has adopted all of the IMO's maritime safety resolutions and conventions.

Secondly, a flag state should have an established maritime organization that is capable of enforcing all international and national regulations. Major flag registries are said to provide comprehensive maritime expertise and administrative services. In addition they are required to conduct annual safety inspections prior to the issuance of a passenger vessel certificate and use recognized classification societies to monitor its vessels' compliance with all international and flag state standards.

SAFETY OF LIFE AT SEA

The International Convention for the Safety of Life at Sea (SOLAS) was first adopted in 1948. It is called a "living" document—that is, one that is continuously amended and updated. SOLAS is concerned with the establishment of international regulations that address maritime safety, including lifesaving, fire protection, and ship stability. According to the US Coast Guard, cruise ships are regulated for safety by government agencies in the following way (US Coast Guard, 2004). While some vessels are registered in the United States, current patterns suggest that most are not, and for these vessels the safety inspection is administered within the country of registration.

The US Coast Guard requires any ship, irrespective of country of registration, to meet the SOLAS convention if they wish to take on vessels in US ports. US law expects that any cruise company advertising in the United States will disclose the country of registration for their vessels. SOLAS is far reaching in its remit and requires compliance with stringent regulations regarding structural fire protection, firefighting and lifesaving equipment, watercraft integrity and stability, vessel control, navigation safety, crewing and crew competency, safety management, and environmental protection.

The Coast Guard, in respect of SOLAS requirements, examines all cruise ships when they first visit US ports. Thereafter, the vessels are inspected, or checked for compliance, quarterly.

Records relating to these inspections (called Control Verification Examinations) are available for public scrutiny. Inspectors involved with these examinations board the ship to verify structural fire safety, ensure that lifesaving equipment is available and located as required in the appropriate condition, witness fire and abandon ship drills as conducted by the ship's crew, and test key equipment such as steering systems, fire pumps, and lifeboats. The Coast Guard has the authority to require correction of any deficiencies before allowing the ship to take on passengers at the US port. In terms of crew member competence, the Coast Guard can suspend or revoke licenses or merchant mariner's documents if a US-registered ship is found to be operating below published standards for experience and training. On foreignflag ships, SOLAS requires that the ships must be efficiently and sufficiently staffed, and this is checked during control verification examinations.. SOLAS is not designed to provide guarantees for health care, and, as a result, it is not a proviso that cruise ships carry a ship's doctor.

SOLAS requires that the ship's captain schedule and implement periodic fire and lifeboat drills. This is intended both to give the crew practice and to show passengers the critical action that may be required in the event of a serious incident or emergency on board.

For this reason SOLAS expects that all passengers participate in these drills. The drills are scheduled according to the duration of the cruise. In a one-week cruise, the first drill would take place as soon as all passengers were on board and immediately prior to sailing. If the cruise lasts more than a week, an additional drill would take place every week thereafter. For a cruise lasting less than a week, the drill takes place within 24 hours of departure from the home port.

Notices are to be posted in clear view in every passenger cabin or stateroom to provide easily understood information regarding safety issues. *This notice includes:*

- How to recognize the ship's emergency signals (alarm bells and whistle signals are normally supplemented by announcements made over the ship's public address system).
- The location of passenger life preservers in that stateroom (special life preservers will be provided for children, if necessary, by the room steward).
- Instructions and pictures explaining how to put on the life preserver, as well as the lifeboat assignment for passengers in specific staterooms. Modern cruise ships carry a variety of survival craft. Passengers are invariably assigned to lifeboats or similar survival craft that can be used in an emergency.

Crew members from the hotel department play an important and potentially critical part in the safety routines and are generally responsible for assisting and directing passengers for emergency drills, although some may have other safety duties. The regulations call for direction signs showing the path to reach lifeboats to be posted in passageways and stairways throughout the ship. The crew member in charge of each lifeboat will gather or muster the passengers assigned to that lifeboat and give passengers any final instructions for properly donning and adjusting their life preservers. The crew should be prepared to help passengers and clarify the emergency procedures, if necessary.

MARITIME ORGANIZATIONS

It is important to recognize certain organizations involved in the maritime industry or the cruise industry. A number of these organizations, some of which have been previously mentioned, are listed and described below.

IMO (International Maritime Organization) The International Maritime Organization (formerly known as the Intergovernmental Maritime

Consultative Organization) was established in 1948 as an agency of the United Nations to set international maritime policy and regulate the shipping industry. In this capacity, it develops a crossgovernmental, consensual approach for safety and practices at sea. The IMO is the glue that binds together the treaties and conventions for international shipping, with responsibility for ensuring compliance with implementation of regulations, although the principal responsibility for enforcing these regulations rests with the flag states, or the country within which the ship is registered. "Port state control" supplements flag-state enforcement by allowing officials from any country a ship may visit to inspect foreign flag ships to ensure that they comply with international requirements. The IMO's slogan, "Safe, secure, and efficient shipping on clean oceans," encapsulates the agency's mission statement. Despite this seemingly mammoth task, the organization remains relatively lean in scale because of the requirement for individual countries to undertake enforcement.

The US Coast Guard represents the United States in this international agency. The IMO has been instrumental in the development and adoption of several important treaties or conventions, including the previously mentioned SOLAS agreement, the International Convention for the Prevention of Pollution from Ships (known as the MARPOL agreement), and the International Safety Management Code (ISM), which is part of SOLAS and the Standards for Training, Certification, and Watch-keeping (STCW).

Classification Societies

These classification societies are mainly organizations whose primary function is to inspect ships at regular intervals to ensure they are seaworthy and regularly maintained in keeping with the classification societies' rules. Classification societies also inspect cruise ships for compliance with international safety regulations, including SOLAS, STCW, and MARPOL.

Major classification societies include the American Bureau of Shipping in the United States, Lloyd's Register of Shipping in the United Kingdom, Det Norske Veritas in Norway, Bureau Veritas in France, and Registro Italiano Navale Group in Italy.

Cruise Lines International Association (CLIA)

The CLIA is a marketing and promotion organization that represents 23 member cruise lines and approximately 19,000 North American travel agencies.

The CLIA was formed in 1975 with the specific intent of promoting the benefits of cruising. The CLIA also undertakes training in line with its mission "to educate travel agents and to promote the value, desirability, and affordability of the cruise vacation experience." The CLIA joined with the International Council of Cruise Lines to establish the Cruise Line Coalition in 2001 to act as an information source for the industry.

International Council of Cruise Lines (ICCL)

The ICCL is a trade association that represents a range of major cruise companies and associate members such as suppliers and industry partners. With its mission to "participate in the regulatory and policy development process and ensure that all measures adopted provide for a safe, secure, and healthy cruise ship environment," the association has an important role to play. To achieve its aims, the association analyzes and interprets international shipping policy and offers recommendations to its membership on a wide variety of issues, including safety, public health, environmental responsibility, security, medical facilities, passenger protection, and legislative activities. In undertaking its role, the ICCL works closely with key domestic and international regulatory organizations, policymakers, and other industry partners and serves as a non-governmental consultative organization to the IMO.

Florida-Caribbean Cruise Association (FCCA)

This is a trade organization that was inaugurated in 1972 to provide a forum for 13 cruise brands to meet and debate operational issues concerning them. The FCCA can highlight legislation, tourism development, port safety, security, and other emerging issues to create solutions that are a product of cooperation and partnership.

The FCCA also undertakes targeted training, such as customer service programmes for taxi drivers in ports, as well as commissioning research looking at the impacts of cruising.

The association has created a charitable foundation to find humaritarian causes and help to improve the laws of people most in need.

North West Cruise Ship Association (NWCA)

The North West Cruise Ship Association is a not-for-profit body that represents nine cruise lines operating in Hawaii, Canada, Alaska, and the Pacific Northwest. The association was established in 1986 initially to focus on security concerns, although later it developed a broader role addressing government relations with respect to legal and regulatory issues. In addition, the association seeks to maintain positive links with the local communities involved in cruising areas in order to work on environmental protection, economic development, and other industry-connected concerns.

SHIPPING INDUSTRY

Shipping, or carriage of goods by water, has played a significant role in the development of human society over the centuries. Shipping has been a crucial link by which commercial relationships have been established between widely separated parts of the world. There are 2 major types of shipping services: shipload services, which move goods in bulk for one or a few shippers; and liner services, which carry relatively small shipments of general cargo on a regular schedule for many shippers. Some ships are owned by firms engaged in the production or processing of goods in bulk. Examples are tankers owned by petroleum companies, and bulk carriers owned by steel companies. Most ships, however, are owned by firms whose prime business is shipping. These owners make their vessels available to importers/exporters through a highly efficient international network of shipping brokers.

History and Development

Shipping is often the least expensive way of moving large quantities of goods over long distances. The existence of reliable water transportation has been a key to the economic and political well-being of most nations throughout history. For example, the merchant fleet of Great Britain during the Industrial Revolution was instrumental in the growth of that nation as a world power. Shipping services have always been an economic lifeline for Canadians. For the first settlers, ships were the source of essential supplies from the Old World, and they provided the means by which fur, agricultural, forestry and mining products could be marketed. In eastern Canada, especially in the Maritimes, a tradition based on SHIPBUILDING, fishing and trade flourished.

In 1840 Samuel CUNARD of Halifax established a transoceanic service that developed into the world-famous CUNARD COMPANY, and by 1878 Canada ranked fourth among the shipowning nations of the world. However, in the last decades of the century, Canadian participation in shipbuilding and shipping diminished, as steel and engineering skills, which Canada lacked, became prerequisites for a successful shipbuilding industry. The 2 world wars caused temporary booms in shipping under the Canadian flag, but since 1949, when the Canadian government decided to sell off its Canadian-registered fleet, the vast majority of Canadian overseas trade has been carried in ships registered in other countries. Most Canadian-registered ships now operate on domestic routes, such as the ST LAWRENCE SEAWAY, the Great Lakes and the coastlines.

ECONOMIC SIGNIFICANCE

Shipping is especially important to Canada because of the importance of trade in the economy (in 1996, exports were 33.5 per cent and imports 29.2 per cent of Gross Domestic Product), and the importance of water transport in facilitating this export and import trade. About one third of exports and over a quarter of imports by value are transported by water, more than half of this by liner vessels. Although trade with the US is dominant and mostly by land transport, shipping is vital to the competitiveness of resource-based products in world markets. Liner shipping accounts for more than one half of the value of exports. However, because of the volume of resource exports and oil imports, the quantity of goods carried by shipload services greatly exceeds that carried by liners.

Although the Canadian-registered deep-sea fleet is small, officers and crews are needed to operate vessels on domestic routes. Vessels arriving from abroad require a variety of services, including Canadian pilots and tugs to bring them into port, as well as repair facilities and supply services in port. The movement of the cargoes themselves also creates considerable employment. For example, longshoremen help load and unload cargoes on the docks, and many persons, such as customs and insurance agents, look after documentary and other related requirements. Shipping agents, located in port cities, sell shipping services and co-ordinate the arrangements for ships and handling of cargo.

Domestic and Transborder Routes

Domestic shipping can be divided into 3 main categories. East Coast traffic consists primarily of fuel, pulpwood and general cargo shipments to Newfoundland and along the coastlines of the Maritime provinces and into the St Lawrence. The St Lawrence-Great Lakes traffic is by far the most important route. The main commodity movements are grain from the Lakehead to the St Lawrence ports, andIRON ORE from Canada to the US. West Coast shipping services include the movement of forest products and other natural resources, often by tug and barge operations.

On both the East and West coasts there is an extensive network of ferry services (seeFERRIES). Other shipping services include occasional intercoastal movements of bulk commodities, barge services on the MACKENZIE RIVER and supply services to Arctic communities. Shipping is a key to the development of Canada's North, a means by which natural resources can be reached (seeTRANSPORTATION IN THE NORTH). The supply lines to many remote northern communities are maintained as the weather permits. In 1969 the American tanker SS Manhattan successfully navigated theNORTHWEST PASSAGE with the aid of a Canadian Coast Guard vessel, thereby proving that mineral and petroleum resources in remote northern areas could be reached by water (seeICEBREAKERS).

Overseas Shipping

Canada's most important overseas trading partners are Japan, Great Britain and other western European nations, so that the busiest shipping routes are the North Atlantic and the North Pacific. Significant ties are maintained with all regions of the world, and bulk shipping services are available as needed. Canada's trade is carried in vessels registered in many different countries. Many of these deep-sea vessels are registered in so-called flag-of-convenience nations, such as Liberia and Panama, where favourable tax and legal environments permit lower-cost operations.

SHIPS AND PORT FACILITIES

Ships and port facilities are efficiently serving Canadian trade. Specially designed ships and port facilities have been built to accommodate particular commodities. In eastern Canada, for example, ships called LAKE CARRIERS are built to the maximum allowable seaway dimensions. Maximum-sized lakers can carry about 29 000 tonnes (28 000 cargo capacity, 1000 fuel etc). On the West Coast, the self-dumping log barge has been developed for use in the forest industry. Roberts Bank, BC, is the site of a large coal superport, specially designed to handle the large volume of coal which arrives by rail for export overseas. Modern container terminals are essential to the liner services of Halifax, Montréal and Vancouver.

Canadian Shipping Today

Few Canadian-flag ships operate deep-sea routes. As of 31 December 1994 the Canadian-flag fleet of vessels over 100 gross registered tons (grt) was 2.5 million grt. By comparison, the three largest fleets were those of Panama, 64.2 million grt; Liberia, 57.6 million grt; and Greece, 30.2 million grt.

The US fleet at 13.7 million grt was eleventh and the UK fleet at 6.5 million grt was sixteenth (Lloyds Register of Shipping). Most Canadian-registered merchant vessels operate on domestic routes, although several vessels constructed for the Great Lakes-St Lawrence Seaway traffic are also capable of transoceanic voyages.

The government implemented the recommendations of the 1985 task force on deep-sea shipping by amending tax regulations so that the management of international shipping could be conducted in Canada without exposing the earnings of the shipping services to corporate tax until distributed. This made Canada competitive with other countries as most ship owners do not pay tax. The result has been an increase in the number of shipowners in Canada and an increase in employment opportunities.

While several existing Canadian companies have retained their prior structure, for example, Canada Maritime (a subsidiary of CANADIAN PACIFIC LTD.) and Fednav Ltd, other companies have been able to expand into ship ownership, for example, Canadian Transport Company (until 1997 a subsidiary ofMACMILLAN BLOEDEL). A number of companies have moved into Canada; the largest is Teekay Shipping, a public company specializing in oil tanker shipping.

Regulation

Most shipping is by nature international - the carriage of goods between countries and across international waters. A ship may be owned, financed, registered, insured, and managed, each in a different country. When a ship is registered in any given country, it becomes subject to the laws of that country at all times. Each country has the right to establish its own shipping laws. International shipping conventions have been reached by a number of intergovernmental organizations, such as the International Labour Organization (ILO) and the International Maritime Organization (IMO). Many of the conventions have been ratified by Canada.

The United Nations Conference of the Law of the Sea (UNCLOS) has established a new regime of international maritime law of interest to shipowners and shippers. UNCLOS defines international maritime boundaries and, therefore, the extent of coastal state jurisdiction in environmental-protection and coastal shipping regulation.

In Canada, shipping falls under the jurisdiction of the federal Department of TRANSPORT. The Canada Shipping Act sets out the basic rules for ships flying the Canadian flag or operating in Canadian waters. The CANADIAN COAST GUARD ensures that ships meet the requirements of the Shipping Act and follow pollution-prevention procedures. The Canada Transportation Agency (formerly National Transportation Agency; CANADIAN TRANSPORT COMMISSION) is responsible for economic regulation: for example, shipping conferences must file their rates with the Agency. The Canada Maritime Act of 1997 proposes to decentralize the management of ports by allowing major ports to form self-funding port corporations.

INDUSTRIAL CARRIERS

Industrial carriers are vessels operated by large corporations to provide transportation essential to the processes of manufacture and distribution. These vessels are run to ports and on schedules determined by the specific needs of the owners. The ships may belong to the corporations or may be chartered. For example, the Bethlehem Steel Corp. maintains a fleet of Great Lakes ore carriers, a number of specialized ships that haul ore from South America to Baltimore, Maryland, and a fleet of dry-cargo ships that transports steel products from Baltimore to the Pacific coast. Many oil companies maintain large fleets of deep-sea tankers, towboats, and river barges to carry petroleum to and from refineries. The ships often operate under contracts of affreightment.

TANKER OPERATION

All tankers are private or contract carriers. In the 1970s some 34 percent of the world tanker fleet, which aggregates about 200 million dwt, was owned by oil companies; the remaining tonnage belonged to independent shipowners who chartered their vessels to the oil companies. So-called supertankers, which exceed 100,000 dwt, are employed to transport crude petroleum from the oil fields to refineries. The refined products, such as gasoline, kerosene, and lubricating oils, are distributed by smaller tankers, generally less than 30,000 dwt, and by barges.

VESSEL TYPES

Merchant ships are classified as passenger carriers, cargo ships, and tankers. During the height of passenger travel by ship, the largest as well as the most glamorous ships afloat were the famed liners of the North Atlantic, which, beginning in the mid-19th century, sailed regular schedules between the Americas and Europe.

Competing in speed as well as in size and appointments, such ships as the Mauretania, the Queen Mary, the Queen Elizabeth, the United States, and the France gradually reduced the time for the North Atlantic crossing to less than four days.

Their size, from about 45,000 to 75,000 metric tons and up to 300 m (1,000 ft) in length, was gigantic by the standards of the first half of the 20th century, but they have been dwarfed by the oil tankers of the 1970s and '80s. Today's passenger liners operate principally in the cruise trade.

CARGO SHIPS

Cargo ships carry packaged goods, unitized cargo (cargo in which a number of items are consolidated into one large shipping unit for easier handling), and limited amounts of grain, ore, and liquids such as latex and edible oils. A few passengers are accepted on some cargo liners. Specialized ships are designed and built to carry certain types of cargo, for example, automobiles or grain.

CONTAINER SHIPS

In the late 1950s container ships set the pattern for technological change in cargo handling and linked the trucking industry to deep-Sea shipping. These highly specialized ships carry large truck bodies and can discharge and load in one day, in contrast to the ten days required by conventional ships of the same size.

The rapid development of the container ship began in 1956, when Sea-Land Service commenced operations between New York City and Houston, Texas. Barge-aboard, or lighter-aboard, ships, also called seabees (sea barges) or LASH (lighter-aboard ships), resulted from an evolutionary development of the container ship. They are capable of carrying about 38 barges, or up to 1,600 containers, or a combination of containers and barges. Their design enables them to deliver cargo to developed or undeveloped ports, without the need for berthing.

TANKERS

Tankers, designed specifically to carry liquid cargoes, usually petroleum, have grown to many-compartmented giants of a million metric tons and more. Despite their great size, their construction is simple, as is, for the most part, their operation. A major problem with the giant tankers is the severe environmental damage of oil spills, resulting from collision, storm damage, or leakage from other causes. Specialized tankers transport liquefied natural gas (LNG), liquid chemicals, wine, molasses, and refrigerated products.

TREATIES AND CONVENTIONS

Many treaties and conventions have been adopted over the years with the objective of increasing the safety of life at sea. One of the most important agreements provided for the establishment of the International Iceberg Patrol in 1913, after the Titanic disaster. Under the International Load-Line Convention of 1930, ship loading was regulated on the basis of size, cargo, and route of the vessel. The International Convention for the Safety of Life at Sea, which governs ship construction, was ratified by most maritime nations in 1936, and updated in 1948, and again in 1960 and 1974.

THE LEGAL ENVIRONMENT

The cruise ship industry has experienced an enormous growth in terms of popularity, size and variety of destinations in the last years, with bigger and more luxurious ships designed to meet the also growing demand for cruising as a holiday option that offers beauty, adventure, relaxation and entertainment to passengers from across the world. The splendour of tourist destinations and their natural beauty are essential to maintain such demand, so the future of the cruise industry depends on and is inextricably linked to environmental performance and compliance.

Although the cruise industry represents just a small portion of the international maritime activity, and environmental issues associated with it is not unique to this sector, cruise ships and their passengers and crews generate a more significant volume of waste and pollutant emissions, both while underway and docked in port, with an also more important effect on the subset of ports and coastal areas along cruise routes.

As cruise ships get larger and more luxurious, they also produce more waste. Recently, U.S. Environmental Protection Agency estimated that, during a one-week voyage, a large cruise ship with capacity for 3,000 passengers and crewmembers can produce around 210,000 gallons (794,850 L) of sewage stream, one million gallons (3.785 million L) of greywater, 25,000 gallons (95,000 L) of oily bilge water, 150 gallons (568 L) of hazardous wastes, 8 tons of solid waste and a difficult-to-calculate quantity of air pollutants, which must be multiplied by the more than 200 cruise ships currently plying the world's waterways 365 days a year.

In fact, it has been suggested that cruise ships constitute about 77 per cent of the marine pollution world wide. These wastes represent a significant source of pathogens and toxic substances that, if not properly treated and disposed of, can have a serious effect on human health, including disturbance and destruction of fishing grounds and precious marine ecosystems such as coral reefs.

The most worrying aspect of this whole situation is that cruise ship waste disposal is highly unregulated, and waste can be dumped just few short miles off shore (returning later to coasts by ocean currents) rather than installing appropriate onboard treatment systems. Formerly, discharges from most cruise ships usually exceed the water quality standards established by national authorities and international associations and organisms in relation to concentration of bacteria, metals, hydrocarbons and plastics. In many cases, there was no monitoring, no enforcement and no recourse for local authorities if cruise companies violate the existing pollution standards.

Nevertheless, the repeated public exposés of environmental abuses committed by cruise companies, which include viral and bacterial epidemics, are a serious problem that have caused these organizations severe embarrassment and lawsuits, indicating the need for more strict monitoring of waste discharges, and pressing the industry to adhere to a new ethical and procedural code in the application of more advanced waste treatment technologies meeting more rigourous environmental control standards and procedures.

In this regard, especial attention must by paid to the pressure from coastal localities and areas without large commercial port infrastructures, which complain about air quality problems derived from gas emissions produced by shipboard diesel engines and incinerators while in port. Although the cruise industry unabashedly promotes itself as environmentally friend, the reality is that there is a long history of breaking the law, seeking all kinds of concessions and non-regulation by lobbying and local regulators; in addition to the progressive accumulation of hundreds of pollution violations, which have resulted in higher-level enforcement actions and the payment of millions of dollars in environmental fines for illegally dumping water waste, garbage and other toxic waste into coastal and international waters. These cases have involved both small and large cruise companies in a diversity of surrounding circumstances and volume of discharge, which also varies widely, from tons of oil and solid garbage to drops of oil-based paint that spilled into the water during painting of a ship's hull.

Regarding the causes, in some cases environmental incidents is accidental, resulting from mere human or mechanical error, such as many fuel-related discharge cases involving cruise ships loading fuel in port. In other cases, environmental damage is caused in circumstances that cannot be determined from the available information. Finally, there have been companies involved in discharges that were judged to be intentional, including a number of cases in which cruise companies pled guilty to the wilful, regular and routine discharge of hazardous waste into the water, use of permanent piping that allowed oily waste to be discharged directly overboard, use of bypass pipes allowing employees to avoid pollution control devices and discharge liquid waste from the ship without first processing it, failure to keep of records of waste discharges, presentation of false record books during environmental pollution investigation procedures, etc.

As an example, we can mention the acknowledgment of guilt by Royal Caribbean executives for several episodes of disposal of toxic waste into the Alaska's Inland Passage waters in 1.999, which unleashed a flurry of activity among citizen-based environmental organizations, and an aggressive effort to legislate compliance to environmental regulations, promoting the development and implementation of diverse monitoring programmes for cleaner air emissions and water and waste effluent from 2.000.

ENVIRONMENTAL IMPACT OF SHIPPING

A cargo ship discharging ballast water into the sea. The environmental impact of shipping includes greenhouse gas emissions, acoustic, and oil pollution. The International Maritime Organization (IMO) estimates that Carbon dioxide emissions from shipping were equal to 2.2 per cent of the global human-made emissions in 2012and expects them to rise by as much as 2 to 3 times by 2050 if no action is taken. The First Intersessional Meeting of the IMO Working Group on Greenhouse Gas Emissions from Ships took place in Oslo, Norway on 23–27 June 2008. It was tasked with developing the technical basis for the reduction mechanisms that may form part of a future IMO regime to control greenhouse gas emissions from international shipping, and a draft of the actual reduction mechanisms themselves, for further consideration by IMO's Marine Environment Protection Committee (MEPC).

BALLAST WATER

Ballast water discharges by ships can have a negative impact on the marine environment. Cruise ships, large tankers, and bulk cargo carriers use a huge amount of ballast water, which is often taken on in the coastal waters in one region after ships discharge wastewater or unload cargo, and discharged at the next port of call, wherever more cargo is loaded. Ballast water discharge typically contains a variety of biological materials, including plants, animals, viruses, and bacteria. These materials often include non-native, nuisance, invasive, exotic species that can cause extensive ecological and economic damage to aquatic ecosystems along with serious human health problems.

SOUND POLLUTION

Noise pollution caused by shipping and other human enterprises has increased in recent history. The noise produced by ships can travel long distances, and marine species who may rely on sound for their orientation, communication, and feeding, can be harmed by this sound pollution The Convention on the Conservation of Migratory Species has identified ocean noise as a potential threat to marine life.

WILDLIFE COLLISIONS

Marine mammals, such as whales and manatees, risk being struck by ships, causing injury and death. For example, if a ship is traveling at a speed of only 15 knots, there is a 79 percent chance of a collision being lethal to a whale.

One notable example of the impact of ship collisions is the endangered North Atlantic right whale, of which 400 or less remain. The greatest danger to the North Atlantic right whale is injury sustained from ship strikes. Between 1970 and 1999, 35.5 percent of recorded deaths were attributed to collisions. During 1999 to 2003, incidents of mortality and serious injury attributed to ship strikes averaged one per year. In 2004 to 2006, that number increased to 2.6. Deaths from collisions has become an extinction threat.

ATMOSPHERIC POLLUTION

Exhaust gases from ships are considered to be a significant source of air pollution, both for conventional pollutants and greenhouse gases.

There is a perception that cargo transport by ship is low in air pollutants, because for equal weight and distance it is the most efficient transport method, according to shipping researcher Amy Bows-Larkin. This is particularly true in comparison to air freight; however, because sea shipment accounts for far more annual tonnage and the distances are often large, shipping's emissions are globally substantial. A difficulty is that the year-on-year increasing amount shipping overwhelms gains in efficiency, such as fromslow-steaming or the use of kites. The growth in tonne-kilometers of sea shipment has averaged 4 percent yearly since the 1990s. and it has grown by a factor of 5 since the 1970s. There are now over 100,000 transport ships at sea, of which about 6,000 are large container ships.

Conventional Pollutants

Air pollution from cruise ships is generated by diesel engines that burn high sulfur content fuel oil, also known as bunker oil, producing sulfur dioxide, nitrogen oxide andparticulate, in addition to carbon monoxide, carbon dioxide, and hydrocarbons. Diesel exhaust has been classified by EPA as a likely human carcinogen. EPA recognizes that these emissions from marine diesel engines contribute to ozone and carbon monoxide non-attainment (i.e., failure to meet air quality standards), as well as adverse health effects associated with ambient concentrations of particulate matter and visibility, haze, acid deposition, and eutrophication and nitrification of water. EPA estimates that large marine diesel engines accounted for about 1.6 percent of mobile source nitrogen oxide emissions and 2.8 percent of mobile source particulate emissions in the United States in 2000. Contributions of marine diesel engines can be higher on a port-specific basis. Ultra-low sulfur diesel (ULSD) is a standard for defining diesel fuel with substantially loweredsulfur contents. As of 2006, almost all of the petroleum-based diesel fuel available in Europe and North America is of a ULSD type.

Of total global air emissions, shipping accounts for 18 to 30 percent of the nitrogen oxide and 9 percent of the sulphur oxides. Sulfur in the air creates acid rain which damages crops and buildings. When inhaled, sulfur is known to cause respiratory problems and even increases the risk of a heart attack. According to Irene Blooming, a spokeswoman for the European environmental coalition Seas at Risk, the fuel used in oil tankers and container ships is high in sulfur and cheaper to buy compared to the fuel used for domestic land use. "A ship lets out around 50 times more sulfur than a lorry per metric tonne of cargo carried." Cities in the U.S. like Long Beach, Los Angeles,Houston, Galveston, and Pittsburgh see some of the heaviest shipping traffic in the nation and have left local officials desperately trying to clean up the air. Increasing trade between the U.S. and China is helping to increase the number of vessels navigating the Pacific and exacerbating many of the environmental problems. To maintain the level of growth China is experiencing, large amounts of grain are being shipped to China by the boat load. The number of voyages are expected to continue increasing.

Greenhouse Gas Pollutants

3.5 to 4 percent of all climate change emissions are caused by shipping, primarily carbon dioxide. As one way to reduce the impact of greenhouse gas emissions from shipping, vetting agency RightShip developed an online "Greenhouse Gas (GHG) Emissions Rating" as a systematic way for the industry to compare a ship's CO_2 emissions with peer vessels of a similar size and type. Based on the International Maritime Organisation's (IMO) Energy Efficiency Design Index (EEDI) that applies to ships built from 2013, RightShip's GHG Rating can also be applied to vessels built prior to 2013, allowing for effective vessel comparison across the world's fleet. The GHG Rating utilises an A to G scale, where A represents the most efficient ships. It measures the theoretical amount of carbon dioxide emitted per tonne nautical mile travelled, based on the design characteristics of the ship at time of build such as cargo carrying capacity, engine power and fuel consumption. Higher rated ships can deliver significantly lower CO_2 emissions across the voyage length, which means they also use less fuel and are cheaper to run.

Fig. Cruise ship haze over Juneau, Alaska

Stress for Improvement

One source of environmental stresses on maritime vessels recently has come from states and localities, as they assess the contribution of commercial marine vessels to regional air quality problems when ships are docked at port.

For instance, large marine diesel engines are believed to contribute 7 percent of mobile source nitrogen oxide emissions in Baton Rouge/New Orleans. Ships can also have a significant impact in areas without large commercial ports: they contribute about 37 percent of total area nitrogen oxide emissions in the Santa Barbara area, and that percentage is expected to increase to 61 percent by 2015. Again, there is little cruise-industry specific data on this issue. They comprise only a small fraction of the world shipping fleet, but cruise ship emissions may exert significant impacts on a local scale in specific coastal areas that are visited repeatedly. Shipboard incinerators also burn large volumes of garbage, plastics, and other waste, producing ash that must be disposed of. Incinerators may release toxic emissions as well.

In 2005, MARPOL Annex VI came into force to combat this problem. As such cruise ships now employ CCTV monitoring on the smokestacks as well as recorded measuring via opacity meter while some are also using clean burning gas turbines for electrical loads and propulsion in sensitive areas.

OIL SPILLS

Most commonly associated with ship pollution are oil spills. While less frequent than the pollution that occurs from daily operations, oil spills have devastating effects. While being toxic to marine life, polycyclic aromatic hydrocarbons (PAHs), the components in crude oil, are very difficult to clean up, and last for years in the sediment and marine environment. Marine species constantly exposed to PAHs can exhibit developmental problems, susceptibility to disease, and abnormal reproductive cycles.

One of the more widely known spills was the Exxon Valdez incident in Alaska. The ship ran aground and dumped a massive amount of oil into the ocean in March 1989. Despite efforts of scientists, managers and volunteers, over 400,000 seabirds, about 1,000 sea otters, and immense numbers of fish were killed.

INTERNATIONAL REGULATION

Some of the major international efforts in the form of treaties are the Marine Pollution Treaty, Honolulu, which deals with regulating marine pollution from ships, and the UN Convention on Law of the Sea, which deals with marine species and pollution. While plenty of local and international regulations have been introduced throughout maritime history, much of the current regulations are considered inadequate. "In general, the treaties tend to emphasize the technical features of safety and pollution control measures without going to the root causes of sub-standard shipping, the absence of incentives for compliance and the lack of enforceability of measures." Cruise ships, for example, are exempt from regulation under the US discharge permit system (NPDES, under the Clean Water Act) that requires compliance with technology-based standards. In theCaribbean, many ports lack proper waste disposal facilities, and many ships dump their waste at sea.

SEWAGE

Carcass of a whale on a shore in Iceland. The cruise line industry dumps 255,000 US gallons (970 m^3) of greywater and 30,000 US gallons (110 m^3) of blackwater into the sea every day.

Blackwater is sewage, wastewater from toilets and medical facilities, which can contain harmful bacteria, pathogens, viruses,intestinal parasites, and harmful nutrients. Discharges of untreated or inadequately treated sewage can cause bacterial and viralcontamination of fisheries and shellfish beds, producing risks to public health. Nutrients in sewage, such as nitrogen and phosphorus, promote excessive algal blooms, which consumes oxygen in the water and can lead to fish kills and destruction of other aquatic life. A large cruise ship (3,000 passengers and crew) generates an estimated 55,000 to 110,000 litres per day of blackwater waste.

Due to the environmental impact of shipping, and sewage in particular marpol annex IV was brought into force September 2003 strictly limiting untreated waste discharge. Modern cruise ships are most commonly installed with a membrane bioreactor type treatment plant for all blackwater and greywater, such as (http://www.gertsen-olufsen.com/Ship-Offshore/Products/G-O_Brands/G-O_Bioreactor.aspx) , Zenon or Rochem which produce near drinkable quality effluent to be re-used in the machinery spaces as technical water.

CLEANING

Greywater is wastewater from the sinks, showers, galleys, laundry, and cleaning activities aboard a ship. It can contain a variety of pollutant substances, including fecal coliforms, detergents, oil and grease, metals, organic compounds, petroleum hydrocarbons, nutrients, food waste, medical and dental waste. Sampling done by the EPA and the state of Alaska found that untreated greywater from cruise ships can contain pollutants at variable strengths and that it can contain levels of fecal coliform bacteria several times greater than is typically found in untreated domestic wastewater. Greywater has potential to cause adverse environmental effects because of concentrations of nutrients and other oxygen-demanding materials, in particular. Greywater is typically the largest source of liquid waste generated by cruise ships (90 to 95 percent of the total). Estimates of greywater range from 110 to 320 litres per day per person, or 330,000 to 960,000 litres per day for a 3,000-person cruise ship.

SOLID WASTE

Solid waste generated on a ship includes glass, paper, cardboard, aluminium and steel cans, and plastics. It can be either non-hazardous or hazardous in nature. Solid waste that enters the ocean may become marine debris, and can then pose a threat to marine organisms, humans, coastal communities, and industries that utilize marine waters. Cruise ships typically manage solid waste by a combination of source reduction, waste minimization, and recycling. However, as much as 75 percent of solid waste is incineratedon board, and the ash typically is discharged at sea, although some is landed ashore for disposal or recycling.

Marine mammals, fish, sea turtles, and birds can be injured or killed from entanglement with plastics and other solid waste that may be released or disposed off of cruise ships. On average, each cruise ship passenger generates at least two pounds of non-hazardous solid waste per day. With large cruise ships carrying several thousand passengers, the amount of waste generated in a day can be massive. For a large cruise ship, about 8 tons of solid waste are generated during a one-week cruise. It has been estimated that 24 percent of the solid waste generated by vessels worldwide (by weight) comes from cruise ships. Most cruise ship garbage is treated on board (incinerated, pulped, or ground up) for discharge overboard. When garbage must be off-loaded (for example, because glass and aluminium cannot be incinerated), cruise ships can put a strain on port reception facilities, which are rarely adequate to the task of serving a large passenger vessel.

BILGE WATER

On a ship, oil often leaks from engine and machinery spaces or from engine maintenance activities and mixes with water in the bilge, the lowest part of the hull of the ship, but there is a filter to clean bilge water before being discharged. Oil, gasoline, and by-products from the biological breakdown of petroleum products can harm fish and wildlife and pose threats to human health if ingested. Oil in even minute concentrations can kill fish or have various sub-lethal chronic effects. Bilge water also may contain solid wastes andpollutants containing high levels of oxygen-demanding material, oil and other chemicals. A typically large cruise ship will generate an average of 8 metric tons of oily bilge water for each 24 hours of operation.

To maintain ship stability and eliminate potentially hazardous conditions from oil vapors in these areas, the bilge spaces need to be flushed and periodically pumped dry. However, before a bilge can be cleared out and the water discharged, the oil that has been accumulated needs to be extracted from the bilge water, after which the extracted oil can be reused, incinerated, and/or offloaded in port. If a separator, which is normally used to extract the oil, is faulty or is deliberately bypassed, untreated oily bilge water could be discharged directly into the ocean, where it can damage marine life. A number of cruise lines have been charged withenvironmental violations related to this issue in recent years.

SAFETY OF LIFE AT SEA

HOW SAFE ARE CRUISE SHIPS?

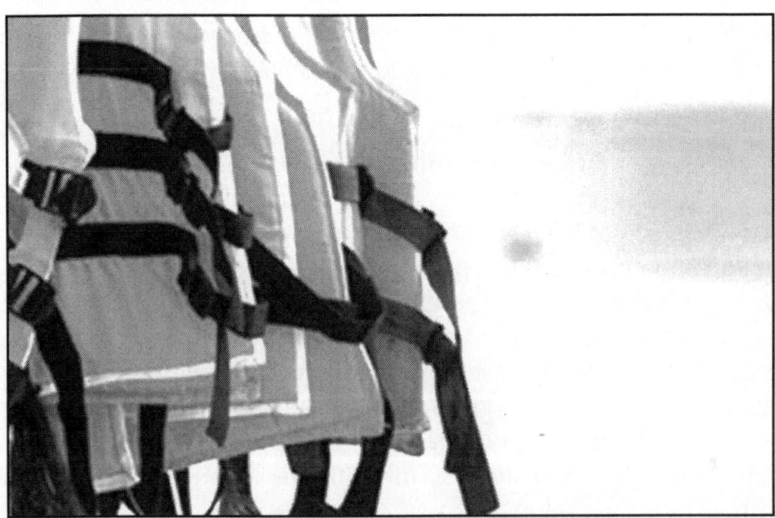

Cruise ships are some of the safest modes of moving transportation you'll ever be on. Cruise lines must follow a surprising number of rules and regulations to protect passengers' (and crewmembers') safety while onboard a cruise ship. Ships operate under international rules, known as Safety of Life at Sea (SOLAS), which regulate everything from fire safety to navigation and maritime security.

Plus, the Coast Guard conducts rigourous inspections of all ships that operate from U.S. ports to ensure they comply with emergency response requirements.

How do I Know what to do in the Event of an Emergency Onboard a Cruise Ship?

International maritime rules require all cruise ships to hold a safety drill before the ship leaves the dock. Called a muster drill (not mustard!), the safety briefing will take place about a half-hour before sail away. You will be required to go to your muster station at the designated time where you will listen to a description of your ship's safety features and the procedures you'll need to follow in case of an emergency. On big ships, the code for your station is printed on your key card and on the back of your cabin door; on small ships, there's usually only one muster station. Before the muster drill starts, the cruise director will make an announcement as to where all the muster stations are, and during the drill crewmembers will guide you in the right direction. As part of the instructions you'll receive, you will learn what signals to listen for, where to go and how to put on a life jacket.

What Type of Emergency Crew are Onboard Cruise Ships?

Most cruise ships plying the oceans have at least one medical doctor and two nurses onboard who can respond to medical emergencies. There also are trained security officers onboard who will respond to complaints of violent confrontations or crimes and unruly behaviour. All crewmembers receive continuous training in emergency procedures and first aid as mandated by the International Maritime Organization.

Are there Lifeguards at the Pools on a Cruise Ship?

Only Disney Cruise Line has trained lifeguards onboard its cruise ships, and they are only stationed at family pools during specified hours. Norwegian Cruise Line has a crewmember that monitors pools during specified hours, but the monitors are not lifeguards. Passengers are responsible for watching their own children and travel companions, and following posted pool rules.

I Am Cruising Alone, what Advice do You have for Me Regarding My Personal Safety?

As with any place with lots of people, you should always take precautions to keep yourself safe. Most general safety rules apply here: don't accept drinks from strangers, be aware of your surroundings, don't go into a stranger's room and keep your cabin door locked at night.

Can My Cabin Room Steward Enter the Room while I'm in there?

As in a hotel, room attendants do have access to your cabin, but receive strict instructions never to enter a passenger cabin except while performing their job duties. Before entering a room, stewards will always knock first and will not enter if you tell them you are inside. If you want to nap, put up the Do Not Disturb notice and stewards will come back later. Keep in mind, if you leave the Do Not Disturb notice up for too many days in a row, they will eventually enter to make sure everything is ok. If your cabin ship door has a deadbolt (most do), you can use that as well to indicate you're inside the room.

Will My Kids be Safe Exploring the Ship on their Own, or do I have to Stay with them at All Times?

Cruise ships carry thousands of people you do not know. Take the same precautions you do at home, at a hotel or resort in any city worldwide. That might mean that you keep the littlest kids with you at all times, allow older kids to leave the kids club on their own only if they go directly to you or your room and let teens have free range — or choose differently. Certainly, you will want to instruct kids or teens allowed to roam freely on using common sense to avoid danger (don't climb the ship's railings, don't go to secluded places with unfamiliar adults, etc.).

Are My Children Safe in the Kids Club?

The kids clubs and nurseries all have gated access, meaning people can't just wander in. Parents must sign the youngest kids in and out; older kids can sign themselves out, but cannot leave without alerting a staff member. Youth counselors are trained to handle food allergies and medical emergencies; but if your child isn't feeling well or is upset, they will contact you or a guardian you've named. Some youth staff are also trained to handle children with special needs, such as autism. But be aware, there is no one-on-one supervision and youth staff are not responsible for the activities of children or teens once they have signed out of the clubs.

6

Hospitality Management

INTRODUCTION

It's important for people to know what you stand for. It's equally important that they know what you won't stand for. The twenty-first century began with a flurry of high-profile scandals involving managers in a wide variety of industries, ranging from high-tech firms to pharmaceutical manufacturers. Many very successful business-people found themselves behind bars for their ethical transgressions. The topic of business ethics is receiving increasing coverage in all media, including newspapers, business periodicals, television, radio, and even the Internet, while the pressures on businesses to perform continue to increase.

With continued technological advancement, political upheaval, increased global competition, changing demographics, and pressure from stockholders, maintaining one's ethical integrity will become both more difficult and more important. In 1993 a large group of hospitality industry executives were asked, "What skills and abilities do students need to obtain to be successful in the hospitality industry?" The number one answer was "business ethics." There is little evidence to suggest the answer would be any different today. One thing is clear: Ethical behaviour is important, and all of you will be facing situations in which you will need to make difficult decisions that you will base on your ethical beliefs and value systems.

Individual Ethics

Ethics is defined as "the system or code of morals of a particular person, religion, group, or profession." As such, ethical beliefs may vary from person to person. There are three basic individual approaches to ethics that are reflected in the behaviour of people. First is the moral rights approach, which judges the consistency of decisions and behaviors with the maintenance of certain fundamental personal and group liberties and privileges such as life, freedom, health, privacy, and property. Second is the justice approach, which judges the consistency of decisions and behaviors with the maintenance of equity, fairness, and impartiality in the distribution of costs and benefits among individuals. Third is the utilitarian approach, which judges the effects of decisions and behaviors on providing the greatest good for the greatest number of people.

THE CHALLENGES OF HOSPITALITY SALES

MIS: The New Challenges

Management Information System is effective when it improves the profitability of an organisation considerably. The new and improvised MIS triggers the decision makers for proactive decision process. Technology has always been associated with quick decision-making that enables businesses to minimise risks and attain quality output. The hospitality industry is now keen to use technology to its full potential to offer the best services.

The management on the other hand has always been using software that played a key role in defining the performance of a hotel. Management Information System (MIS) has been one of them and has played a potent role in this industry. With time, it has become the most dependent tool, having gone through some changes apart from being customised to a company's needs. These changes in a way enabled the hospitality sector to view MIS as a complete networked platform upon which performance of a company can be viewed and dissected easily.

The competitive culture has crept into the Indian scenario as well, where constant perfection is vital to keep the revenue graph moving upwards. Hence, the new genre of MIS is all about division of departments, being web-based and offering single platform for all information across the network.

MIS Operational Platform

MIS is undertaken to take account of the day-to-day operations and the aberrations that need to be quickly addressed. It works on client-server architecture and facilitates maintenance of necessary data as well as generation of reports and queries. This software explicitly expresses the operation in a format that is conceived easily and enables quick understanding of various levels of operations. MIS is like a report card of an organisation but, experts feel, it needs to be more refined in order to figure out where the performance diversion is taking place.

This is a crucial aspect which a few software solution providers have incorporated in its software where customers (hotels) can directly pin-point the areas where things are going wrong, thereby bringing about immediate rectification. Today, hoteliers are even extending the use of MIS for keeping a bank of guest information and feedback using this real data into bringing about changes in service styles, menus, etc. An in-depth analysis can therefore be possible with the kind of information available through customisation, feeding the right inputs and evaluating the output generated.

Vital Factors

MIS primarily focuses on the soft skills of the operations. But there has to be a synergy of information flow within the managerial, operational and the top management of a hotel. To address this issue companies try to attain exactly that feature through their MIS module. In a hotel, there are different departments and MIS is made on a platform where work is divided and managed according to the departments.

MIS will be more beneficial and effective only when it considerably improves the profitability of an organisation. This will happen only when it triggers the decision-makers to be proactive, which in turn benefits the bottom line. Also, each hotel goes about customising the software according to their needs.

However, there are a few factors that are making MIS a more potent tool. Focusing on the hotel sector we have introduced a Drill Down feature. If Drill Down is provided on MIS (displaying up to voucher level data which is composed of the MIS) the management can get down to the minute details of any abnormal behaviour and can take instantaneous corrective actions. Further, we tend to forget the expense part in the budget set for each department where the emphasis is on sales. Identifying and then reducing these expenses or core areas of concern through MIS is a big boon for the management.

Going the Web Way

MIS operations have become more complex and challenging in this sector because of chain hotels which need to be linked to each other when it comes to finding out the performance of each unit. Therefore, MIS is presently being upgraded for Web-based operations too. Here, a central system is created - central MIS - that takes into account the reports generated by each property (through MIS) at the end of the day after the completion of night audit. This is done by uploading the day's report at the central Web server.

The idea is to reach the root of any discrepancy quickly and keep the profitability of the business at the optimum. This tabulation brings the performance of all properties on a single platform - single window information system - for evaluation and appraisals. Here one can figure out reasons for lacklustre performance through links provided for report generation. This also enables a company to study past trends to predict future trends. Also, MIS going the Web way not only secures data from possible theft but also ensure quick recovery from any part of the world for reference and future planning, which gives this software a status like never before.

Drivers of change

Globalisation dictates the shape of the future; it reduces artificial barriers and creates the practicalities of business thereby necessitating alliances. The protagonist of this change is primarily the traveller himself who will dictate what alliances should take place in the future. The opportunity to seize and dominate a marketplace, distribution networks, introduce new products, technologies and international management talent, with the specter of competition looming overhead will require alliances to mould their collective fortunes. Rapid growth in the marketplace without ancillary support of third party services and a free economy to spur consolidation will spearhead strategic alliances.

Understanding customers will become critical to establishing competitive advantage. The modalities in place will shift in angle in the age of intense competition and retaining customers will become as important as acquiring them in the first place.

In what ways will a traveller evolve to enter the next decade? In India, firstly, he will move up the value chain, creating a segment that has been there, seen that, and doesn't want the same experience anymore. But at the same time, a whole new mass will be drawn up the same value chain, taking the place of the first time traveller, for which the market and communications, and befitting alliances has already been developed.

Research will lead to the better understanding of the target consumers and their behaviour, leading to more precise identification of customer segments and sub-segments, and basing alliances on the basis of this, which will further open opportunities for data mining, between different cross segments and verticals, targeting the same demographic group. Focused strategy and communication, targeted at the right persons and alliances with the right people will precede mass media as an option.

This opens a whole new untapped market - of the luxury, wellness and the experienced traveller, who's looking to combine convenience with comfort. Raymond Bickson, MD of Indian Hotels Company, elaborates, "The globetrotting wealthy traveller today is intensely important. One must understand the intricacies and subtleties for luxury clientele. These travellers influence global issues and look for value for money but one must not mistake them for bargain hunters." This will reveal new tourism products and marketing strategies to evolve, with worldwide trends moving towards shorter breaks and short haul travel during off-season.

The Way Forward

The two-edged sword of globalisation has not only made the world accessible but also brings the threat of being obsolete along with it. To stretch marketing rupees, groupings will develop to undertake joint marketing and research efforts. Cross-sector alliances will prove to be effective marketing formats, with access to database and direct marketing tools, with verticals looking at other segments to associate with. This will increase the retail, arts, cultures and others on a bigger framework and canvas than it is today. Global opportunities will create more openings for health and wellness tourism and medical tourism - a market that the Indian government has already realised as a growing one.

Its worldwide medical tourism campaign is proof enough. And not without reason; according to market statistics, the medical tourism market in India is touching US $300 million (with an estimated 1.5 lakh foreign patients visiting India every year) and growing into a US $2 billion business by 2012. The Leela Palaces & Resorts, according to its president, Peter J Leitgeb, is the first five-star hotel group in the world to offer special packages to travellers from the UK at its Kerala property after having tied-up with Globe Health Tours.

Meanwhile, hotels will try to differentiate their products even more, and expand through the management cum franchise route by integrating marketing synergies. Standalone properties are bound to integrate under the umbrella of a known brand. Alliances to differentiate the product, both with consumer brands and retail in addition to marketing alliances worldwide, will become a compulsion for Indian brands to compete against the giant franchises and managed brands.

While evolving into the next decade, it would be the visibility of a brand and its penetration into the marketplace that will be the first step to forge an alliance. Accordingly, a hotel will select the right fit for furthering its growth through the right associations, since one-size no longer fits all. And it would be the right partnership. This, in some cases, might lead to inorganic growth but nonetheless will be a win-win situation for all.

HOSPITALITY DIRECTIONS

The hospitality sector has adopted numerous strategies, approaches and measures in response to the challenge of sustainable development. The sector has particularly used environmental management systems and tools to demonstrate commitment to an environmentally friendly work ethic. Many multinational and independent hotel companies have introduced environmental management practices at the property level. These include:

- Environmental management systems and tools
- Education, awareness creation, training and information dissemination
- Voluntary initiatives
- Multi-stakeholder communication and consultation
- Environmental reporting
- Implementation of the Rio principles

Ideally, the framework for this involves defining an environmental policy and building a management system to measure environmental impacts and compliance with the policy and local regulations, as well as documenting the system's performance for inspection and auditing purposes.

Such environmental management systems (EMS) help businesses to evaluate manages and reduces their negative environmental impacts by providing a methodology to integrate environment management into business operations in a systematic manner.

Connected Thinking

Businesses are increasingly being asked to shoulder responsibility for their social, ethical and environmental impacts, with this pressure particularly keenly felt in consumer-facing industries. While for many hospitality companies interest in the sector started with environmental management issues, the focus has now widened to include social and economic impacts, more broadly defined as Corporate Responsibility.

The travel industry of course drives demand for hotel accommodation and between 1950 and 2000 the number of journeys taken by international tourists, including business travellers, increased nearly 28 fold. This year alone 840million tourist arrivals are forecast globally, and by 2020 the figure could reach 1,580 million.

Fears that numbers of this size are unlikely to be sustainable have led to calls for less air travel and for more personal and Corporate Responsibility. However, despite some progress, Jonathon Porritt, Chair of the UK Sustainable Development Commission, recently commented on the travel industry:

"The industry cannot begin to claim that it's even remotely responsible. Our collective efforts to date are hopelessly inadequate".

In January 2006, PricewaterhouseCoopers undertook new research into 14 of Europe's leading hotel groups, accounting for some 1.5 million rooms globally. We tested these hotel companies against 11 key components of Corporate Responsibility to assess the relevance of Corporate Responsibility to their businesses, the expectations of key stakeholders, and how well the sector is performing. This article presents the results of this research and also assesses some of the future challenges the sector must tackle. Overall, our research shows that:

- Some progress has been made, but the sector lags behind other European industries in responding to Corporate Responsibility challenges;
- Because of the complexity of the sector it is not easy for hotel companies, and others in the industry value chain, to respond too many of the issues without engaging with their business partners;
- Long term, there is a clear business advantage for those who get their Corporate Responsibility response right but real risks for those who don't.

"The industry creates buildings full of air conditioning and there's no comment on how waste is being disposed of. For an 'eco' agenda to be meaningful, hoteliers have to look at the repercussions of what they're doing from the beginning. Yes, a large number of hotels now have light-saving devices.

They ask us to hang up our towels. But that's not enough. Let's be honest: these are often just mechanisms for the hotelier to manage costs".

Mark Banning-Taylor, owner of upscale hotel and lodge development, Moonlight Head, Australia.

While consumer awareness of Corporate Responsibility in the hospitality industry is still in its inception, consumers are becoming more active in directing their spending towards goods and services that meet their ethical expectations and boycotting companies and brands which they view as exploitative. This is particularly apparent in the clothing and grocery sectors.

Corporate Responsibility

Over the past few years, a wide range of stakeholders have become increasingly interested in the social, ethical and environmental performance of the hospitality industry, including the media, investors and rating agencies, consumers, employees, governments and non- governmental organisations (NGOs):

The media is paying ever-greater attention to sustainability issues. Much of this interest has previously focused on the retail sector, for example, with headline- grabbing statements on issues such as child labour. Such exposes have had a considerable impact and in some cases have led to boycotting of certain consumer brands with a consequent impact on shareholder value. The hospitality sector cannot shy away from these issues any more than the retail sector can.

Current headlines are focusing on topics such as climate change, the impact of global travel, worker exploitation, binge drinking and obesity. This media attention has amplified the need for companies in the sector to not only establish systems and controls to monitor supplier performance, but also to develop reporting mechanisms to demonstrate to external audiences what actions they are taking to ensure high standards of Corporate Responsibility.

Governments across Europe are also taking an increasing interest in Corporate Responsibility, although they are not currently a key driver for change in the sector. Initiatives in place include, for example, at the EU level, the European Commission's White Paper on Corporate Social Responsibility, which contains guidance on labour standards.

Many corporate investment companies are now screening their investments according to a range of social and environmental criteria. Additionally, rating indices such as FTSE4Good and the Dow Jones Sustainability Indices (DJSI) include ratings on hospitality companies on the basis of their performance in this area. For example, the DJSI has an assessment category covering "hotels, restaurants, bars and recreational services". As of September 2005, DJSI had identified Accor, Compass Group, McDonald's, Sodexho and Starbucks as sustainability leaders. The Socially Responsible

Investment (SRI) market is expected to expand significantly in the next decade with a greater scrutiny of performance in this area.

A November 2005 report on Responsible Tourism from First Choice, based on more than 1,000 people questioned by market research firm Mintel, found that a quarter of respondents were concerned about the impact of tourism on the environment of the countries they visited and 28 per cent were prepared to pay a small supplement to offset the carbon emissions of their flights. One in five said that it was important that their visit benefited local communities. More than half said they would be happy to take more public transport to explore on holiday (54 per cent), half said they would recycle on holiday (50 per cent), and four out of 10 said they would accept local drinks if this meant fewer imports (44 per cent). Other suggestions included:

- Reducing the changes of towels and bedlinen (34 per cent)
- Buying locally produced souvenirs (32 per cent)
- Borrowing brochures from travel agents to avoid wastage (30 per cent)
- Accepting a smaller range of food in hotel buffets to reduce wastage (20 per cent)
- Reducing the number of holidays taken (14 per cent)
- Spending a couple of hours to help with local projects such as beach cleaning (11 per cent)
- Paying more for a holiday so a higher proportion can benefit the local community (11 per cent).

First Choice Mainstream Sector managing director Dermot Blastland commented on the findings that:

"We and other travel companies need to make it as easy as possible for people to do the right thing while they are away. It also means we need to show our customers how, with their help we can make a positive difference and preserve holiday destinations for future generations".

Increasing numbers of travel companies appear to be responding to consumer concerns. Several mainstream companies now include information or advice about ethical, social or environmental issues in their brochures, and niche companies specialising in 'eco-friendly' or 'responsible' travel have sprung up in recent years. For example, Earth, a London-based travel company focusing on luxury properties. The company has made a soft environmental impact, by being small and respectful of the landscape and local culture. Amanresorts follow ecologically sympathetic architectural principles and tend to be small and sensitive developments.

Additionally, the travel industry is starting to respond. British Airways has recently launched a scheme where its customers can choose to offset the carbon dioxide emissions created during their flights. Customers can pay via a link from the airline's website for the cost of the emissions created by their journey. For example, a return flight to Madrid will cost £5 and a return flight to Johannesburg will cost £13.30.

The money raised will be used by an organisation called Climate Care to invest in sustainable energy projects that tackle global warming by reducing carbon dioxide levels. Climate Care's projects include a scheme in South Africa that has distributed 50,000 energy efficient lamps this year via school groups as part of an environmental awareness campaign. In India, Climate Care's support means schools are able to use stoves that run on renewable energy briquettes made from crop waste rather than liquid petroleum gas. Customers can offset their carbon emissions via the booking confirmation form when they book British Airways flights.

Responsible Organisations

Employees are increasingly demanding assurances from their employers regarding the management of a broad range of Corporate Responsibility issues. Employee concern is the most commonly cited reason for companies producing Corporate Responsibility reports. This is supported by research by the Work Foundation and the Virtuous Circle Ltd, 'Achieving High Performance: CSR at the heart of business', which found a strong positive correlation between companies that are seen to take their responsibilities towards society seriously and those seen as a good employer to work for.

NGOs are increasingly looking at the practices of the hospitality industry. Although such organisations do not have any direct power to force change in the sector, the publicity that NGO campaigns can generate is an important driver of business behaviour. In the summer of 2004, Tourism Concern started a campaign looking at working conditions in the tourism sector. They conducted research in five popular holiday destinations – Bali, Mexico, the Dominican Republic, Egypt, and the Canary Islands. The research revealed examples of exploitative labour conditions.

These included over-dependence on tips, long working hours, unpaid overtime, stress, lack of secure contracts, poor training and almost no promotion opportunities for locally employed people. Their research also found that tour operators often use their considerable purchasing power to force down prices in much the same way as supermarkets do when imposing price cuts on farmers.

The result is invariably cost-cutting and longer hours for the lowest paid workers. Those who suffer most are the socially weaker and less skilled staff members, a high proportion of whom are women. In response to this research, Tourism Concern is now calling on all tour operators to 'audit' labour standards across the tourism supply chain.

The industry is currently considering its Europe Edition response to this specific campaign. Additionally, Federation of Tour Operators (FTO) members last year signed a statement of commitment to sustainable development and management of tourism. The statement commits members to making a positive contribution to the natural and cultural environment and to generate benefits for host communities. Members are committed in the future to following the FTO Integrated Responsible Tourism Programme, which is currently under development.

Challenges Facing the Hospitality Industry

Irrespective of wherever individual hospitality companies have got to in their thinking on Corporate Responsibility, the issue is clearly here to stay, indeed with issues such as climate change coming further to the forefront in 2006, many are likely to become more pressing. In the hospitality industry, it will affect daily activities including location and site decisions, employment issues, management of the supply chain, and customer treatment and management. Sustainable tourism is about preserving popular destinations, the environment and its resources. We have got to get it right for this generation and beyond.

Within the hotel and travel sector, various initiatives and standards have been established to try to better define what Corporate Responsibility means for the sector. Such initiatives include the International Tourism Partnership and the International Eco-tourism Society. In addition, various award programmes now exist to recognise good performance in Corporate Responsibility in the sector. For example:

- International Hotel & Restaurant Association's Environmental Award: launched in 1990 and conducted with the UNEP, the United Nation's Environment Programme and sponsored by American Express. Judges include Conservation International, Green Globe 21 and ITP. The award recognises the efforts being made to 'green' the hotel industry from within.
- British Airways Tourism for Tomorrow awards launched in 1991 by British Airways and, since 2004, under the auspices of World Travel and Tourism Council (WTTC), Tourism for Tomorrow recognises and promotes best practice in travel and tourism development around the world.
- Conservation International & National Geographic Traveller: Traveller magazine and Conservation International together launched the 2004 World Legacy Awards, a global campaign to promote environmentally, culturally, and socially responsible tourism practices across a wider spectrum of the tourism industry, with the goal of "protecting the Earth's natural and cultural heritage".
- Conde Nast Traveller's Ecotourism Awards: These awards have been set up to recognise properties, tour operators, and destinations committed to preserving the local environment, assisting and

employing the people who live there, and educating the guests who visit. Organisations can nominate themselves for entry to the awards, after which a panel of industry judges vote on the finalists.

What do stakeholders expect from companies who are serious about addressing Corporate Responsibility? Leading companies follow the same broad principles, although these may differ in their application and emphasis. First, stakeholders, be they staff, customers, shareholders or the community at large, expect to see commitment from the top of an organisation – this means leadership and advocacy. If employees, communities and customers do not actually see repeated evidence of this commitment, then the organisation will lack credibility.

"My priorities for 2005 are to continue our focus on generating shareholder value through further disposals of hotel assets, returning additional funds to shareholders, and retaining and enhancing our powerful brand positions and infrastructures. We will also maintain our focus on Corporate Social Responsibility, where we seek to be an industry leader." - Andrew Cosslett, CEO of IHG.

They view their contribution and buy-in as essential in assessing environmental, social and economic dimensions of hospitality management, and in balancing short-term priorities against long term needs.

The ITP is a programme of The Prince of Wales International Business Leaders Forum (IBLF) and exists to inspire and provide global leadership for responsible business in hotels, travel and tourism. The initiative builds on the success of the International Hotels Environment Initiative (IHEI) launched in 1992. Organisations including airlines, car hire companies and tour operators through to existing hotel chain members and non government organisations (NGO) all work together within ITP to promote responsible practical actions that ensure sustainable solutions. Partners are drawn together to work on specific projects to drive actions and awareness in areas that affect responsible travel and tourism. The ITP also assists hotel, travel and tourism companies define and build a leadership role in responsible business by contributing to policy dialogues, pioneering new approaches to changing business and development agendas and by providing practical business solutions.

The ITP has developed "BenchmarkHotel" - an environmental benchmarking tool designed to help hotels around the world improve their environmental performance.

The International Eco-tourism Society (TIES)

TIES was founded in 1990 and is the largest and oldest ecotourism organisation in the world dedicated to generating and disseminating information about ecotourism. It currently has members in more than 70 countries. The organisation membership includes academics, consultants, conservation professionals and organizations, governments, architects, tour operators, lodge owners and managers, general development experts, and ecotourists. TIES provides guidelines and standards, training, technical assistance, research and publications to foster sound ecotourism development.

This is a very tricky process for a company to get right. All too often, "engagement" is a one-way dialogue, with the company telling stakeholders the decisions that it has made. This risks engendering alienation and, potentially, opposition from stakeholders who feel insulted rather than consulted. Effective engagement, by contrast, is invaluable in shaping corporate strategy, understanding upcoming risks and opportunities, and providing a suitable response and feedback.

It is best practice, for example, to refer directly to stakeholder concerns and corresponding actions in corporate reports. Publishing your Corporate Responsibility strategy and defining priorities for action is also a key part of best practice. Corporate commitments should then be enshrined in "policy" – which could be a formal sustainability policy, code of practice or some guiding principles. This policy should be effectively communicated and implemented, for example through objectives and performance targets/indicators. It should be monitored through appropriate control processes and management systems, such as the ISO 14001 environmental management standard.

Performance indicators should be determined, with regular reports disclosing performance. Best practice is to have these reports assured by an independent third party. Corporate Responsibility is still a relatively new concept for the hospitality industry. However, by taking action now and reporting to stakeholders on progress made, forward- looking companies do have the opportunity to gain a leadership position in this respect. Adopting such a leadership position would have corresponding potential long term beneficial impacts on critical business areas such as customer and staff recruitment and retention, ultimately translating into shareholder value.

In order to look at how the industry is currently responding to the Corporate Responsibility agenda, PricewaterhouseCoopers conducted new research into the Corporate Responsibility activities of Europe's 14 largest publicly listed hotel companies in January 2004.

Together these hotels accounted for more than 1.5 million hotel rooms across the world in 2004. Our research examined how each company was responding on 11 key components of Corporate Responsibility, such as their overall level of disclosure, policies in place, management systems and stakeholder engagement.

The research was based solely on publicly available information, for example, through company websites, investor briefings and annual reports. This research builds on previous work by PwC in 2001 to examine the implementation of environmental policies in European hotels.

PwC's research found that 10 out of 14 of Europe's leading hotel companies provided at least some information relating to Corporate Responsibility in their published information. For example, Accor's website contains an interactive web-based Corporate Responsibility report.

Research results: how well are Europe's leading 14 hotel groups responding to the Corporate Responsibility agenda? Accor's website contains interactive sections on its responsibilities towards shareholders, For example, while most companies did have Corporate Responsibility, environmental or social polices in place, only three of the 14 companies stated that they had conducted a Corporate Responsibility risk assessment. Additionally, only four of the companies had made a clear link between their Corporate Responsibility activities and business strategies. This lack of risk assessment and connection with broader business strategy could mean that many of these companies are not currently deriving real business benefits from their Corporate Responsibility activities.

Environmental Policy

In terms of policy disclosure, nine out of the 14 companies had environmental policies in place. Accor, Hilton Group and Whitbread all disclosed a significant amount of information on their environmental performance.

- Hilton Group reported on the use of the Hilton Environmental Reporting tool (HER) and staff training (15,000 staff to date). Hilton group also publicly report their target of a 10 per cent reduction in utility consumption across the UK and Ireland by 2006
- Accor publicly disclosed that, in 2004, 26 properties were awarded ISO14001 certification. Significant disclosure was also provided in areas such as water and energy consumption, waste, biodiversity, and environmental building design
- Whitbread published a stand alone environment report, which received third party assurance. The report contained considerable disclosure on environmental performance, e.g. reductions in C02 emissions, water, energy consumption, and recycling was also provided.

Whitbread refer to their Environment Management System (EMS) in their report. Detailed information on how Accor sees its responsibilities towards customers, employees, suppliers, the environment, local communities and shareholders. Likewise, Hilton Group plc has published a detailed "Responsible Business" report for the last three years. This report contains information on Hilton's vision and core values, corporate governance and key Corporate Responsibility issues, defined as people, equal opportunities and diversity, human rights, health and safety, environment, business practice, customers, products and services, business partners and supply chain and communities/ charities.

For companies that did not produce standalone Corporate Responsibility reports, disclosure was usually focused on case study examples of particular developments or initiatives that were initiated with Corporate Responsibility in mind. These ranged from employee volunteering schemes, to monitoring working conditions across the supply chain, to providing details of community impacts in terms of working with local people to provide employment opportunities. These examples demonstrate how, to some extent, all hotel companies are actively considering Corporate Responsibility in their operations, and in doing so, are focusing on the full range of issues – not simply environment, health and safety.

Once we dug below the surface, we found the organisations we benchmarked had markedly different levels of Corporate Responsibility activity. In terms of disclosure on 'social' areas of Corporate Responsibility, ten out of the 14 companies benchmarked publish information on policies in this regard. Areas covered by many included:

- People issues
- Diversity
- Equal opportunities
- Community/charitable donations

However, fewer companies reported their activities in emerging issues such as:

- Human rights and
- Supplier management

One exception to this was Intercontinental Hotels Group (IHG), who have publicly stated their commitment to the Universal Declaration on Human Rights and the International Labour Organisation's (ILO's) core conventions. Another notable exception was Accor's significant disclosure on its programme in place to monitor the social and ethical performance of its key suppliers.

However, where applicable, none of the hotels covered within the survey disclosed any significant information on the environmental or social performance of their franchised hotels. Rather, the sector is currently focusing on the activities of directly owned and managed properties. Looking to the future, it is likely that stakeholders will expect the sector to also disclose the performance of franchised hotels.

In addition, it would be prudent for companies to include coverage of these franchised properties in Corporate Responsibility programmes as franchised hotels do have the ability to cause significant reputation and brand damage if found lacking in sensitive Corporate Responsibility issues, such as child labour and minimum wage payments.

In terms of Corporate Responsibility board sponsorship, the research found that only 4 of the 14 companies publicly articulated a board level commitment to Corporate Responsibility. Such board level sponsorship is critical to Corporate

Responsibility programmes being taken seriously by external audiences. IHG is a good example of a company that has made a clear, board-level, commitment to Corporate Responsibility:

"We need to build an IHG culture. A culture that's focussed on driving returns for our owners and on supporting each other in a more collaborative way. Part of the culture will be about raising our commitment still further to helping the communities in which we operate. As an organisation we will increase our commitment to Corporate Social Responsibility and ensure that we are industry leading in this area. Not just because it helps to drive the culture which it does, but because it increasingly helps attract talented people to the business." - Andrew Cosslett CEO IHG.

Looking at the implementation of management systems to actively monitor and control elements of Corporate Responsibility such as environment, health and safety, only five organisations claimed to have established management systems, and three more were in the process of developing them.

One company that does disclose details of its Corporate Responsibility management systems are Rezidor SAS, which has an established Responsible Business (RB) programme. The programme focuses on three key areas: taking Responsibility for the health and safety of employees and guests, respecting social and ethical issues in the company, as well as in the community, and reducing negative impacts on the environment.

The operational responsibility for the RB programme lies with the Hotel Managers, who are supported by the RB co-coordinators at each hotel. In 2003, a regional structure was added, supporting the hotels at a regional level and providing a liaison between the hotels and the Corporate Director of Environmental and Social Affairs. The local RB action plans guide the hotels in what measures and actions they will implement during the year to improve performance.

Six companies within the benchmark provided details of their stakeholder engagement plans and a further two provided limited details with a commitment to future activity in this area. However, even for these six companies that did disclose information on engagement, the level of disclosure was limited. It is increasingly expected that companies will publicly disclose who they believe their key stakeholders are and what activities/processes they have in place to engage with these key stakeholder groups. The hotel industry is significantly behind other sectors in this area, for example, British Telecom has a highly established process of stakeholder engagement.

Looking at disclosure on actual performance, just four of the 14 organisations were able to publish meaningful data on Corporate Responsibility type parametres (e.g. health and safety, resource use, waste production, community consultation); while four more produced some limited data. For example, the Hilton Group plc reported in its most recent Corporate

Responsibility report that 'team member satisfaction scores have increased across the world by up to 7 per cent from 2003, averaging at 75 per cent.' Hilton was also the only company in the survey to have third party assurance over their reported information on Corporate Responsibility, although three other companies did provide assurance in some limited areas.

What conclusion should we draw from this information? Perhaps the majority of hotel companies are focusing on Corporate Responsibility, but not publicly talking about it? Or, alternatively that they recognise that Corporate Responsibility is important but have not fully implemented the necessary processes or controls throughout their business. Alternatively, there could be a more complex explanation. Perhaps the industry's current response results from the complex value chain and business partner relationships in the hospitality sector generally.

Individual companies may not always be responsible for the direct buying relationship with the customer, often being dependent on other companies up and down the value chain in terms of Corporate Responsibility related impacts. Whatever the explanation, it is clear that progress has been made in terms of implementing environmental policies for many in the sector since PricewaterhouseCoopers examined this issue of Hospitality Directions. However, the sector is behind other European industries, e.g. the retail sector, in terms of Corporate Responsibility reporting, and faces a challenging agenda to catch up and respond effectively to the concerns of stakeholders.

Indeed, in the 2004 Business in the Community Corporate Responsibilty Index, of the top 100 quoted companies from a Corporate Responsibilty perspective, only four came from the leisure and hotels sector. By comparison, a sector such as Banks and Utilities had 11 apiece. However, this could partly be explained by relatively few hotel companies being quoted on the FTSE 100 and FTSE 250.

Looking Towards the Future

Many companies in the hospitality industry are currently not making the most of the Corporate Responsibility agenda. While it can easily appear to business as a threat and a recipe for extra burdens, the reality is that Corporate Responsibility related issues present real business opportunities. In a recently published report by the leading global business organisation, the World Business Council for Sustainable Development, "From Challenge to Opportunity: the role of business in tomorrow's society", business leaders in a number of major companies have produced a model for tomorrow's global business. It is based on recognising and capturing the opportunities that are presented by societal and environmental concerns.

By focusing on the issue strategically, companies which address Corporate Responsibility are likely to achieve better community relationships, save money through operational efficiencies and differentiate themselves as responsible and accountable companies. Transparent and accountable behaviour helps to build stakeholder trust and enhance corporate reputation, both long-term drivers of value. Other sectors such as the European retail, telecommunications, pharmaceutical and extractive industries have already started to yield such benefits through established Corporate Responsibility programmes.

There are several steps that the hospitality industry will have to take to embed Corporate Responsibility into the way it does business day-to-day. The most immediate steps include instituting the right policies, processes, and systems for monitoring and reporting performance. Additionally, for such Corporate Responsibility programmes to be credible, it is important to ensure the following:

- A serious commitment to Corporate Responsibility is shown from the top of the organisation;
- Stakeholders are actively involved in decision making;
- Corporate Responsibility strategy is published, with defined priorities for action;
- Corporate commitments are enshrined in policy; and
- Performance indicators are determined, with regular reports disclosing performance.

Overall, the biggest challenge for the sector will be to win over the 'hearts and minds' and thus the behaviour of the company. This is a longer term and more complex process, and will demand cross industry collaboration, but is essential for Corporate Responsibility to really 'stick'. Many leading hospitality companies have made a start, but achieving maximum value from Corporate Responsibility will be far from simple. It will require a clear sense of direction, a commitment from the organisation, robust planning and strong implementation to deliver.

"All this talk about jumping on the green bandwagon has died down. Being 'green' is no longer fashionable or glamorous, it is a fact of life. Now considered by all industries to have a direct impact on profitability, it has been absorbed in business practice. Having left the glamour and excitement, we are now at stage two – the detail of implementation." - David Henderson, Former Marketing Manager of Plysu Containers, UK

STATUS OF HOSPITALITY MANAGEMENT IN INDIA

There has been no data, and no research has been conducted in India on the status of hospitality management or hotel management education. Although a large number of Government and private sector institutions are working in this area, there is no data about the number of students passing out from different programme every year. More than that, there is no data about the demand for trained manpower in the hotel, restaurant and catering industry in India. This research study has attempted to fill this gap and provide the necessary data and qualitative information on hospitality management education in India.

A questionnaire was sent out to 1200 FHRAI hotel members in different cities to provide the necessary data on the various parameters on which research was conducted. The research revealed:

- There are, on the average, 2.28 staff members, including managers, supervisors and staff, per room in 5 star deluxe hotels in India. This staff to room ratio goes down to 1.84, 1.82, 1.84 and 1.30 in 5 star, 4 star, 3 star and 2 star hotels respectively.
- There is a ratio of 1 manager to 1.22 supervisors, 1 supervisor to 5.40 staff and 1 manager to 6.58 staff in the 5 star deluxe hotels. These ratios go up on the higher side, which means that there are more staff members and lesser number of managers and supervisors, as we go down the ladder to lower category star hotels. The ratio is 1 manager to 1.75 supervisors, 1 supervisor to 8.59 staff and 1 manager to 15.04 staff members in 2 star hotels.
- In India currently there are 13937 managers, 20707 supervisors and 128077 staff, all 3 categories totaling to 162721 employees in 1722 star category hotels (from 1 to 5 star deluxe) in the hotel industry in India.
- The average staff turnover in 5 star deluxe hotels in India is 24.14 per cent, going up to 28.96 per cent, 31.64 per cent, 42.97 and 45.63 per cent in the case of 5 star, 4 star, 3 star and 2 star hotels respectively.
- Figures on the number of trained manpower working in star category hotels in India indicate that there are total of 4668 trained persons working in 2 star to 5 star deluxe category hotels. (The definition of trained manpower is those persons who have qualified with a minimum of 1-year educational certificate or diploma in hotel management, which is mostly obtained before joining the service). Trained persons working in 1 star, government approved/ unapproved hotels, restaurants and other catering establishments and made the estimate that there are currently about 80,000 trained persons working in the hospitality and catering industry in India.
- There is a requirement of about 15000 additional trained persons in the star category hotels in India, which includes about 2700 managers, about 2500 supervisors and about 1000 staff members. The requirement given for manager and supervisor categories which totals to 5200 and will be filled by 3 or 4 years diploma and degree holders. In 1 star, government approved/unapproved hotels, restaurants and

other catering establishments, it is estimated that there is an additional requirement every year for about 7500 diploma/degree holders in the country and about 15000-20000 one year certificate holders.

- In trained manpower, which means certificate/ diploma/ degree hotels coming out of hotel management institutions, 5171 students passed from 3 or 4 years diploma/degree courses in private hotel management institutions in 2004. In addition 1658 students passed from the 25 institutes of hotel management (IHMs) under the National Council of Hotel Management and Catering Technology under the Ministry of Tourism. This makes a total of 6829 such graduates who came out in the market for jobs in 2004. Similarly 989 students passed from one or two years postgraduate diploma courses from private institutions and a much smaller number of 218 qualified from Government institutions, making a total of 1207 numbers passing out from such programmes.
- Many institutions that offer one year certificate courses where the entry qualification is 10th grade, these persons are absorbed in lower level jobs in hotels, restaurants and catering establishments. The data shows that 3786 persons qualified from private institutions through such courses in 2004 and 1275 persons passed out from 12 Food Craft Institutes of the government, making a total of 5061 students who qualified with certificate in hotel management in 2004.
- Although the numbers passing out from diploma/degree courses match with the demand side statistics collected, there is a strong evidence, that not more than 60 per cent of diploma/ degree holding students are joining the Indian hospitality industry.

For a qualitative assessment of the status of hospitality education in India and to obtain certain estimated data from the key players, FHRAI also conducted field interviews among the three key stakeholders - the hotel managers, faculty of hotel management institution and students.

- 21 managers from hotels and restaurants in Delhi, Bangalore and Kolkatta stated that the current status of hospitality management education in India and faculty is poor or that it is satisfactory but needs tremendous improvement. A lot of emphasis is laid on theory rather than practical training of hotel operations.
- Many interviewees felt that the objective of majority of private sector institutions is to make money and they are not spending enough funds in providing the basic infrastructure, qualified faculty and quality education.
- Mushrooming of private sector institutions in hotel management and additional numbers are opening up every year. They usually do not have any infrastructure or labs and have poor faculty and standards.

A number of them also said that there should be a curb on such institutions from the Government, who should only allow quality institutions to come up

- On the question on the quality of students joining the hotel management institutions, many managers said that it is still the last resort or a low priority programme, and bright students go for medical, engineering, IT, business management and other programmes. However, the situation is improving. This is because of opening up of job opportunities for hotel management graduates in many other sectors like call centres, airlines, banks, shopping malls, cruise ships, multiplexes and others. A large number of them are also able to find jobs abroad.
- On the complaints from the institutions on the quality of industrial training for students in the hotels, majority of the interviewed managers said that there are problems in this, and the fault lies on both sides. While many hotels consider such trainees as cheap labour and fill more seats than they can manage, some fault also lies with the institutions. They do not monitor the training and do not make sure that the students are sent only to such hotels which have a training department and have also earned a high reputation for imparting good industrial training in the past. This is also a numbers game as the number of aspiring students is much more than the reasonable number of slots which can be filled in good hotels and restaurants.
- Faculty members of some Government and private institutions of hotel management contradicted the views of the hotel managers and felt that the standard of hotel management education in India is satisfactory and is going up over the years. This is because of better job prospects for hotel management graduates, not only in hotels and restaurants but also in many other sectors and abroad.
- Many faculty also said that the quality of industrial training in the hotels is poor. They all squarely blamed the hotels for it, which treat these students as cheap labour and do not give them satisfactory training or a comprehensive exposure to the operations. There are just a few hotels that take good care of the students and have structured and meaningful training programmes for them. Many faculty members said that these practices are lowering the image of the industry in the eyes of the students and this spreads far and wide through word of mouth. Many of these disenchanted students leave their education before finishing it.
- Many faculty members felt that hotels should co-operate more with the institutions in areas like curriculum development, guest lecturers

and training of faculty members in the hotels. They appreciated some of the hotels who are inviting the faculty members for a brief exposure of about two weeks where they get to see the working in key departments of the hotel and also get exposed to latest trends in operations, equipment and procedures.

- It is now a known fact that hotel management graduates and certificate holders have much wider job prospects and less than half of them join hotels and restaurants after passing out. Some faculty members said that only about 15 per cent of those passing out from diploma/ degree programmes are joining any hotels and restaurants in India. This appears to be too small a number and could perhaps apply to a few upper end institutions from where majority of students are able to afford higher studies or go abroad or have the personality profile to join the higher paying jobs in other service sectors. The other view expressed by some faculty members, which could perhaps apply to majority of the institutions was that about 60 per cent of students passing out from hotel management institutions are joining the hospitality industry in India and the remaining numbers are accounted for by jobs in other sectors like call centers, higher studies and going abroad. It was the general view that a much higher number of students who do one year certificate courses in India, are able to go abroad for jobs as there is a greater demand for such persons in cruise ships and places like the Middle East. Some interviewees said that about 70 per cent of certificate holders are able to go abroad after passing out and a brief job in India.
- Majority of interviewed faculty members felt that there is a over capacity in students passing out of diploma/ degree programmes in India. A majority of them are not able to get good jobs and feel frustrated after doing an expensive professional course. Some persons also felt that there is an over capacity in certificate holders also, but most of them felt that there is a need for more seats in the certificate courses and training of larger numbers in this segment.
- Majority of students said that they were happy with their studies and the institute. On the question as to whether they would still join hotel management education after seeing the working conditions in hotels, particularly in terms of long hours and low pay, majority of them said that they had known about this in advance and were enthusiastic about doing their careers in the hospitality industry. Some of them were happy that such a course had helped them in personality development, communication skills and grooming, which they would not have received from an ordinary BA course. These remarks and those appearing in the following paragraphs may again be taken in

the context that we did the interviews only in a small number of upper end institutions in India.

- While hotel managers and faculty members were critical of the state of industrial training for students for different reasons, surprisingly the students all appeared to be happy with their industrial training. They said that this gave them a rare insight into operations in the hotels, which they could not have received while studying in the institute. Majority of them considered the exposure and training in the hotels to be highly valuable to their education and for their job prospects
- While hotel managers said that institutes have a theoretical curriculum and many of the things they taught are not in keeping with modern trends in hotels operations, the students did not mind it. They said that they were getting good and useful education, even if it was theoretical. They were getting some practical training in the hotels during their education and they would get more of it when they joined the industry. Some of them did feel that the institutes should revise their curriculum, add more practical hours and also buy some new and latest equipment being used in the hotels.
- While hotel manages and some faculty members said that many institutions have poor faculty with low skills and practical exposure, the interviewed students did not agree with this view. Majority of them praised their faculty and said that they were getting good education. Many of them said that their faculty had past experience of working in the industry and this was not an issue. As clarified earlier, this could perhaps apply to a few upper end institutions in India.
- On the question of fees being charged in the institutions and whether they were satisfactory or high, the students gave the reply on the basis of where they were studying. Those who were in Government IHMs said that the fees were adequate and should not be increased further.

Through this survey on hospitality management education in India, it was found that many institutions are stuck in the syndrome of low fee, low quality of faculty, lower infrastructure and standards resulting in lower quality of students. In some cases the fee is being mandated by institutions like AICTE and Universities to which the institutions are affiliated. In other cases it is competitive market pressures that influence the fee structure. They are also essentially playing a numbers game. Such inadequate fee revenues lead to poor infrastructure, lab facilities and lower emoluments for faculty. For example a senior lecturer (even in Government IHMs) gets a salary in the range of Rs 8000 to 12,000. Hotel management institutions are thus getting teachers who are unable to find a job in good hotels and restaurants or in other service sectors. Such teachers, mostly without any working experience in hotels, are providing poor quality of teaching and academic inputs. This is leading to a situation where a majority of students passing out from the institutions are not considered employable by the hotel industry. This scenario is also leading to lower quality of students coming into these programmes, most of whom cannot get admission in good colleges, either for normal degrees or professional courses. It is indeed becoming a vicious circle.

There is a need for serious thinking on this matter whereby the institutions should be willing to increase their fees by a substantial margin and spend more money on infrastructure, operational expenses and hiring of faculty. Once the overall fee level goes up, the students and parents will gradually accept it. Moreover, loans are easily available from the banks and paying a higher fee for good education should not be a problem.

However this will only be possible with a change in the mindset of officials in the affiliating institutions like AICTE, universities and the concerned agencies/ departments in the government.

However this may be read with a caveat. Even with current level of fees, many institutions are still making good surpluses. This is also true of many government IHMs where the surpluses are visible on the records. Some IHMs have reserves of many crores of rupees piled up with them, but they still pay a pittance as salary to the faculty and have a dismal placement record.

Therefore, it is also a question of vision and commitment of management, in private or Government sector institutions, to analyse the reasons for their near failure and do something about it.

As our solution, if top 50 institutions in the country, both government and private, raised their faculty salaries to the level of managers in 5 star hotels, and concurrently raised expenses on other things, the face of hospitality management education in India will change drastically for the better, over the next five years.

BEING A HOSPITALITY PROFESSIONAL

The hospitality industry can offer a promising future for IT professionals wanting to make an exciting career. In recent years, the scope of IT professionals in this industry has been on the upswing. International brands are coming to India bringing along state-of-the-art technologies, which other local brands will need to match up to. This has begun to open up new avenues for the IT professional to implement, learn and to develop.

The accelerated infusion of computerised systems and sub-system transactions sweeping the hospitality industry has spurred IT professionals to look at the industry as a potential workplace. The challenge to integrate computer interface and the need to accelerate upgradation of technology usage so as to lower costs has added allure to this industry.

Just six years ago, all the IT professionals wanted to do was set base within the IT industry. But today the non-IT companies, including hotels, are proving to be equally lucrative. Jobs that are being targeted are in the areas of database management and administration, security and technical support. In fact, the hospitality industry holds sway over other industries as well. It is one sector which cannot choose to outsource simply because of the security aspect and a dedicated in-house team is considered to be better equipped to solve problems.

The worth of IT professionals is well recognised by the industry and an IT job is as important in hotels as in any other industry. No hotel can run without IT support these days. Moreover, the hotel industry offers unique challenges that make it more attractive to the IT professionals.

EDP Domain

The basic responsibility of the EDP or IT department in a hotel is to maintain all the computer systems, cater to troubleshooting of all hotel management software such as Fidelio, Point of Sale (POS) management system, Materials Management System (MMS), BOSS, etc, over and above managing the hotel's website. From the guests' point of view, IT should solve any frustrating computer-related problems.

Information management plays a very important role in hotels on a daily basis for successful management requirements of internal and external customers. With automation coming to the fore, there are packages used to support the needs of a unit or a group. This package may either be customised or taken off the shelf. To oversee the smooth functioning of the software package being used, most hotels have an EDP department where the manager is required to enhance the usability of the package. But this can be a remote requirement since in most cases the package bought by the unit comes with an after-sales service option. Indeed, the management laps up any form of automation, which may support the hotel's cause to generate customer satisfaction and retention.

IT requires constant upgradation and bringing in new advancements which involves the finance department at every step. Moreover, IT being in the know-how of valuable and confidential information related to finance, it is the finance department in many hotels that oversees the IT department.

The Right Man

The industry considers certain qualities as necessary for becoming a successful head of the hotel industry. These include job knowledge in becoming a successful IT head, knowledge in setting up networks, experience with various software packages (Micros, Fidelio), familiarity with different types of servers, switches, routers, etc. One should be in a position to work under pressure and meet timelines. The IT professional must be up-to-date and aware of new technologies introduced in the market. Other than this, he must be an effective listener, a team player and a quick learner.

An IT professional can grow in the hotel industry starting as an executive and moving up to become head of the department. There are various growth positions, but it calls for total dedication and continual improvement. When selecting candidates, hotels generally look for persons with good personality traits - the ability to communicate, educational qualification to match the post and experience. Other than the candidates' qualifications and personality traits, we also look for resourcefulness, his ability to keep abreast with new developments with in-depth knowledge of the technicalities and the ability to solve problems not just over the phone but attend to the needs personally. The aspirant should have good management skills and be a team player.

Growth Potential

This is one industry that makes an effort to constantly utilise its funds for upgradation and introduction of new technologies. Every IT professional wants to be associated with and learn about new technologies. The hotel industry gives such IT professionals a chance to broaden their horizons thus making it an attractive option.

One's growth is determined by one's capability and willingness to work. The pay is very rewarding. One's remuneration does not stop at the monthly pay package - there are hosts of incentives given while on the job. Over and above this, performance-based benefits and schemes provided make working for the hospitality industry that much more rewarding.

Marketing Basics for the Small hotel Business

The essence of marketing is to understand your customers' needs and develop a plan that surrounds those needs. Let's face it anyone that has a business has a desire to grow their business. The most effective way to grow and expand your business is by focusing on organic growth.

You can increase organic growth in four different ways. They include:

- Acquiring more customers
- Persuading each customer to buy more products
- Persuading each customer to buy more expensive products or up selling each customer
- Persuading each customer to buy more profitable products

All four of these increase your revenue and profit. Let me encourage you to focus on the first which is to acquire more customers. Why? Because by acquiring more customers you increase your customer base and your revenues then come from a larger base.

How can you use marketing to acquire more customers?

- Spend time researching and create a strategic marketing plan.
- Guide your product development to reach out to customers you aren't currently attracting.
- Price your products and services competitively.
- Develop your message and materials based on solution marketing.

The Importance of a Target Market

When it comes to your customers keep in mind the importance of target marketing. The reason this is important is that only a proportion of the population is likely to purchase any products or service. By taking time pitch your sales and marketing efforts to the correct niche market you will be more productive and not waste your efforts or time.

It's important to consider your virtual segmentation by selecting particular verticals to present your offerings to. Those verticals will have the particular likelihood of purchasing your products and services. Again, this saves you from wasting valuable time and money.

Marketing Differs between Small hotels and larger hotels

If you are like the majority of small hotel business owners your marketing budget is limited. The most effective way to market a small hotel business is to create a well rounded programme that combines sales activities with your marketing tactics. Your sales activities will not only decrease your out-of-pocket marketing expense but it also adds the value of interacting with your prospective customers and clients. This interaction will provide you with research that is priceless.

Small hotel businesses typically have a limited marketing budget if any at all. Does that mean you can't run with the big dogs? Absolutely not. It just means you have to think a little more creatively. How about launching your marketing campaign by doing one of the following:

- Call your vendors or associates and ask them to participate with you in co-op advertising.
- Take some time to send your existing customers' referrals and buying incentives.
- Have you thought about introducing yourself to the media? Free publicity has the potential to boost your business. By doing this you position yourself as an expert in your field.
- Invite people into your place of business by piggybacking onto an event. Is there a concert coming to town, are you willing to sell those tickets? It could mean free radio publicity. If that is not your cup of tea, how about a walkathon that is taking place in your area, why not be a public outreach and distribute their material?

When you do spend money on marketing, do not forget to create a way to track those marketing efforts. You can do this by coding your ads, using multiple toll-free telephone numbers, and asking prospects where they heard about you. This enables you to notice when a marketing tactic stops working. You can then quickly replace it with a better choice or method. By being diligent in your marketing and creating an easy strategy such as holding yourself accountable to contact ten customers or potential customers daily five days a week you will see your business grow at an exceptional rate. The great thing is it will not take a large marketing budget to make it happen.

Prospect

For people who think this is the industry for them, they really think about their personality and be sure they can thrive (and survive) in the atmosphere. It truly is different from anything else. It is critical that they work for a hotel while they are still in school, preferably in a few different hotels, and departments, so they can get a feel for it and know where they would be the happiest and most successful. The growth in the services sector of the worldwide economy has been phenomenal in the last 25 years. In the United States, services currently account for more than 75 percent of the gross domestic product (GDP), which is a popular measure of an economy's productivity.

Similarly, on an international scale, services continue to account for an ever-increasing percentage of economic activity. Most new jobs are created in the service sector, and the growth in the hospitality and tourism industry is a major contributor. Until the mid-1980s, the emphasis within the marketing community was on products. Now services have surpassed products and have taken on a more important role in marketing. Services, such as those offered by providers in the hospitality and tourism industry, have developed marketing strategies and practices that are unique. It has been established that the strategies, tactics, and practices that have been used successfully for product marketers do not always work successfully for those who market services. With the distinct differences between products and services in mind, the field of services marketing has evolved.

Services Defined

Unlike products, which are tangible, services are usually intangible. A service is not a physical good; rather, it is the performance of an act or a deed. This performance often requires consumers to be present during the production or delivery of the service. Service industries, including hospitality and tourism, are actually selling consumers an experience. Services have been defined to "include all economic activities whose output is not a physical product or construction, is generally consumed at the time it is produced, and provides added value in forms (such as convenience, amusement, timeliness, comfort or health) that are essentially intangible concerns of its first purchaser."1 Service employees such as front desk agents, housekeepers, hostesses, wait staff, car rental agents, flight attendants, and travel agents are responsible for creating positive experiences for customers. These frontline employees are critical to the success of service firms and play boundary-spanning roles because of their direct contact with customers. These roles are important because customers' perceptions of service firms are formed as a result of their dealings with the boundary-spanning employees. Several reasons underlie the remarkable growth in services.

The numerous reasons for this growth:

Changing patterns of government regulation: The reduction in government regulation has spurred the growth of services. In recent years, there has been a very noticeable shift toward the government taking a much less active role in the regulation of business activities. The most noteworthy of these shifts have been in the airline, trucking, telecommunication, and electrical generation and distribution industries. All of these industries have seen significant changes, as the barriers to entry have been removed and regulations governing such marketing elements as price have also been relaxed or entirely removed.

Relaxation of professional association restrictions on marketing: A new element of competition has been introduced into professions such as law and medicine as more of the practitioners in these areas advertise their services. Bans or restrictions on promotion have been largely removed. Within the hospitality and tourism industry, standards have also changed. We have seen an increase in advertising focusing on direct comparisons, or attacks, on competitors' products and services. This type of advertising strategy creates, or sustains, the perception of superiority in the mind of the consumer in favor of the brand being advertised.

Privatization of some public and nonprofit services: The term privatization was first used in Great Britain when the government adopted the policy of returning national industries from government to private ownership. This transformation has resulted in a greater emphasis on cost containment and a clearer focus on customers' needs. Later, in Central and Eastern Europe, following the fall of communism, we witnessed a continuing transformation from planned or government-run economies to market-driven economies fueled by private companies. Many of these countries' governments have released the control of airlines and travel agencies to private firms.

Technological innovation: Technology continues to alter the way firms do business and interact with consumers. In all types of businesses, consumers take a more active role in the service delivery process. For example, airlines, in an effort to reduce labour costs and increase speed of service to customers, have aggressively promoted self-check-in, both at the ticket counter and through their Web sites prior to arrival at the airport. Customers print boarding passes, receipts, and other documents without intervention by an airline employee. Express checkout for hotel guests has been in place for many years, but hotel chains continue to experiment with ways to enhance the service, thereby reducing labour costs and/or increasing the customers' perceived value.

In other settings, touch-screen computers collect feedback from guests, in much the same manner that comment cards have been used previously. The ease with which a company can maintain and access a database has permitted the development of sophisticated reservation systems and has led to more sophisticated frequent traveler Programmes. The use of more sophisticated reservations and property management systems has allowed hospitality and tourism firms to improve the level of service provided to guests. Guest history data serve as another example of how a hospitality organization can use technology to gain a competitive advantage. If a hotel guest requests a specific type of pillow, staff can record this preference within the individual's guest history file. When this guest checks into another hotel operated by the chain, the items that were previously requested can be waiting, without the guest even having to request them.

Growth in service chains and franchise networks: Much of the growth in service firms, including the hospitality industry, has been the direct result of franchising efforts by some of the major companies. Franchising represents a contractual arrangement whereby one firm (the franchisor) licenses a number of other firms (the franchisees) to use the franchisor's name and business practices. Notable lodging organizations such as Choice Hotels International and Marriott International, as well as food service firms such as McDonald's, Burger King, Taco Bell, and Wendy's, have all used franchising as a major vehicle for growth. The continued growth of the hospitality industry by means of franchising has put additional stress on independent owners and operators. In fact, each year the percentage of hospitality and tourism operations that are independently operated decreases.

Internationalization and globalization: Increasing shareholder value often remains directly associated with increasing company sales and profits, and globalization is one means of achieving this. As more and more of the prime locations are developed domestically, companies look internationally for expansion opportunities. This has been particularly true for fast-food franchisors: a significant proportion of their expansion during the last few years has occurred outside of their traditional domestic markets.

Pressures to improve productivity: In many industries within the service economy, competition stays very intense. This factor, when combined with the pressure from investors for higher returns on capital, has resulted in pressure to increase productivity and reduce costs. In many cases, managers seek to reduce labour costs by running leaner operations or using technology to replace humans for some tasks An example of this was when Delta Airlines encouraged passengers to check in via the Internet, thereby reducing the number of passengers who wanted to check in at the airport. They offered an incentive of 1,000 extra frequent-flyer miles to any passenger who used this service. While increasing productivity and profits remains a highly desirable goal, it must not be done at the expense of longterm customer satisfaction. Without long-term satisfaction, future profitability may exist in jeopardy.

The service quality movement: With the advent of consumerism, the public's perception is that service quality has declined. In response, successful firms are using the customer's perception of quality to set performance standards, rather than relying solely on operationally defined standards for service quality. They often conduct extensive research to determine the key elements that impact the customer's perception of service quality. When Ritz-Carlton won the Malcolm Baldrige National Quality Award, this was tangible evidence that paying careful attention to customers' service expectations can have a dramatic impact on the firm.

Expansion of leasing and rental businesses: The expansion of businesses that lease equipment and personnel to firms has been a contributing factor in the growth of the service sector. More and more firms are looking to outsource some elements of their operation, and they often start with elements that are not part of the firm's core product or business. For example, most hotels that host meetings and conventions have outsourced the servicing of the audiovisual needs of groups to a company that specializes in that type of business. The company in turn leases the audiovisual equipment to groups that are holding meetings in the hotel.

The company is able to provide more up-to-date and specialized equipment to groups than the hotel might if it provided the service itself. The hotel does not have to maintain an inventory of equipment, and therefore capital costs are reduced.

Manufacturers as service providers: Some of the firms that traditionally manufactured and distributed tangible products have found it profitable to provide services as well. For example, most automobile manufacturers have consumer credit agencies to facilitate the leasing and purchasing of automobiles. In the hospitality industry, PepsiCo decided to enter the restaurant industry and distribute its products through acquisitions such as Taco Bell and KFC, but the company later reconsidered this strategy and sold these brands to Yum! Brands, Inc. In the computer industry, firms such as IBM and Hewlett-Packard provide services in addition to hardware and software. In most cases, the profit margins on services are higher than on products, contributing significantly to the bottom line of the firm.

Pressures on public and nonprofit organizations to find new income sources: All organizations are under pressure to increase sales, which often becomes difficult within the traditional products that a firm sells. There are many reasons for this, but increasing competition and mature industries are often contributing factors. In an effort to find new sources of income, firms often seek new services that will generate new net sales, without cannibalizing sales of existing products. For example, a limousine company might expand its city tour business in addition to the other services offered.

Hiring and promotion of innovative managers: In the past, managers in the service industries often spent their entire careers within a single industry, or perhaps even with the same firm. This situation no longer reintroduction to services marketing mains the same, especially at the corporate level of management. Firms often hire individuals from other industries to provide a fresh perspective and fresh ideas.

The results can become dramatic. One such individual is Steven Bollenback, president and CEO of Hilton Hotels. Prior to his very positive impact on Hilton Hotels, he had engineered innovative financing at both Marriott International and Trump Hotels and Resorts.

CUSTOMER RELATIONSHIP MANAGEMENT

Customer relationship management (CRM) covers methods and technologies used by companies to manage their relationships with clients. Information stored on existing customers (and potential customers) is analyzed and used to this end. Automated CRM processes are often used to generate automatic personalized marketing based on the customer information stored in the system.

Customer relationship management is a corporate level strategy, focusing on creating and maintaining relationships with customers. Several commercial CRM software packages are available which vary in their approach to CRM. However, CRM is not a technology itself, but rather a holistic approach to an organisation's philosophy, placing the emphasis firmly on the customer.

CRM governs an organization's philosophy at all levels, including policies and processes, front-of-house customer service, employee training, marketing, systems and information management. CRM systems are integrated end-to-end across marketing, sales, and customer service.

A CRM system should:

- Identify factors important to clients.
- Promote a customer-oriented philosophy
- Adopt customer-based measures
- Develop end-to-end processes to serve customers
- Provide successful customer support
- Handle customer complaints
- Track all aspects of sales
- Create a holistic view of customers' sales and services information

There are three fundamental components in CRM:

- Operational - automation of basic business processes (marketing, sales, service)
- Analytical - analysis of customer data and behaviour using business intelligence
- Collaborative - communicating with clients

Operational CRM provides automated support to "front office" business processes (sales, marketing and service). Each interaction with a customer is generally added to a customer's history, and staff can retrieve information on customers from the database as necessary. According to Gartner Group operational CRM typically involves three general areas:

Sales force automation (SFA): SFA automates some of a company's critical sales and sales force management tasks, such as forecasting, sales administration, tracking customer preferences and demographics, performance management, lead management, account management, contact management and quote management.

Customer service and support (CSS): CSS automates certain service requests, complaints, product returns and enquiries.

Enterprise marketing automation (EMA) : EMA provides information about the business environment, including information on competitors, industry trends, and macroenvironmental variables. EMA applications are used to improve marketing efficiency.

Integrated CRM software is often known as a "front office solution", as it deals directly with customers.

Many call centers use CRM software to store customer information. When a call is received, the system displays the associated customer information (determined from the number of the caller). During and following the call, the call center agent dealing with the customer can add further information.

Some customer services can be fully automated, such as allowing customers to access their bank account details online or via a WAP phone.

Analytical CRM

Analytical CRM analyses data (gathered as part of operational CRM, or from other sources) in an attempt to identify means to enhance a company's relationship with its clients. The results of an analysis can be used to design targeted marketing campaigns, for example:

- Acquisition: Cross-selling, up-selling
- Retention: Retaining existing customers (antonym: customer attrition)
- Information: Providing timely and regular information to customers

Other examples of the applications of analyses include:

- Contact optimization
- Evaluating and improving customer satisfaction

- Optimizing sales coverage
- Fraud detection
- Financial forecasts
- Price optimization
- Product development
- Programme evaluation
- Risk assessment and management
- Strategic Marketing
- Operational marketing

Data collection and analysis is viewed as a continuing and iterative process. Ideally, business decisions are refined over time, based on feedback from earlier analyses and decisions. Most analytical CRM projects use a data warehouse to manage data.

Collaborative CRM

Collaborative CRM focuses on the interaction with customers (personal interaction, letter, fax, phone, Internet, e-mail etc.)

Collaborative CRM includes:

- Providing efficient communication with customers across a variety of communications channels
- Providing online services to reduce customer service costs
- Providing access to customer information while interacting with customers

Driven by authors from the Harvard Business School (Kracklauer/Mills/ Seifert), Collaborative CRM also seems to be the new paradigma to succeed the leading Efficient Consumer Response and Category Management concept in the industry/ trade relationship.

In its broadest sense, CRM covers all interaction and business with customers. A good CRM programme allows a business to acquire customers, provide customer services and retain valued customers.

Customer services can be improved by:

- Providing online access to product information and technical assistance around the clock
- Identifying what customers value and devising appropriate service strategies for each customer
- Providing mechanisms for managing and scheduling follow-up sales calls
- Tracking all contacts with a customer
- Identifying potential problems before they occur
- Providing a user-friendly mechanism for registering customer complaints
- Providing a mechanism for handling problems and complaints

- Providing a mechanism for correcting service deficiencies
- Storing customer interests in order to target customers selectively
- Providing mechanisms for managing and scheduling maintenance, repair, and on-going support
- Scalability: the system should be highly scalable, as the volume of data stored in the system grows over time
- Communication channels: CRM can interface with a variety of different channels (phone, WAP, Internet etc.)
- Workflow - a company's business processes need to be represented by the system with the ability to track the individual stages and transfer information between steps
- Assignment - the ability to assign requests, such as service requests, to a person or group.
- Database - the means of storing customer data and histories (in a data warehouse)
- Customer privacy considerations, such as data encryption and legislation.

Improving Customer Relationships

CRM applications often track customer interests and requirements, as well as their buying habits. This information can be used to target customers selectively. Furthermore, the products a customer has purchased can be tracked throughout the product's life cycle, allowing customers to receive information concerning a product or to target customers with information on alternative products once a product begins to be phased out.

Repeat purchases rely on customer satisfaction, which in turn comes from a deeper understanding of each customer and their individual needs. CRM is an alternative to the "one size fits all" approach. In industrial markets, the technology can be used to coordinate the conflicting and changing purchase criteria of the sector.

The data gathered as part of CRM raises concerns over customer privacy and enables persuasive sales techniques (see persuasion technology). However, CRM does not necessarily involve gathering new data, but also includes making better use of customer information gathered as a result of routine customer interaction.

The privacy debate generally focuses on the customer information stored in the centralized database itself, and fears over a company's handling of this information. For example, there is virtually no way a consumer can determine if the company shares private (personally identifiable) data with third parties. Furthermore, companies may not always accurately declare to the consumer the types of information collected by CRM systems and the specific purposes for which the information is used.

CRM is also important to non-profit organizations, which sometimes use the terms "constituent relationship management", "contact relationship management" or "community relationship management" to describe their information systems for managing donors, volunteers and other supporters. salesforce.com, a popular CRM service that is on demand, offers its products for free to nonprofit organizations.

MANAGEMENT AND SUPERVISION IN HOSPITALITY SERVICES

There are a variety of views about this term. Traditionally, the term "management" refers to the set of activities, and often the group of people, involved in four general functions, including planning, organizing, leading and coordinating activities. (Note that the four functions recur throughout the organization and are highly integrated.) Some writers, teachers and practitioners assert that the above view is rather outmoded and that management needs to focus more on leadership skills, *e.g.*, establishing vision and goals, communicating the vision and goals, and guiding others to accomplish them. They also assert that leadership must be more facilitative, participative and empowering in how visions and goals are established and carried out. Some people assert that this really isn't a change in the management functions, rather it's re-emphasizing certain aspects of management. Both of the above interpretations acknowledge the major functions of planning, organizing, leading and coordinating activities — they put different emphasis and suggest different natures of activities in the following four major functions. They still agree that what managers do is the following:

1) *Planning:* including identifying goals, objectives, methods, resources needed to carry out methods, responsibilities and dates for completion of tasks. Examples of planning are strategic planning, business planning, project planning, staffing planning, advertising and promotions planning, etc.

2) *Organizing resources:* to achieve the goals in an optimum fashion. Examples are organizing new departments, human resources, office and file systems, re-organizing businesses, etc.

3) *Leading:* including to set direction for the organization, groups and individuals and also influence people to follow that direction. Examples are establishing strategic direction (vision, values, mission and / or goals) and championing methods of organizational performance management to pursue that direction.

4) *Controlling, or coordinating:* the organization's systems, processes and structures to effectively and efficiently reach goals and objectives. This includes ongoing collection of feedback, and monitoring and adjustment of systems, processes and structures accordingly. Examples include use of financial controls, policies and procedures, performance management processes, measures to avoid risks etc.

Another common view is that "management" is getting things done through others. Yet another view, quite apart from the traditional view, asserts that the job of management is to support employee's efforts to be fully productive members of the organizations and citizens of the community. To most employees, the term "management" probably means the group of people (executives and other managers) who are primarily responsible for making decisions in the organization. In a nonprofit, the term "management" might refer to all or any of the activities of the board, executive director and/or programme directors.

There are several interpretations of the term "supervision", but typically supervision is the activity carried out by supervisors to oversee the productivity and progress of employees who report directly to the supervisors. For example, first-level supervisors supervise entry-level employees. Depending on the size of the organization, middle-managers supervise first-level supervisors, chief executives supervise middle-managers, etc. Supervision is a management activity and supervisors have a management role in the organization.

Supervision of a group of employees often includes:

1. Conducting basic management skills (decision making, problem solving, planning, delegation and meeting management)
2. Organizing their department and teams
3. Noticing the need for and designing new job roles in the group
4. Hiring new employees
5. Training new employees
6. Employee performance management (setting goals, observing and giving feedback, addressing performance issues, firing employees, etc.)
7. Conforming to personnel policies and other internal regulations

Introduction to Contemporary Hospitality Industry

The word hospitality can generate rich mental images depending on whether you are a recipient or a provider of its services. The *Oxford Dictionary of Current English* (1993) defines hospitality as the friendly and generous reception and entertainment of guests or strangers. Receivers of hospitality might imagine friendly social occasions enhanced by good food and drink and the warmth of the welcome.

Those who provide these services, however, may recollect the drudgery of producing this fare and serving it to people who are often fussy and ungrateful. Whether giving or receiving, the hospitality industry has touched the lives of everyone and has developed, over time, from a domestic to a commercial activity. This overview article seeks to set out some of the ways in which hospitality has become more professional as it becomes a major international business. Further, a framework is proposed through which hospitality may be reviewed and its future activities speculated. The hospitality industry has grown from its roots of welcoming strangers away from home and its practices are still the major focus for those who are involved with it. As hospitality practice became more complex and widespread, it requires theoretical frameworks by which strategic practitioners might conceptualise problems and better understand the emerging complexities.

These theoretical paradigms also provide learning frameworks by which students can be taught so as to supply the increasing need for better-trained and more competent managers and skilled workers. It is fitting that the hospitality industry's professional body, the Hotel and Catering International Management Association (HCIMA) has adopted the symbol of Janus as the embodiment of its activities. Janus is one of the oldest Roman deities, depicted with two faces, one facing forward and the other facing to the rear. He was a god of vigilance and wisdom who knew the past and looked to the future. Hospitality too has a proud tradition but it needs to develop its practices, theories and education for what promises to offer a flourishing future in the new millennium.

Careers and Jobs in Hospitality Industry: An Introduction

The hospitality industry is the largest, fastest growing industry in the world. More people work in the hospitality industry than any other retail profession in the United States. The hospitality industry supports more than 21.1 million jobs. Career opportunities are varied with positions from entry-level to senior executive and continued strong employment growth is forecast for these fields during the 2003-2010 period. According to the Department of Labour, opportunities to fill job openings are expected to be best for those with a college degree. Better-trained workers are needed in greater numbers to fill employment growth and the new job openings created from replacement needs in this large industry. Think of yourself running a convention hotel in an urban environment, cooking gourmet dinners for international dignitaries, preparing a convention hall for 1,000 doctors attending a training seminar or more. The opportunities are endless. Jobs in the hospitality industry are everywhere. You can choose to work in the U.S. or think about working internationally. Your choice.

Nature of Hospitality and Hospitality Management

The question; "What are hospitality and hospitality management?" is one which generates a number of varied and interesting responses, depending upon the nature of the constituency to which it is put. On the one hand, this could indicate the presence of a lively and invigorating debate over the very essence of the phenomenon researchers are attempting to study and practitioners seeking to provide. On the other, it could equally suggest a lack of clarity and/

or the uncritical acceptance of "handed down" truths about the fundamental nature of the phenomenon. Which of these extremes constitutes a more accurate interpretation of the current state of affairs, if indeed either does, is arguable. However, what does appear to be clear in much of the contemporary hospitality-related research literature is the rather variable and fluid use of the terms "hospitality" and "hospitality management". Perhaps one, if not the, key question faced by hospitality management researchers is; What is hospitality? The term, let alone the concept of, hospitality, is defined and used by most, if not all, hospitality management researchers in a quite indistinct and unsatisfactory manner. Precisely what different researchers mean when they use the term hospitality is rarely defined or explained in either a clear or an acceptable way.

Indeed its common usage by this research community is a relatively recent phenomenon, and one which most seem to have drifted into from the prior focus of hotel and catering in the UK or lodging and foodservice in the USA. It is also rarely clear where the boundaries of hospitality are drawn in relation to "near neighbours" such as tourism and leisure (Brotherton, 1989), or the structural and behavioural characteristics of other service industries such as retailing, financial services etc., and whether hospitality should be conceived as a product, a process, an experience, or all three!Thus, hospitality management researchers face a fundamental problem; how can the epistemological aspects of the field be developed and strengthened if it has not been adequately defined and delimited in the first place? (Taylor and Edgar, 1996).

How can we have a theory of hospitality knowledge if we are unclear over what constitutes the very essence of hospitality? As we approach the millennium perhaps what is even more surprising about this fundamental shortcoming is that it is hardly a new revelation. Other commentators (Nailon, 1982; Slattery, 1983) in the early 1980s have raised similar questions. Similarly, Cassee ventured; "What we need is a sound theory of hospitality based on research"; with others, such as Middleton observing that; "There is a definitional problem from the term 'hospitality industry' [and] it may be surprising that, in the 1980s, one must contemplate educational programmes for the hospitality industry without agreement on what the industry comprises". An observation which is perhaps as relevant today, as we approach the new millennium, as it was in the early 1980s!

Towards the end of the 1980s other hospitality management researchers (Lewis, 1988; Khan and Olsen, 1988; Edgar and Umbreit, 1988; Litteljohn, 1990) have also called for the hospitality management research community to raise the profile and importance of hospitality and hospitality research. More recently Jones has suggested that; "there is certainly no commonly shared paradigm of what we mean by 'hospitality' ... Reference to the research literature would indicate that there has been little or no discussion of what we mean by hospitality ... I would propose that the idea of hospitality research exists more in form than in substance".

Also Taylor and Edgar (1996, pp. 218, 215), in reflecting on the current state of development of hospitality research, have pointed out: "An essential first step ... is to decide what the scope of hospitality research should be [and] if academic research in hospitality is to develop satisfactorily it is our view that it must do so within a coherent framework". In the light of the available evidence it would therefore seem clear that the hospitality management research community has been content to promulgate the supposed, but rarely successfully articulated, "mystical" qualities of hospitality in very much a "head-in-the-sand" manner to both the wider academic and hospitality practitioner communities it interfaces with. If hospitality is indeed distinct and has unique properties a definition to reflect these is urgently required in order that its essence be identified and the field delimited, or the mythical creature be laid to rest.

Though historically this has been an issue hospitality management researchers have shown a virtually zero propensity to explore, there may be some hope for the future. A group of hospitality management researchers (including the present author), drawn from a number of universities and colleges in the UK involved in hospitality management education and research, have initiated a more serious and systematic discourse on the essence of hospitality and hospitality management.

Although this work is in its early stages, with unpublished working papers currently being circulated between the members of the group for discussion, it is important to acknowledge the contribution that all the colleagues involved in these discussions have made to the arguments expressed in this paper, whether they would all agree with them or not!More specifically, the unpublished working papers produced by Roy Wood and Alison Morrison (University of Strathclyde), Rosemary Lucas (Manchester Metropolitan University), Yvonne Guerrier (South Bank University), Conrad Lashley (Leeds Metropolitan University), and Judie Gannon (University of Huddersfield) have been invaluable in stimulating the thinking behind the views expressed here.

New Interpretation of "Hospitality"

"To put it simply, both hospitality and hostility imply the possibility of the other" . The notion that both hospitality and hostility share an equal amount of sway on the development of a relationship between one human being and another is undoubtedly an intriguing one. At a time when hostility seems to be the theme of almost every news bulletin and newspaper across the globe, could a better understanding as to the nature of its opposing virtue, hospitality, provide the solution that those in search of world peace have long been looking for?

Quite possibly, although discovering the solution for world peace is not the aim of this article. Discovering a truer meaning of *genuine* hospitality, and whether or not a better understanding can help to steer the hospitality industry in the right direction in the future, on the other hand, is this article's aim. It is suggested that the most practical way for achieving this goal is to investigate the history and origins of hospitality. Only once an understanding of hospitality's origins and its place in human nature is achieved can one expect to discover what hospitality means today, and more importantly what it will mean to those entering the industry in the future.

Defining "Facilities Management

For many academics in the field, the definition of "facilities management" (FM) remains a vexatious issue. It is made all the more vexatious (and, it might be argued, even more interesting) by the evident growth of facilities management practice and international FM organizations dedicated to research and the dissemination of best practice. It is thus legitimate to inquire as to how facilities management can be practised in the absence of any definition as to what it is that is being practised.

This is no mere sophistry, as will be demonstrated shortly. The principal objective of this paper is to explore issues in the definition of "FM" while drawing parallels with similar debates in other fields of vocational education, specifically hospitality management. The choice of hospitality management as a comparator is not arbitrary. Like FM education, it is, in Europe, a relatively recent presence in institutions of higher education. Hospitality management is, like FM, a broadly vocational field with its origins in other, more established disciplines (many FM courses have their roots in professional engineering). Hospitality management has also faced problems of definition and acceptance within the wider academic community. Comparisons can thus potentially be instructive.

In the film of Umberto Eco's *The Name of the Rose*, competing religious factions meet in a remote monastery to debate whether Christ owned the clothes he wore. This situation finds resonance in academic life where, periodically, various disciplines and subject areas have experienced debates over the legitimate focus of their study. In the UK, for example, Carr's (1961) book *What Is History?* had a profound influence upon discussions of no less than what should be constituted and taught as history. In the 1980s, Cambridge's English Faculty was riven by debates over the relevance of "structuralism" to the curriculum that led to the departure of a young academic, Colin McCabe. Nor are such controversies confined within disciplines. Various academics in the so-called "social studies of science" movement have challenged, or been perceived as challenging, the very basis of scientific theorising and technique (Collins and Pinch, 1993). For the most part, these subjects are established "traditional" areas of the university curriculum. FM is not. One of a number of relatively new "vocational" subjects, there is debate over not only the definition of the subject, but also its scope. One suggested way of overcoming this lack of clarity is suggested by Jorna who confidently asserts that: Although there is a common understanding about core competencies of FM, harmonizing educational programmes around them will be neither easy or, perhaps, necessary. The precise balancing of competencies could be a distraction. Facilities management is still very new and still ill defined.

This lack of definition is better seen as, not fluidity, but diversity. Perhaps a more productive approach would be to concentrate on understanding the essentials of facilities management. How do they translate into practical skills and individual qualities? The "core competencies" to which Jorna alludes are those developed and disseminated by the EuroFM organization Education Group. Derived *inter alia* from a review of existing FM course provision and professional pronouncements (from organizations such as the British Institute for Facilities Management) (Jorna, 1999, p. 43), there are six of these, namely:

(1) understanding business organization;
(2) managing people;
(3) managing the work environment;
(4) managing resources;
(5) managing premises; and
(6) managing services.

Careful consideration of these semi-official observations by Jorna highlights three problems of logic. The first has already been mentioned – how is it possible to talk meaningfully about facilities management if it remains impossible to define? Second, following Jorna's suggestion, how is it possible to concentrate on the "essentials" of FM if no agreement exists as to what is constituted by the study and practice of FM? Third, it seems that the second problem is to be overcome in terms of elaborating core competencies, which may or may not be the same as the "essentials of facilities management" to which Jorna (1999) alludes.

The problem here is that the first four core competencies developed by EuroFM are generic business and management competencies. Only in the management of premises and services is anything distinctive mooted. Even here, the competencies described could apply equally to managers in almost any service industry, for example retailing or hospitality. The difficulties are compounded when considering van Wagenberg's (1997) seminal paper on this topic. Reviewing various definitions of FM he contrasts US and Dutch approaches (the Dutch having played a major role in Europe in promoting the development of FM education). Two of the US definitions cited by van Wagenberg are of interest. FM is: The practice of co-ordinating the physical workplace with the people and work of the organization; it integrates the principles of business administration, architecture and the behavioural and engineering sciences (Cotts and Lee, 1992, p. 3, cited in van Wagenberg, 1997, p. 3). … responsible for co-ordinating all efforts related to planning, design and managing buildings and their systems, equipment and furniture to enhance the organization's ability to compete successfully in a rapid changing world (Becker, 1987, p. 82, cited in van Wagenberg, 1997, p. 4).

The emphasis of both definitions is on co-ordinating but both definitions imply more than this – specifically that FM is a "throughput process" – it is invoked and implemented at the start of a building project and is an ongoing concern. Yet, as van Wagenberg (1997) demonstrates, such concerns have only relatively recently become a feature of FM practice – in short, historical evidence for FM as a throughput process is lacking. A further issue in van Wagenberg's (1997, p. 4) analysis arises from the aforementioned act of contrasting these US definitions with Dutch ones. The main difference emerges in the Dutch (and since, more broadly European) tendency to encompass all services within definitions of FM (*e.g.* reception, catering, security and mail handling).

This produces very nearly the opposite of the problem thus far considered. It moves us from considering a term ("FM") in search of a meaning to defining that term in a manner so all-inclusive that it is nearly meaningless. In the case of the definition recorded by van Wagenberg (1997) above, there is little that FM is not about. It is clear that existing debates over the definition of FM and its core competencies are flawed. Should we care? It might be argued that all new subject areas evolve organically and that facilities management is an emerging paradigm in any Kuhnian sense, one characterized by gradual growth interrupted by occasional, determining, revolutions (Kuhn, 1962). To have any hope of proposing an effective answer to this question, it is first necessary to examine what benefits might descend from greater clarity over the meaning of "facilities management". This exercise will be performed in three parts. First, the general academic environment in which FM and other vocational subjects operate will be considered. Second, parallels with a slightly more mature field of study – hospitality management – will be investigated. Finally, the possible lessons and future lines of enquiry to be drawn from such analysis will be considered.

7

Customer Service Management in Hospitality Industry

INTRODUCTION

In order to achieve rationality the models of business excellence also, in a way, determine whether the criteria have been met, but the evaluation of business excellence is based not only on the fulfilment of the set criteria but also on the determination of the level up to which the criteria have been fulfilled (systems of points).

When analysing the quality of service it is desirable to analyse the largest possible number of companies supplying the same type of service. As we already mentioned, if a company carries out a research and finds that the results are negative, it can interpret this information in the wrong way and conclude that it provides services in a totally wrong way. On the other hand, when analysing a large number of companies, it is possible to compare data and obtain a realistic picture of the position of an individual company compared to others regarding quality.

The upper part of the model includes phenomena tied to the consumer, while the lower part shows phenomena tied to the supplier of services. The expected service is the function of earlier experiences of the consumer, their personal needs and oral communication. Communication with the market also influences the expected service.

Experienced service, here called perceived service, is the result of a series of internal decisions and activities.

The management's perceptions of the consumer's expectations is the guiding principle when deciding on the specifications of the quality of service that the company should follow in providing service. If there are differences or discrepancies in the expectations or perceptions between people involved in providing and consuming services, a "service quality gap" can occur, as shown in image 1. Since there is a direct connection between the quality of service and the satisfaction of clients in hotel industry, it is important for the company to spot a gap in the quality of service. The first possible gap is the knowledge gap. It is the result of the differences in managing knowledge and their real expectations. This gap can lead to other gaps in the process of service quality and is, among other things, caused by:

- incorrect information in market researches and demand analysis;
- incorrect interpretations of information regarding expectations;
- lack of information about any feedback between the company and the consumers directed to the management;
- too many organizational layers that hinder or modify parts of information in their upward movement from those involved in contact with the consumers.

The second possible gap is that of standard. It is the result of differences in managing knowledge of the client's expectations and the process of service provision (delivery). This gap is the result of:

- mistakes in planning or insufficient planning procedures;
- bad management planning;
- lack of clearly set goals in the organization; and
- insufficient support of the top management to service quality planning.

The management can be right in evaluating the client's expectations and develop business methods to satisfy these expectations, without the employees being correct in providing service. For example, a restaurant can order the waiters to serve the customers in two minutes after they sit at the table. Nevertheless, the waiters can ignore that specification and talk between them on the side. The fourth possible gap is the communication gap arising when there is a difference between the delivered service and the service that the company promised to the clients via external communications. The reasons are:

- the planning of communication with the market is not integrated with the services;
- lack or insufficient coordination between traditional marketing and procedures;
- organizational performance not in keeping with the specifications, while the policy of communication with the market abides by the given specifications; and
- tendency to exaggerate in accordance with exaggerated promises.

Should any of the mentioned gaps arise, the "service gap" will also appear because the real service will not satisfy the client's expectations. Hotel companies try to detect the "service gap" with survey questionnaires. Gap analysis is the file conducteur for the management to find the causes of problems regarding quality and to find suitable ways to remove such gaps. For this reason the first four gaps are also called organizational or internal gaps. Although there are several models (scales) for the measurement of service quality and the satisfaction of customers, they are often too generalized or ad hoc, and as such hard to apply in the hotel industry. As opposed to TQM, which began before all in companies that dealt with products, due to the specificities of services (the basic are: impalpability, inseparability from provider and receiver of service, impossibility of storage), a specific concept called Servqual (SERVices QUALity Model) was created. 8 The Servqual model offers a suitable conceptual frame for the research and service quality measurement in the service sector. The model has been developed, tested and adapted during various researches in cooperation with the Marketing Science Institute from Texas and numerous companies operating in the service sector.

THE IMPORTANCE OF THE SMALL HOTEL

Boutique Hotel

Boutique hotel is a term popularised in North America and the United Kingdom to describe intimate, usually luxurious or quirky hotel environments. Boutique hotels differentiate themselves from larger chain/branded hotels and motels by providing personalized accommodation and services/facilities. Sometimes known as "design hotels" or "lifestyle hotels", boutique hotels began appearing in the 1980s in major cities like London, New York, and San Francisco. Typically boutique hotels are furnished in a themed, stylish and/or aspirational manner. They usually are considerably smaller than mainstream hotels, often ranging from 3 to 50 guest rooms. Boutique hotels are always individual and are therefore extremely unlikely to be found amongst the homogeneity of large chain hotel groups. Guest rooms and suites may be fitted with telephony and Wi-Fi Internet, air-conditioning, honesty bars and often cable/pay TV, but equally may have none of these, focusing on quiet and comfort rather than gadgetry. Guest services are often attended to by 24-hour hotel staff. Many boutique hotels have on-site dining facilities, and the majority offer bars and lounges that may also be open to the general public.

Despite this definition, the popularity of the boutique term and concept has led to some confusion about the term. Boutique hotels have typically been unique properties operated by individuals or companies with a small collection. However, their successes have prompted multi-national hotel companies to try to establish their own brands in order to capture a market share. The most notable example is Starwood Hotels and Resorts Worldwide's W Hotels, ranging from large boutique hotels, such as the W Union Square NY, to the W 'boutique resorts' in the Maldives, to true luxury boutique hotel collections, such as the Bulgari collection, Kimpton Hotels & Restaurants, SLS Hotels, Thompson Hotels, Joie De Vie hotels, The Keating Hotel, and O Hotel, among many others. There is some overlap between the concept of a small boutique hotel and a bed and breakfast.

In the United States, New York remains the centre of the boutique hotel phenomenon, as the original Schrager-era boutique hotels remain relevant and are joined by scores of independent and small-chain competitors, mainly clustered about Midtown and downtown Manhattan. The French Quarter and Garden District, New Orleans have several dozen boutique hotels, most of which are located in old homes or inns. These usually provide an ambience based on 19th-century antiques, artwork with New Orleans themes, vintage or reproduction furniture and decor and/or interesting historical associations. Miami and Miami Beach also have several boutique hotels, found mostly along the beachfront streets Ocean Drive and Collins Drive. Most of these are in buildings from the heyday of the Art Deco period. Their attractions include the Art Deco ambiance, beach access, nouvelle and Latin cuisines, and tropical-themed interior decor.

The concept of boutique or design hotels has spread throughout the world. Including European countries like Spain, and East Asian countries such as Thailand, where many boutique or design hotels are sprouting, especially in resort locations, such as Phuket and Hua Hin. Other Far Eastern cities in which boutique and design hotels are becoming increasingly popular include Bangkok, Singapore, and Hong Kong. Boutique hotels are even appearing in such places as Indonesia, mainland China, Iceland, Peru, and Turkey, demonstrating that the concept has penetrated beyond the typical design capitals of the world and is entering new markets.

CUSTOMER EXPECTATION OF SERVICE

As the consumer market segment of the Internet economy continues to grow, the role of customer service in the emerging logistics supply chain systems will continue to change. Therefore, the need to improve logistics customer service (LCS) to consumers is greater than ever before. Finding meaningful ways to meet consumer service expectations requires LCS programmes that strategically blend website service activities (e.g., online ordering procedures) with offline logistics supply chain activities (e.g., order delivery). This balance may be a key strategy in satisfying and maintaining loyalty relationships with online consumers. Yet very little is understood about the nature of website-enabled LCS and the impact on online customer loyalty, although the level of e-logistics service expectations is often thought to be higher than that demanded by customers in brick-and-mortar environments.

The purpose of this study is to examine:

- The factors that determine the level of perceived LCS quality in the Internet-enabled logistics supply chain, and
- The impact of LCS quality on customer loyalty towards online retailers'websites.

Internet-enabled logistics supply chain refers to the total logistics system of transportation, warehousing, inventory, order processing, information flow, and website-enabled order processing procedures that drive the level of perceived quality of LCS in this system. Perceived LCS quality is defined as the level of expectation-minus performance gap and customer intended loyalty is defined as the tendency of online consumers to repurchase from the same website, as reflected in repurchase intentions or intention to recommend a website to peers. Following conventional practice, LCS was defined as the total output of the logistics system, but with emphasis on cognitive impact: perceived service speed and consistency of service speed, perceived availability of merchandise on the retailer's website and in the supply chain, and perceived responsiveness of the retailer.

This study contributes to the literature on two levels. At the conceptual level, the study provides an empirical validation of the logistics customer service-customer loyalty linkage in the online environment. While this linkage has been widely established in traditional business-to-business markets, it remains to be established in the online environment where the impersonal and self-service nature of customer service may raise doubts about the validity of the LCS-customer linkage.

At the managerial level, the study suggests ways to create a consumer-oriented online logistics customer service strategy by identifying the relevant web-based and traditional supply chain logistics activities that are important in creating and maintaining loyalty relationships with online consumers. As with all service activities, not all website features are likely to be relevant to consumer perception of online LCS quality. Moreover, different website features are likely to play different roles in consumer perception of LCS quality. Thus, this study provides insight into which website features should be emphasized in the different phases of the Internet-enabled logistics supply chain.

The following discussion presents an overview of the influence of website design strategy on LCS quality assessment among online consumers. Using the consumer disconfirmation theory as a theoretical foundation, a conceptual framework is proposed including the hypotheses isolating influences of key website design features on LCS quality, followed by the field study that was conducted to specifically examine the service encounter evaluation of 373 online transactions. Finally, analysis and findings are discussed followed by a discussion of the managerial implications and suggestions for future research.

DIMENSIONS OF QUALITY

At the time of exchange information concerning features, aesthetics, perceived quality and tangibles are observable while performance, conformance and serviceability are available with additional effort on the part of the customer.

However, reliability and durability are largely unknown for the specific product, but can be identified for the category of product. Experience with the product or service is required to establish the extent of those latter dimensions. Further, responsiveness, assurance and empathy are generally available but are still under the on-going control of the seller, and therefore are subject to change over time. The"Customer's Perception of Quality Dimensions over Time"was compiled by a focus group of several academics/consultants to industry. The level of each dimension's importance and the information available to the customer were determined based on the focus group members'many years of experience. A series of empirical research projects are necessary to determine if these findings are generally held to be true by companies in one or more industrial SEC codes.

Further evaluations of these patterns and their availability would afford insight into the customer's level of satisfaction with its product or service purchases over the expected period of usage. A service provider may be chosen based on evident embedded dimensions, promised supporting dimensions and the price charged. However, repeat business comes from satisfaction

Satisfaction: A Model of Quality Dimension's Desirability Over Time

The desirability/importance of quality dimensions could be depicted from the time of exchange to the end of the product/service usability.

Each of the three groups of quality dimensions can be classified respectively by:

Dimensions embedded in the product/service, support dimensions for the product/service, and price. The correct combination and/or level of these three groups of quality dimensions would contribute vastly to any particular customer's degree of satisfaction derived from the transaction.

Certain EB1 dimensions (performance, features, conformance, serviceability and aesthetics) will be prime contributors to customer satisfaction at the time of the transaction due to the immediacy of sight, feel, sound, smell and taste of the product/service itself. These will diminish as the product loses its feel of newness. EB2 will become more important to the customer's satisfaction as the positive or negative value of the product's reliability and durability play out. The second component (support), depicted by (SP), can increase or decrease in importance due to the continuing presence or absence of the supporting quality dimensions.

Quantitative Methodology for the General Model

Traditionally, managers of the selling firm tend to view quality as inherent (embedded) in the product and/or service being sold. This leads to the mindset that quality has been established when the product and/or service has been delivered to the buyer. Therefore, if the product did not live up to the advertised, expected levels of quality, the buyer was stuck with it and the seller's reputation"takes the hit".

This chapter takes the position that some of the dimensions of quality are still under the control of the seller and therefore can still be augmented after the point of sale or delivery. If some of these embedded dimensions do not live up to their billing, then other dimensions can be modified or enhanced to preserve the perception of overall quality of the product and the provider.

For example, if an auto manufacturer found that an unusually large percentage (i.e., 5% versus 1%) of their transmissions developed a significant problem that required those transmissions to be replaced within 75,000 miles of use, the auto manufacturer could do one of four things:

- Do nothing;
- Test all transmissions currently in stock before installing (if possible);
- Remove all the transmissions in stock from the assembly process; or
- Enhance the warranty on all transmissions.

The first option would create a frustrated, angry customer that most likely would not become a repeat customer for the auto manufacturer. The second and third options would be very expensive, and while the cost of these actions could be passed along to the customer, it may place the auto manufacturer at a price disadvantage. The fourth option would be the best for the auto manufacturer as it would require action only on those transmissions that failed and would preserve their quality reputation while the problem was researched, resolved and incorporated into the transmission's design.

This quick, no-questions-asked service, would create a customer that is confident in the auto manufacturer's ability to handle future problems (they would be WOWED!). The enhanced warranty would represent a modification of a controllable dimension of quality that would allow the auto manufacturer to preserve the customer's perception of the overall quality of the purchased product (automobile) and the provider (auto manufacturer).

CUSTOMER VALUE OPPORTUNITIES

An understanding of the role that the firm's product plays in the customer's value chain could open up value-creating opportunities. A customer-focused firm has a detailed picture of the customer's consumption domain. When a firm views value consumption activities, it can see if there are other value creating opportunities that it can leverage from its assets. The watchmaker Swatch, for example, offers wrist watches with the technology that allows them to function as electronic passes at ski resorts in Switzerland or for public transportation in Finland.

Wrist gadgets can now serve not only the function of telling time, but also making phone calls, playing music and videos, browsing the Internet, or sending email. This example defies categorization of product. What is the product? It is a wallet or a pocketbook, as well as a telephone, a personal stereo, a personal VCR, and an Internet communications device! The exercise of determining what revenue opportunities Swatch's value-creating assets would offer forces a complete redefinition of the product.

The (product) solution is conceived to take advantage of opportunities to meet the needs in the customer's life with the assets that the firm has. Swatch has found a way to provide value to a recreational activity—skiing—and a functional activity—public transportation. It is contributing to the "customer access" components of the ski resort's and public transportation's product. By enabling customer access, information technology provides a whole range of supplementary benefits to a variety of products.

Contrast this with the example of a firm that does not understand the value of complementary product components and the customer's value chain. A customer came out of a movie theater in Kendall Square, Cambridge, and experienced a 40-minute ordeal trying to leave the theater's parking lot. She spent 30 minutes standing in line in frigid weather to pay the $2.50 parking fee and a further 15 minutes to exit the parking lot. When complaining to the management of the movie theater, she asked if she could pay the parking fee as she bought the movie ticket. She was told that the parking lot was owned by a different company and the theater would not take responsibility for the customer's bad experience at the parking lot.

In contrast, the airline SAS has been known to provide an annual dinner to taxicab drivers in Stockholm because the SAS management wants the drivers to treat passengers on the way to and from the airport with professional courtesy and respect. Clearly, firms that are customer-focused conceive their product differently from other firms, because of their intimate knowledge of the customer's consumption activities.

Information about the customer's consumption cycle, therefore, is a key prerequisite to exploring the opportunities that might be tapped. An understanding of how the customer actually benefits from the solution and the information of how, when, where, and with whom the customer consumes the product should provide some interesting revelations of what the firm is doing and can be doing in the composition of the total product solution for customers.

Thus, Procter & Gamble sends its researchers to homes to observe how people actually use laundry detergent. When Samsung was trying to break into the microwave business in the late 1970s and early 1980s, their design engineers observed homemakers shopping for microwaves at the retail store. You can stay ahead of the curve by offering value through supplementary product that your customer information tells you customers will be willing to pay for.

Even if the value-producing feature or activity cannot be priced separately, you may be able to command a premium for your superior customer value. Being customer-focused is critical in identifying opportunities for establishing superiority in customer value.

Conceiving and Designing

All decisions about the product and, therefore, the value-creating activities of the firm are based on an understanding of the value-consumption activities of its customers. What are the decisions and what are the issues to be considered in determining the total product by a firm? The three major decisions constituting the product strategy are: the product concept, the operations design, and the value creation and delivery process. The *product concept* defines the customer to be served and what value is to be provided. The *operations design* defines the productive assets of the firm required to create and deliver that value for that customer.

Together, the product concept and the operations design define the scope and configuration of the productive assets that can be leveraged to produce the specific customer value that maximizes profits to the firm. The *value creation and delivery process* executes the product concept with the operations design. In developing the product strategy, the firm makes a fundamental decision in answering the question of how the product will be positioned among all potential solutions to the customer's need.

This positioning question poses an asset- and market-based decision that comprises two perspectives.

- The *market-based perspective* looks outward at the market and asks what customer needs can be most profitably served by the firm.
- The *asset-based perspective* looks inward, at the firm's assets, and asks what assets of the firm can be most profitably leveraged by the firm.

The market-based perspective drives the product concept and the asset-based perspective drives the operations design. Thus, the initial step in developing product strategy involves two critical analyses. The product concept requires analyses of the various segments in the marketspace, while the operations design requires analyses of the firm's productive factors.

These two sets of analyses are essential to determining what value-creating activities the firm should engage in to generate the maximum revenue from its assets.

The Market-Based Perspective

A market analysis to determine what would be the most profitable segment mix for a configuration of the productive assets of the firm is the foundation for product strategy. First you need to identify the segments and the solutions that are currently available to the segments. The target market selection or the selected market segments to be served can be based on the profitability and size of each segment that the firm's assets are best positioned to serve.

Here, a formal comparison of all the current solutions from the customer's perspective is necessary. Based on this analysis, the firm is able to determine what it can provide better than the alternative available to the appropriate target market, thus framing the firm's competitive advantage. Only after such customer needs analysis is it possible to specify what would be the desired customer value in the product offering.

The intended customer value in the product offering can now be translated into a detailed picture of the product concept—what the core and supplementary product ought to be.

Remember that the customer value also reflects the customer's implicit assessment of the firm's solution compared to competitive offerings and, indeed, all solutions that are available to customers in the segment. To ensure that the product concept can effectively be superior customer value, the core product should combine the imperatives that have become commodities in the product category with the appropriate features in the supplementary product to reflect superiority in customer value. Thus, the product concept embodies the product differentiation and the superiority in customer value.

The Asset-Based Perspective

The operations design decision rests on how best the assets of the firm can be most profitably leveraged and follows a sequence of questions that pertain to the productive assets and capabilities of the firm and how they should be deployed: What people, facilities, equipment assets are needed to create and deliver the product? Which employees' skills and knowledge would be needed? When and where would specific human capital be needed and for how much time? Similar questions are asked about the facilities and equipment of the firm. Of course, when the asset or resource is not available within the firm, it seeks suppliers or outsources that part of the value creation. Ultimately, the question is what competitive advantage the firm is capable of and how the assets needed should be configured.

Value Creation and Delivery Process

The process decisions are about determining the specific activities of the value creation and delivery. The process of making the product and delivering it to the customer must be detailed. The value creation and delivery activities required are set in a specific sequence. The firm must deliberate on the structure, content, and process of creating and delivering the product to the customer.

No product differentiation from supplementary product can be seen in isolation. If the total benefits from the product are not worth the costs that the customer incurs in acquiring and using the product, the product is likely to fail. The more carefully the firm designs the process with the customer in mind, the more likely the process ensures ease, convenience and quality for the customer. Thus, the customer-focused firm designs the creation and delivery process with the customer's perception of benefits and costs in the value consumption process.

Ensuring Customer-focused Value Creation

Firms must also recognize that since customer value is dynamic, they need to continually monitor and improve this customer value. Ignorance of the need to innovate to sustain competitive advantage is a common mistake committed by the complacent firm. The argument is sometimes made that the firm's priority of customer focus minimizes the attention to innovation. Customer focus and innovation are not contradictory, an either/or strategic decision. Indeed, to be customer-focused would mean that the firm is continually looking for new ways and solutions to meet customer needs—and to be aware that customer needs evolve as well.

Visualize what the firm needs to do to ensure that it is creating and delivering customer-focused value that can be sustained. To sustain superiority in customer value the firm must ensure that management continually assess its market and its assets to ensure that the choice of customer and the value being created and delivered by the firm maximizes the profit goals of the firm.

How well is the customer value in the product concept translated to the operations design and the value creation and delivery process? Is the superiority in customer value being executed. The answer lies in the customer's judgment. Customer-focused firms will let the customer decide whether the firm's value creation and delivery is customer-focused.

Continual customer satisfaction assessment information needs to be available for the customer-focused firm to improve by changing the product concept, the operations design, and the value creation and delivery process, or to continually reassess whether its assets and capabilities are being leveraged to realize the maximum profit potential. To ensure customer-focused value creation and delivery, firms must assess customers' perceptions of the benefits they receive as well as the costs incurred by them.

As an ongoing assessment of customer value, firms must continually assess customer needs and customer satisfaction. As customer needs change, the value bundle needs to be reviewed in terms of its product concept, operations design and delivery. An assessment of customer satisfaction presents an opportunity to improve customer value. The smart firm will continually monitor customer satisfaction to understand what customers perceive as the benefits they are getting from product compared to the costs that they incur. Based on customer satisfaction, does the value bundle need to be modified and redesigned? Are the assets and capabilities of the firm being leveraged for maximum sustainable profits? If the expected customer value cannot be delivered with the existing value-creating assets, then the firm has two choices. Either it acquires or outsources the required value-creating assets and capabilities, or it determines that the target market decision needs revisiting. These questions are posed as a frame for a customer-focused analysis of the value creation and delivery of the firm.

Managing Customer Interactions

The process of delivering value is a tricky and detail-rich exercise; it requires careful planning, using techniques such as blueprinting to visualize the entire customer experience. From the customer perspective, some service encounters are critical incidents requiring more attention than others. All service encounters must be staged for a customer-focused experience just as in the production of theater. Why does Kimberly-Clark manage the discount retailer Costco's inventory of its diapers? The firm has a salesperson live near the Costco headquarters, and a data analyst responsible for overseeing stock at 155 Costco stores in the western United States. Similarly, Procter & Gamble stations 250 people near Wal-mart's headquarters in Bentonville, Arkansas. Large retailers are asking suppliers to more actively manage the movement of products from factory to retail store shelves. P&G estimates that stock-outs amount to 11 percent of an average retailer's annual sales.

When firms like Kimberly-Clark pay more attention to how its immediate customers—the retailers—create value to their customers, they demonstrate that they are being customer focused. In fact, the Kimberly-Clark salesperson passed on information on how customers place packages in their shopping cart that played into package design for diapers. Wayne Sanders, chairman and CEO of Kimberly-Clark, attributes this change to the information age.

Prior to the industrial revolution, a service orientation and the individual-to-individual interaction was the predominant mode of competitiveness. Assembly-line production distanced the firm from the customer due to the sheer number of customers and the physical distance between the customers and the firm brought about by the wonders of modern transportation. Manufacturing goods became the engine of individual and collective (national) economic growth.

Mechanization far outpaced services and replaced producer-customer interaction, relying instead on intermediary institutions to provide a specialized set of competencies that the producing firm lacked. Businesses lost sight of the customer. Now, information technology has brought this full circle, back to the customer.

We call it the information age because what has changed in our time is that new technology has revolutionized the way information is handled. Another equally significant revolution is the change in the customer's domain. Customers not only have access to more information on products and service offerings, they also have the ability to interact with the providers of products and services in ways not previously possible. Providers can also present enhancements to customer experiences from the functionalities presented by technology. Service providers must, however, also manage customer participation when they utilize technology. When firms take advantage of online marketplaces, it might be necessary to make changes in organizational structure so that value creation and delivery processes are adjusted to the addition of the online delivery. Two key technologies underlie this information age technology phenomenon: the Internet and wireless communications. What customer access to these technologies has done is to bring customer interactions to a new level and to the front and centre in how a firm deals with the customer. These interactions are essentially service encounters with the customer.

Much has been said about the service encounter—customer interactions with the firm. In a way, all customer relationship management (CRM) solutions are basically technology support to ensure that the firm maximizes returns from customers by enabling customer-focused interactions. The service encounter is truly "where the rubber hits the road"—where the prospects of customer loyalty are materialized or lost. It is where promises made in advertising are honored or reneged on, and where expectations of customers are disappointed or met. It is where all the assets of the firm need to be brought to bear.

Service encounters with the customers are also laden with the challenges of a product that is produced and consumed in real time, where failures are bound to happen. When the firm designs the value creation process with the customer in mind, it will be prepared for all predictable eventualities. When the service fails, smart firms have smart processes, that recover and learn from the failure. They have service recovery and knowledge management processes in place. As firms compete more and more on services, the management of the customer interaction becomes critical to ensure superiority in customer value. As the core product is a commodity, and most facilitating services approach the commodity state, the competitiveness comes from how the customer is treated by the firm at each and every encounter. This discusses a method for designing the value delivery process with special attention paid to the service encounter and the critical incidents in the value creation and delivery process. A framework for designing the service encounter based on the theatrical metaphor is offered as a way to examine the customer focus of value creation and delivery.

THE SERVICE ORIENTATION IMPERATIVE

The traditional view of services is to treat products dichotomously, in two categories—*either* services *or* (physical) goods. Sometimes the term *product* is even used interchangeably with packaged goods but not with service. Not only has this usage caused unnecessary confusion, but it has also encouraged the flawed approach that services and packaged goods are separate and mutually exclusive entities. Scholars have gone as far as to suggest that "most product manufacturers and service providers alike are largely service operations."

They asserted that the role of services is critical for any organization in providing value in the form of "technological improvements, styling features, product image, and other attributes that only services can create." The fact is that all products come with some services. As a matter of degree some products have more services than others and are therefore more intangible than others.

Picture a continuum ranging from products that are most tangible (and least intangible in proportion) at one extreme to products that are most intangible (and least tangible in proportion) at the other extreme. At one end of the continuum, services such as education, consulting, and financial services have very few physical goods that customers take title to. At the other end, packaged goods such as a bar of soap or table salt come with no apparent service unless, for example, the customer initiates a customer service phone call.

In the middle of the continuum are products such as fast food restaurants and custom-made clothing that have an almost equal proportion, with no real predominance of tangibles or intangibles. In products that are predominantly intangible, where the customers don't take title to anything physical, such as in banking services, the service provider might use tangibles such as documentation, statements, and billing. The value for the customer is in the information contained in them.

As a proportion of what the customer is getting in the total product, the predominant source of customer value is from the intangibles in the total product. For physical goods, services enhance the core product and provide opportunities for competitive advantage. Thus, any product has some proportion of services attached to it, and this part of the product has a special nature that needs to be handled differently. If all firms provide some proportion of service components as part of the total product, it behooves them to have an understanding of the nature of services.

Only with such an understanding can we truly get into the service-orientation frame of mind. Take for example, the table salt manufacturer, Morton's. For this firm to look at itself as a packaged goods firm and therefore not concerned with services is a mistake. The fact that Morton's makes the product available at the retail store through the appropriate distribution channels is a service to the customer.

Morton's has essentially outsourced its distribution and retailing to channel intermediaries. To be truly customer focused, Morton's needs to view all the value-added it provides the customer, over and above the product of the production process—the salt—as services it provides to the customer. Morton's cannot manage its service components in the same way that it manages the production of its table salt. Most B2B manufacturing firms intuitively recognize the importance of the service component in enhancing its product. Caterpillar, the earth-moving equipment manufacturer, recognizes that prompt and reliable service is critical to its success and organizes the whole firm around customer locations. You need a service orientation to see such product enhancements as service dimensions that add value to the core product. Service orientation is

- A philosophy or frame of mind reflected in the firm's culture
- An attitude to serve the customer reflected in the firm's treatment of its customers, and
- A view of services as necessary enhancements to any core product to make a complete solution.

To provide complete and competitive solutions to the customer, one needs to understand and adopt the service orientation. The service-oriented frame of mind requires a grasp of the fundamental nature of services (whether as the product or a component of a product).

Once the inherent characteristics of services are clear, it becomes apparent that their implications for the customer and the provider offer a number of opportunities and pose a variety of challenges.

As a preface to a discussion of these issues, it would be useful to note the evolution of interest in the concept of service. Prompted by the frustrations of practitioners in the service sector who were finding that marketing practices from the packaged goods world did not make sense for services, scholars began to get interested in the problem. In the late 1970s and early 1980s, for a number of reasons, the academic research community in business disciplines, particularly in marketing, operations, and human resources, began a serious intellectual debate as to whether products that were services, compared to products that were packaged goods, needed to be studied differently.

For example, could you study the marketing of hospitality services the same way as you would the marketing of toothpaste? Some scholars maintained that marketing is marketing regardless of *what* you are marketing. Either way, they argued, one had to go through the tasks of segmenting the market, positioning a product, and making product, pricing, distribution, or promotion decisions. Others argued that although that might be true, one would need to approach these tasks very differently; and they proceeded to offer the rationale for this argument.

There was a great deal of interest in this effort, especially among those who recognized the tremendous growth of the services sector.

Around the same time there were environmental changes in the economy and in the competitive landscape. Services sectors such as airlines, telecommunications, and, later, banking and insurance were going through deregulation in the United States. Manufacturing was moving to cheaper labour markets in the Far East and in Latin America. Meanwhile, by the late 1980s in the United States, even professional services such as health care and legal services began to recognize the need to employ marketing practices.

Not surprisingly, even manufacturing firms were being forced to add service components to their product offerings. As these changes occurred and services were being established as an integral aspect of doing business, the United States had become a service economy. Ultimately, the debate over whether services were really different from physical products produced the rationale that the skeptics demanded. The evidence and essence of this argument epitomizes the service orientation.

Characteristics of all Services

There are certain fundamental characteristics that are inherent in all service products and in the service components of any product. Let us begin by defining service as *a deed, performance, or action.* Thus, by definition, services are intangible. The product that is a service or that component of the product that is a service cannot be seen, touched, or felt. As a deed, performance or action, a service is consumed as it is produced, such that the acts of production and consumption are inseparable. Thus, services are also perishable, in that they cannot be inventoried or produced and stored for later use. Nor can they be produced without some level of customer interaction.

Since services are produced and consumed in real time, they are inherently variable—from customer to customer, from provider to provider, and from time to time for the same customer and/or the same provider. These statements describe features that are fundamental and are inherent in products or components of products that are deeds, performances, or actions, and may sound very simplistic until you delve into the meanings and consequences of these inherent characteristics to the customer and to the provider.

It is generally accepted that services are different from physical goods along four fundamental characteristics labeled as intangibility, simultaneity or inseparability, perishability, and variability. These characteristics are conceptually inherent in all services or in the service component of any product. Although this framework is more useful as a pedagogical vehicle rather than a framework for research or practice, it is powerful in fully capturing the concept of service orientation and accomplishes the objective of placing the reader in the necessary frame of mind.

This mindset is grounded in the appreciation of the fundamental nature of services necessitating appropriate managerial decisions and actions. The fundamental character of services and the associated consequences may play out for the manager. A service orientation requires a thorough understanding of how these inherent characteristics of services are manifested for the customer and the manager.

Intangibility—Services

Services are performances. Services cannot be seen but they can be experienced. The product is a process. As a service provider, you cannot show your product as you could if you were the marketer of a packaged good. Yes, services are the result of value-creating activities, just as physical products are, and may employ tangibles or physical products in producing the service. However, the product being purchased is an experience and not a physical good. Customers cannot take ownership or title to a service. For example, hotels provide the service of overnight stay as their core product. The customer does not take title to the room that is being rented.

The hotel provides the use of the room for the duration of the time that the customer has paid for. Similarly, customers don't take title to anything in air travel or in entertainment.

When office copiers come with service, there is no ownership involved with the service component unlike with the copier itself. When your automobile comes with free service under warranty, unlike the automobile itself there is no real ownership of the service component.

Now, as a manager, you might say: "All this is well and good, but if it doesn't change the way I manage the product, its production, or its marketing, whether it is a packaged good or service, why should I care? Services are intangible and service components in products are intangible—yes! But so what?" Let us examine this question from the customer's point of view. For customers, one immediate consequence of the intangibility is increased perceived risk. When you cannot see the product or what you are going to get before the purchase, customers have to acknowledge a certain amount of risk they are taking. While there is perceived risk in the purchase of a packaged or physical good, you cannot return a vacation as you can a defective lawn mower.

Thus, you accept a certain amount of risk as unavoidable in the case of a service. When you book your vacation, do you really see the product? If you have previously been to the locations, you may have seen the facility, but your product was the experience.

Complicating the perceived risk is the fact that the evaluation of services or the service component of the product is inherently subjective. Compared to packaged goods, customers find it harder to evaluate services before the purchase. In some cases, services are harder to evaluate even during and after their performances.

In the case of health care, for instance, you use several proxy elements, such as the cleanliness of the facility, the medical professional's "bedside manner, " and the process you had to go through. What you are evaluating is a lot more than the core product, the medical treatment itself. Being intangible, services cannot be produced until you have purchased (whether you pay before, during, or after) the service.

Simultaneity—Services

The acts of production and consumption occur simultaneously in services. This is primarily because services are produced and consumed in real time. There is a great deal of interaction before, during, and/or after the service between provider and customer. Some sort of customer interaction is necessary even if customer physical presence is not. At the very least, customers have to specify their needs and their need situations. In most if not all cases, it can be argued that production and consumption cannot be temporally separated. (Thus, this characteristic is also termed "inseparability.") A related complication for services is that in services, the provider is part of the product.

As a customer, the frontline personnel you interact with are a part of the product. In professional services, for instance, the lawyer is part of the (legal service) product, the doctor is part of the (medical care) product, the professor is part of the (education) product.

Comparing this to packaged goods: Do you have to interact with Procter & Gamble and the shop floor employee who made your particular tube of Crest toothpaste? You do interact with the retailer of the toothpaste, but remember that the retail store that makes the toothpaste available to you is a service. What you are consuming from the retailer as it is produced by the retailer is a service. In fact, you interact with the provider of the service component of the packaged good. If you interacted with P&G, it was with customer service.

Once again, let us confront the question: "So what?" To understand what difference it makes for the manager, the customer-focused firm must examine the consequences to the customer from the customer's perspective. The customer has to interact with the provider at some stage or at all stages of the production process. The customer is in the service factory in the case of an amusement park. Sometimes the service factory comes to the customer, as in the case of the landscape contractor. Sometimes the interaction is at arm's length, such as in the case of an online travel agent like Expedia.com. In each case, there is some interaction that the customer usually initiates. Thus, there is some effort on the part of the customer for the product to be produced.

The customer takes on a role in the production process. To perform the expected role, customers have to be educated and sometimes socialized into the process. For example, at a fast food restaurant, the customer needs to get familiar with the process of ordering and picking up the food. When you call your long distance phone company for a question on your bill, you need to have some information ready for the service to be performed. These days you have to be familiar with complex automated voice menus before you can get anything done over the telephone. Since consumption and production are simultaneous, the customer is consuming as the product is being produced. The product cannot be produced ahead of time and then consumed. This means that the product cannot be inventoried.

Perishability—Services

Since services cannot be produced and stored for later use, as physical products can, services are said to be perishable products. What actually perishes? In fact, what perishes is the productive capacity of the service, or more precisely, the opportunity to produce a product. A hairdresser's time is wasted or unproductive when he or she is not serving a customer. The customer service personnel ready to handle customer enquiries is not producing a service unless there is a customer to serve. An empty airline seat perishes without a passenger in it on takeoff. The factors of production such as labour, facilities, equipment, and billable time are the value-creating assets for the service provider.

The opportunity to produce the product from these assets perishes without the adequate number of customers for which the capacity is designed. And the service provider needs to maintain a certain level of capacity that is not easily adjustable. Some services are more capacity-constrained than others. A hotel cannot reduce the number of rooms in its facility when there are not enough guests. A management consulting firm with fulltime employees would be hard pressed to release its staff when there are not enough clients to fill the capacity.

For the customer, service products need to be available and accessible when and where they are needed. When the productive capacity is sometimes not able to meet the demand, customers are likely to have to wait in queues or find another provider. Whether it is on the phone for customer service, at the doctor's office, or in line for a ride in an amusement park, customers will have to get used to waiting. In some services, customers need to plan ahead of time and place reservations. That is how managers instinctively manage the utilization of capacity in the operation.

Conversely, when there is more productive capacity than there are customers to be served, service providers have to look for other customer segment opportunities for their value-creating assets. Service providers have to manage that balance between capacity and demand. They employ methods to anticipate and manage the pattern of demand and to manage the capacity accordingly.

Variability—Services

Service products as experiences vary from one experience to the next, from customer to customer, as well as for the same customer from one occasion to the next. In fact, this variability is compounded with differences among frontline personnel. When there are several steps in the service process where the customer interacts with several different personnel of the service provider, there could be variation from one interaction to another. In some cases, customers will prefer specific frontline personnel with whom they have become familiar and comfortable. Since services are produced and consumed in real time, it is clear that customers will likely see a great degree of variation in product quality.

Customers can receive a different experience each time, even at a standardized operation like McDonald's. Service managers attempt to deliver consistently high quality with frontline training and technology and to customize where possible and standardize where necessary. Customers expect customization even when it is not feasible. Managers have to balance the economics of standardization with the quality issues around customization.

Thus, the fundamental characteristics of services force their implications on the customer. The manager of services and products that involve a significant degree of tangibles are forced to orient themselves to these implications. The complexity of managerial situations as a consequence of these characteristics is manifested as opportunities and challenges. Consequently, the services manager must analyze these consequences, and be prepared to take some actions to address them.

CUSTOMER VALUE AND SERVICE ORIENTATION

Customers buy solutions, not products. Every firm needs to understand what it is providing the customer in terms of customer value, not by focusing on the product but by focusing on the customer. In doing so, the firm is able to assess whether it is providing superior customer value and whether it has a sustainable competitive advantage. Competitive advantage cannot be sustained unless it can be protected from competitor matching. Any aspect of the product can be matched by the competition. What is most difficult for the competition to match is how the firm approaches and treats the customer. The firm *serves* the customer by providing product enhancements in the form of service. When other firms can provide the same service, the differentiator is in the service orientation of the firm.

Customer Value

Many firms focus on the product rather than on the customer. When the focus is on the customer, the business is defined in terms of customer value, not in terms of product. The product is viewed as a customer solution and experience. That is, for any firm, the most fundamental definition of its business.

Try this one. What business is Amazon in? That you can buy just about anything on Amazon may not be too much of an exaggeration. The company abandoned or at least cut back on its strategy of buying up companies, as it did with Drugstore.com in 1999. It now handles retail for such established brands as Toys 'R' Us, Target, and Circuit City. Amazon shocked everyone in early 2002, when they announced their first operations profit of $59 million and a net profit of $5 million in the previous quarter. What value does Amazon provide its customer? Customers don't buy products. They buy solutions. If firms are focused on the customer, they ought to see themselves in the role of providing solutions, not products. The information technology sector has popularized the term "solutions providers, " with labels such as application service providers (ASPs, as they are called) or technology solutions providers. These labels may be appropriate at the very general level and allow people to gloss over and take for granted the real meaning of the term *solutions.* The label has no real meaning as a concept unless it can be translated into customer value terms. Customers buy value in the solutions. Thus, customer value defines the primary purpose of any business.

This presents an approach to conducting a critical analysis of this fundamental question of "defining the business of a firm." In doing so, it defines "customer value" and redefines "products" in the customer-focused perspective. Finally, this briefly indicates the fruits of a customer-focused organization providing superior customer value.

Management guru Peter Drucker said in his 1954 book, *The Practice of Management,* "to know what a business is we have to start with its purpose." He goes on to say: "There is only one valid definition of business purpose: *to create a customer.*" Drucker reiterates this concept in a number of different ways, always emphasizing that "it is the customer who determines what a business is." It is not important what the business thinks it is producing.

The customer determines the value of what the business produces based on what the customer thinks he or she is buying. Such a perspective places the final result in focus—what the product *does* for the customer. Thus, the purpose of a business is what it creates for the customer. The first and foremost question for any firm to ask is, what business are we in? How many firms diligently confront this question? And, when they do encounter this question, whose perspective do they take? Taking the customer's perspective to answer this fundamental question forces a number of thought processes that benefit the firm in different ways. In fact, businesses will find that approaching the question of *what business are we in?* in so fundamental a manner not only allows the firm to understand its existing customers, but will also help open up new market potential. It forces the analysis of value-creating assets, including the firm's skills and knowledge sets. The question also opens up the analysis of who the competition is. When firms strive to beat rivals, they typically end up competing within the confines of existing business.

Firms sometimes do not realize that they compete with firms in other industries. They are able to see this if they articulate their business from the customer's perspective. When customers consider their options in meeting a need, they don't limit themselves to one industry. Without realizing it as such, their solutions may involve different industries. Firms are forced to redefine their competitive landscape when they take the customer's perspective because they will find themselves competing outside their well-defined spaces. Kim and Mauborgne call it competing in a "market space.

They urge firms to expand their view of their business by looking "across substitute industries, across strategic groups, across buyer groups, across complementary product and service offerings, across the functional-emotional orientation of an industry and even across time." They argue this point with examples of how Home Depot cultivated the do-it-yourself market from homeowners using contractors, how Intuit saw that people managing personal finances using a pencil and paper calculation actually competed with their software, how overnight package delivery firms FedEx and UPS competed with telephones and fax machines, and how Southwest Airlines competed with driving. This argument illustrates the definition of a business from the perspective of the customer. Not only does it underscore the value that the customer places on what the firm delivers, but it also reveals that the customer's perspective redefines the business.

Well-known Harvard scholar Ted Levitt expanded on Drucker's thesis of defining a business from a customer's perspective when he popularized the concept "marketing myopia, " where firms and entire industries (such as buggy-whip makers) could perish when inwardly focused. He used the example of railroads as an industry that suffered from marketing myopia because it did not see itself in the business of transportation, but rather in the railroad business. Contrast this with a firm like the Williams Companies, one of the world's largest pipeline builders. Until a few years ago, it built steel pipes to move oil and natural gas. Today, it also builds fiber-optic pipes for the big cable companies. Clearly, Williams did not see itself as being in the oil and gas business, but as being in the business of serving big companies that needed to move material (or data) through pipes. Would Williams have seen this opportunity if it had been focused on competing within the oil and gas industry?

To expand your opportunities, you need to look beyond the product horizon and into the customer's space. For example, if a family was looking for something to do on a Saturday, consider their options: have some friends over for dinner, go out for dinner, go to a nearby mall, go to the movies, go to a play or a show, go bowling, go to a miniature golf course, go for a drive to the lake or the beach—and many other options. Now, look at these options in terms of all of the different industries that are competing with each other. If you were a firm in any one of these industries, you could be defining your business the same way as any of the other industries, depending on who your typical customer is. The customer's perspective broadens your own view of your product. Taking the customer's perspective helps firms identify what they are about—their mission and their values. They are better able to understand their strengths and sources of competitive advantage. Firms are better positioned and more effective in allocating resources and efforts, both strategically and operationally. They are better situated to understand what would be considered superior customer value.

Products as Solutions

Where do you even begin when you want to define your business? Let us consider the basics. What *do* businesses sell, at the most general level? In what terms will your response be made? Do you see services and goods as solutions to a customer problem—a need to be met? Customer needs are problems searching for solutions and firms are providers of solutions to customer problems. When seen this way, firms draw focus away from products and orient themselves to the customer with the sole purpose of delivering solutions to problems. The business is defined in terms of customer solutions. Firms suffering from a product focus define their product by its capabilities in terms of product features and promptly lose sight of the customer. The solutions-to-problems approach emphasizes the customer rather than the product. It emphasizes product benefits rather than product features.

Firms must align processes, people, and their entire culture to serving the customer rather than on making and selling products. In customer-focused firms, processes are designed with customers in mind. The output of the processes, the product, is defined by the customer need it serves. In serving the customer, firms offer a combination of benefits or values. Are all products, therefore, a service to the customer? In a sense, yes! The solution represents the value that the firm is providing customers by serving their needs.

Firms' activities produce solutions as value bundles that we call products. All products involve a mix of value producing components—tangibles and intangibles—in value bundles. The proportion of tangibles and intangibles in the entity that the customer takes title to prompts the artificial distinction between services and products. This unfortunate dichotomy detracts from the necessary customer focus in the conception of the product. Regardless of whether the total product is predominantly a packaged good or a service, in a business-to-business (B2B) or business-to-consumers (B2C) context, all solutions to customer problems can be seen as bundles of benefits or value bundles designed to deliver value by meeting customer problems or needs. This book adopts the approach that all products are a mix of physical goods and services in some proportion.

Some solutions employ more tangibles (physical goods) than intangibles (services) in meeting customer needs, while others may provide an intangible (service) involving physical objects. The important question is, what is that total solution from the customer's perspective? It is more important to understand what the value bundle *does* for the customer than what the bundle *is*. To identify the value bundle, one needs to identify and understand the customer.

Identifying the Customer

To understand the customer is to understand your business. To understand the customer's perspective is basic to defining a business. The first obvious question is, who is the customer? If the firm defines the customer too narrowly or without context, any subsequent analysis is flawed. Firms either focus on their end users as packaged-goods firms tend to do, or as in the case of industrial firms, the focus is on the immediate customer. Both cases reflect a narrow view and a lack of understanding of the context. To determine who the customer is, the question to ask is, how does what we produce or provide add value to the client's value creating process?

Most important, what do customers see as the value we are providing to their value creation process? This point is central to what we know as the "value chain" concept. An understanding of customers requires an understanding of the customers' value chain that includes the set of their value consumption activities. If the value created by the immediate customer creates value for a subsequent customer, that customer is also an indirect customer of the firm. We really need to identify the customer as a first step to determine whose perspective we should take and to understand the customer value that we are providing. Performing the analysis of the customer sometimes forces the redefining of the customer. For Bright Horizons, a workplace child care and early education service company, it made a huge difference in how they went about their business when they viewed employers, and not parents, as their primary customers. The company could now tap into the financial and other resources of corporations and gain access to a much wider pool of parents. The value they were providing to the employer became the focus of the company. Chase Manhattan, for example, figured that its child care centre was yielding 110 percent return on investment through reduced absenteeism. Similarly, Merck found that its employee retention rate among those who were young parents went up dramatically.

The customer-focused perspective blurs the boundaries between entities in the value chain. Take the case of Aramark Corp., a firm that caters special events and runs cafeterias for big corporate clients. Nancy Naatz, resident district manager for business services for Aramark, has an office in the premises of her customer, Sears, in Chicago. Since Ms. Naatz is on location at her client's company, she is able to observe and interact with the local vendors Aramark has contracted to supply and serve Sears. Ms. Naatz is able to understand Sears executives' and employees' nutritional needs and interact with the vendors to ensure that the appropriate choices are made available. In this case, Aramark matches the food vendors' solution with the needs of the Sears employees who are the real customers. So, who is the customer? The perspective of *which* customer I inspect and analyze, so as to help determine the business of my business, is the question. This question also raises the fundamental marketing decision of what or who our target market should be. It is a logical place to start before making any marketing or operations decision. Of all the potential customers that make up the market, which particular type of customer is most appropriate for our solution? The analysis involves segmentation, and the decision involved is one of targeting.

We are able then to determine which particular type of customer from the universe of all customers for this product would find most value in what our value-creating assets can produce. We thus segment the market and target those segments for whom our value-creating assets can provide differentiation and a cost advantage. To know who the customer is necessitates an understanding of the typical customer in that segment at a general or aggregate level. Traditionally, customer profiles have come out of the segmentation exercise. Segmentation variables in the B2C context have included demographic, psychographic, and behavioural variables. For customer-focused management we need information on all of the characteristics of the need or problem or use-situation that the customer is involved in, encompassing all of the activities of the customer that the product is a part of. Consequently, the question, who is the customer? You want to know how the customer purchases and uses the product.

Similarly, the profile of the customer in a B2B context involves understanding the business of the organizational customer. For either the B2C or the B2B context, an understanding of the customers requires analysis of their use-situations, and the contexts within which a product helps them in what they do. Of what value are you to them? Now we begin to hint at the notion of what customer value really is. The answers lie in the *consumption* of the product, not in its production.

Customer Value

Customer value is what the customer thinks he or she is getting in return for what the customer has to part with, reflecting an implicit comparison akin to "give and receive." It has been described as the quotient of quality over price. Understanding the customer is about understanding customer value. Customer value is a complex concept and measuring it is complicated. But in the exercise of trying to understand customer value, the manager benefits from a better understanding of the customer and of the opportunities for a superior solution. Here are some characteristics of customer value that any manager should examine in an analysis of the firm and its activities: Customer value

- Is what the customer believes that a product or service provides in a certain use situation.
- Is an implicit comparison between what the customer receives from the provider and what the customer provides in time, effort, and money. The frame of reference is not just the price tag on the product,

but also the ease and convenience in the acquisition and use of the product and the whole interactive experience the customer has with the firm.

- Is the customer's rather than the provider's perspective. It has to do with customer perceptions of the product and the firm, and not the provider's perspective of what the firm is delivering.
- Is dynamic, in that it can change over time before, during, and after the purchase, use, over repeated use of the product, and during all the various stages in the relationship with the providing firm.
- Can vary over different use situations. Your automobile may provide less or more value in transporting a group of kids to the ballpark compared to taking the spouse to the boss's house for a party.
- Can be shaped by attitudes, opinions, and behaviours of others, such as friends, family, media, the providing firm, and other competitors in the industry as well as in substitute industries.
- Determines customer satisfaction and the likelihood of brand or firm loyalty. This cause-effect relationship could be affected by comparisons with competitors and other substitutes.

Your Value to the Customer

In order to determine what business a firm is in, therefore, the fundamental and imperative exercise is to understand customer value. Let us begin the analysis with the question, what exactly does customer value consist of? It is not easy to determine what the customer is getting as value from a product or service. To understand customer value, you really need to get into the customer's way of thinking about products. In a recent *Harvard Business Review* article, Chase and Dasu urge the use of behavioural science to get into the head of the customer, to understand their total experience with the product or service. Only then can you grasp all the components of customer value.

Examining the components and determinants of customer value is a critical step in the analysis. It requires analysis of the benefits as well as costs to the customer. The benefits seen are evident in the perceptions of the product performance. Perceptions of product performance are framed in the context of customer expectations. The expectations are shaped by past experience with the product and by messages about the product received from a variety of sources such as friends and family as well as from the marketer. From an analytical perspective, product performance comes from functional (core) benefits and supplemental benefits. Functional benefits arise from the core attributes of the product. For instance, you buy a set of golf clubs. How the golf clubs affect your game is a core and functional benefit, as in the primary benefit from the product. The prestige of the brand image, the product return policy, and other customer service features would translate into supplemental benefits.

Every customer value analysis requires that we identify and examine core and supplemental benefits. Similarly, we need to identify the costs to the customer—both monetary and non-monetary costs. Monetary costs include costs incurred in the acquisition, use, and disposition of the solution. Non-monetary costs could include the time and effort in acquiring and benefiting from the solution and the opportunity costs where the product failed. Tom Wright, Buy.com's vice president of operations called his company's old way of handling returns "almost embarrassing." To return a product that a customer bought from Buy.com, the customer had to telephone Buy.com to generate a return authorization, which led to a shipping label from the package delivery firm (UPS) to be mailed to the customer, who then used that label to send the product back to Buy.com. It was weeks before the customer got credit for the product return! Imagine the non-monetary cost of aggravation to that customer.

Many firms that focus on acquiring customers do not retain customers because of their shallow understanding of customer value. Customer value includes interactions with the firm before, during, and after the consumption of the product. Smart firms are focusing on the whole customer and defining their business in terms of market spaces. The market space is the actual set of customer solutions defined by the consumption activities to which the firm caters. In recognizing that customer value is dynamic, we need to place this analysis in the context of different use situations and how they are changed over time by various influences. Customers' concepts of what to expect from a provider change with each consumption experience. They learn from their own experiences with the product as well as vicariously from others. Competitor offerings and marketing messages continually shape their expectations. Therefore, implicit in the assessments made by the customer is a comparison with expectations based on the alternative—that is, the competition. Customer value analyses can be performed at a qualitative level and with some difficulty can be quantified as well.

Data-driven representations of monetary worth of what a firm does for a customer are what Anderson and Narus called "customer value models." Such models are useful in assessing the customer value of your product and comparing it with the competition to determine whether you are providing superior customer value or not. The next fundamental question is, Can you provide this superior customer value at a sustainable profit by commanding revenues to cover costs and profits?

Mutual Value of Customer and Firm

Just as the customer value analysis requires an examination of the benefits versus the costs, the firm makes a similar analysis to determine its profit potential. In providing the customer value, what does the firm get in return? How do the monetary and nonmonetary benefits from the customer compare with what it cost the firm to provide that solution to that customer? Can we sustain these profits in the long term? A firm creates value for itself by creating value for the customer.

In many ways, the value of a firm is reflected in the profits it provides its investors and the value of the customer to the firm is reflected in the profits that the customer provides the firm. The greater the values of the customer to the firm, the greater are the profits. This means that the surplus from the revenues after costs is greater if you can attract and retain profitable customers in the long run. Part IV in this book covers the valuation of the customer by the firm. Firms can attract and retain customers if they can provide superior value. It could boil down to, can we command a premium on our solution? If you can, it turns out that the margins are not in the commoditized part of the product, it is in the services provided by the firm.

The margins increase when you are able to extend your role in the customer's space. This may come in the form of "cross-selling" or "up-selling." It may be the case that the total solution provides such value to the customer that the customer is better off with you than with the competition.

As the firm gets more valuable to the customer, the customer gets more valuable to the firm. The value from a customer is derived not only from purchases. Customers can become advocates for the firm, the benefits of which are frequently less understood. The value of the customer in terms of purchases and referrals over the lifetime of the customer should be an imperative calculation for firms who are focused on the customer. It appears that in the final analysis, it is the customer-focused firm that can provide a complete solution through a service orientation that succeeds in providing superior customer value and in return enjoys sustainable profits. So, how is it that a firm is able to provide superior customer value? What gives them a sustainable competitive advantage, such that the firm has sustainable profits?

HOSPITALITY SERVICE

The concept of Hospitality Services, also known as "accommodation sharing", "hospitality exchange", and "home stay networks", refers to centrally organized social networks of individuals who trade accommodation without monetary exchange. While this concept could also include house swapping or even time share plans, it has come to be associated mostly with travellers and tourists staying with one another free of charge. Since the 1990s, these services have increasingly moved away from using printed catalogs and phone trees to connect users towards Internet websites. These have grown exponentially since 2000 and today it is estimated that well over 100,000 people are registered users of these networks. These vary in operational structure, place different emphasis on graphical vs. textual formatting, and cater disproportionately to specific geographic regions. In 1949, Bob Luitweiler founded the first hospitality service called Servas Open Doors as a cross national, non-profit, volunteer run organization advocating interracial and international peace. The next earliest began in 1965 when John Wilcock set up the Traveller's Directory, originally as a listing of his mutual friends willing to host each other when traveling. This later became the Hospitality Exchange in 1988 when Joy Lily rescued the organization from imminent demise.

Hospitality Club is the direct successor Hospex, the first Internet-based service, operating out of Poland since 1992. It is currently the largest hospitality exchange network, growing rapidly. CouchSurfing is a newer but also rapidly growing hospitality exchange organization founded in 2004. Just as all the individual services have their own individual creation stories and organizational histories (often including demise and resurrection), many also have specific niche markets that they cater to including students, activists, religious pilgrims, and even occupational groups like police officers. However, the trend in recent years points to a greater consolidation of users in networks without a specific group, value, or lifestyle affiliation. In essence, these systems employ reciprocity – users gain access to other users' information only by posting their own. Required fields normally include name and contact information, though newer services encourage users to include more detailed personal material, including likes and dislikes, hopes and dreams, and even photographs.

Of course, more information included tends to improve the chances that someone will find them trustworthy enough to host or stay with while traveling. It is very much akin to online dating services.

Staying in private homes means that travellers can save lots of money on accommodation that they would usually be spending on hotels or hostels. Used over a long period of time (2 to 4 weeks), this strategy can cut overall travel budgets in half, or even more combined with hitchhiking. These savings can then be passed on towards more generously patronizing local establishments or simply staying abroad for longer periods of time.

Many tourist vacations today are sold in package form, often including flights, hotels, rental cars, sightseeing tours, and coupons for chain restaurants and bars. While this makes purchasing more convenient, it also puts more money in the hands of large multinational corporations exploiting the synergy strategy of marketing their products in the context of their subsidiary companies operating in other markets. Many years ago, this might have been termed collusion; today, however, it is the norm. This comes at the expense of locally owned independent businesses. Accommodation sharing helps to break apart this monopoly and hopefully redirects some of the tourist revenue back to the local or national economy.

While this is especially important in more rural travel venues where hotels are often built in very picturesque, though fragile environments, every night stayed at a local's home means that much less demand for such hotel rooms.

Also, if accommodation sharing does in fact increase the length of average stays, it may reduce the amount of trips to and from different locations and back home again, thus reducing the overall fuel expenditures in the process.

Ostensibly, one of the primary reasons we travel is to experience what life is like for people living in other countries. Making interpersonal connections and fostering understanding of different cultures may in the long run also be important to international relations. However, even in our increasingly globalized world supposedly rife with diversity, in many popular travel destinations we find tourists milling around "tourist enclaves" where the companies they patronize back home have set up shop to cater to their desires while they are abroad. Sociologist George Ritzer has referred to this phenomenon as the "McDonaldisation of society" and the more recently, the "globalization of nothing". The location of hotels near these centres only fosters more convenient envelopment of the tourist dollar. During hospitality exchanges, hosts want to show off their local knowledge and exciting "off the map" venues. Not only may travellers get a distinctly different experience, but they will also get a feel for the everyday lives of local residents.

These systems foster richer and more convenient travel experiences not so much on the premise of altruism, but on the basis of social exchange theory. Implicit in the agreement to host travellers is the ability to ask to be hosted by them in the future. If one enjoys having interesting guests in their home, this works out well for both parties. It works comparatively better if you are visited by travellers from a locale you find particularly attractive. Thus, hosting someone from New York City in Gainesville, FL seems to be an unbelievable opportunity. Moreover, if you are a Westerner visiting someone in a developing nation, your stay might be the only way that this individual or family could afford a trip to a rich nation. This may mean more than just a relaxing vacation for such disadvantaged parties. Tourism has always searched for these two qualities, but much like Midas and his golden touch, the reach of tourism has to a large extent destroyed the opportunity to encounter them in most places. Unluckily, the experience has been thoroughly commodified by everyone who wanted to secure their opportunity to make a buck in the process. Accommodation sharing offers a way out of this bind and a viable alternative to having one's desires manipulated by corporate conglomerates who never had the best interests of the place or the people foremost in their minds. There is no contractual agreement between users in these systems. Reservations are made, but if they are for some reason broken, there is no higher authority to which one could plead for a refund or other compensation. The only repercussion will be the poor rating you give that user and your only consolation will be that your warning will deter others from visiting or hosting them. For those who feel insecure unless their travel arrangements are written in stone before departure, this system will not be comforting. There is a chance that guest and host will not get along. Perhaps there will be scheduling or ideological conflicts. Maybe you will find that hosts or visitors have misrepresented themselves. Perhaps the experience will not live up to your expectations. Intense interpersonal communications in advance and a flexibility once you have arrived is your best bet. These experiences require additional planning and courtesy towards the demands of your host. Thus, your living conditions, length of stay, and overall experience will be circumscribed by the living conditions you enter into. The average user is a young white person who speaks English and lives in a developed nation. While there are many users who do not fit this description, the more different they are, the less likely they will be involved. This is especially true for persons living in the developing world who likely do not have easy access to the fundamental prerequisite for using these services: computers and the Internet. Thus, the sample population found in searches of these databases are really much less diverse than a geographical representation of worldwide users might suggest.

There is a distinct possibility that someone will abuse the system and that innocent users (especially women) will get hurt. All services include disclaimers that require users to waive their rights to hold anyone but themselves responsible for any harm that may come to them in using the system. They advise that the best defence mechanism is to only involve oneself with users that have extensive personal information and interpersonal networks within the system that have been verified by others. It does seem entirely plausible that someone clever and patient enough might be able to invent an entire group of complex user identities and build histories convincing enough to fool even more cautious patrons. Still, the difference between these systems and the other social networking platforms popular nowadays on the web (such as MySpace, Tribe, Orkut, LiveJournal and Ebay) is that any agreement reached through the accommodation sharing medium is contingent on actually meeting other people face-to-face. Other web scams are easier because interpersonal interactions rely so much on putative identities that are never actually verified in the real world. However, this does not diminish the greater risk to physical well being that this kind of traveling by definition must entertain. The best advice is to meet unknown persons in public spaces first, and try to meet some of their acquaintances in person before agreeing to a hospitality exchange.

Bibliography

Pierre Chenet and Jon Ivar Johansen: *Beyond Loyalty: The Next Generation Of Strategic Customer Relationship Management* : , PHI Learning.

David A Po Chedley: *Client Relationship Management : Using Relationship Management and Project Service Excellence to Create a Competitive Advantage*, Jaico, 2003.

Bhavi Chhaya: *Customer Relationship Management*, Centrum Press, 2013.

VSR Murty Dinabhai: *Customer Relationship Managemen* , Surendra, 2009.

R. Ramachandran: *Customer Relationship Management*, Serials Publications, 2011.

Ekta Rastogi: *Customer Relationship Management*, Excel Books, 2003.

T Vetrivel: *Customer Relationship Management*, Discovery Publishing House, 2011.

Debasis Mukherjee: *Customer Relationship Management* : , Adhyayan, 2011.

Maksud A. Madraswale: *Customer Relationship Management*, Mittal Publications, 2015.

Arvind Gautam.: *Critical Analysis of Hospitality and Tourism Industry*, Axis Publications, Delhi, 2010.

Jitendra K. Sharma.: *Contemporary Tourism and Hospitality Management*, Kanishka Publications, Delhi, 2006.

Arvind Gautam: *A Concise Course on Hotel and Hospitality Management*, Axis Publications, Delhi, 2010.

B.K. Chakravarti: *Hotel and Hospitality Management*, A.P.H. Publications, Delhi, 2011.

P C Sinha: *International Encyclopaedia of Hotel and Hospitality Management Ethics*, Anmol Publications, Delhi, 2007.

Shambhu Dayal: *Ethical Foundation of Hotel and Hospitality Management*, Akansha Publications, Delhi, 2006.

Amrik Singh Sudan.: *Encyclopaedia of Hotel, Tourism and Hospitality Management in Twenty-First Century (6 Vols)*, Anmol Publication, Delhi, 2001.

Anil Kathuria.: *Hotel Management*, Sonali Publication, Delhi, 2008.

Arvind Gautam.: *A Concise Course on Hotel and Hospitality Management*, Axis Publication, Jaipur, 2010.

B K Chakravarti.: *Hotel Management*, APH Publication, Delhi, 2008.

B.K. Chakravarti.: *Hotel and Hospitality Management*, A.P.H. Publication, Delhi, 2011.

B.K. Chakravarti.: *Hotel Management Theory, Vols. I and II*, APH Publication, Delhi, 2009.

Bal, P K.: *Tourism Industry In New World Order : Focus On Hospitality Management*, Cyber Tech Publications, New Delhi, 2008.

Gagandeep Singh.: *Global Aviation and Hospitality Management*, Book Enclave, Jaipur, 2008.

Gaurav Gandhi.: *Hotel Management Diet and Nutrition*, Random Publications, Delhi, 2012.

Gaurav Gandhi.: *Hotel Management Food and Food Services*, Random Publications, Delhi, 2012.

H.C. Chaturvedi.: *Hotel Management : Current Issues and Practices*, Akansha Publication, Delhi, 2006.

J Mathews.: *Hotel Management*, Pointer Publication, Jaipur, 2008.

J. Mathews.: *Hotel Management and Hospitality*, Aaviskhar Publication, Delhi, 2006.

Jagmohan Negi and Gaurav Manoher.: *Project Report Preparation : Hospitality Management and Tourism Development*, Aman Publications, Delhi, 2010.

Jagmohan Negi, Gaurav M.J., Suniti and Ritushka.: *Communication Skills for Hospitality Management*, Kanishka Publication, Delhi, 2012.

Jagpradeep.: *Hotel Management*, Murari Lal & Sons, Delhi, 2008.

Jitendra K. Sharma.: *Contemporary Tourism and Hospitality Management*, Kanishka Publication, Delhi, 2006.

K.S. Negi.: *A Textbook of Hotel Management*, Wisdom Press, Delhi, 2011.

Lalita Sharma.: *Tourism and Hospitality Management*, Centrum Press, Delhi, 2011.

M C Metti.: *Advertising and Hotel Management*, Anmol Publication, Delhi, 2008.

M C Metti.: *Catering : Housekeeping and Hotel Management*, Anmol Publication, Delhi, 2008.

M C Metti.: *Customer Service and Hotel Management*, Anmol Publication, Delhi, 2008.

M C Metti.: *Hospitality and Facilities in Hotel Management*, Anmol Publication, Delhi, 2008.

M C Metti.: *Hotel Management and Catering*, Anmol Publication, Delhi, 2008.

M C Metti.: *Operation in Hotel Management*, Anmol Publication, Delhi, 2008.

Madhulika Bhatnagar.: *Encyclopaedia of Catering Technology, Food Service and Hospitality Management, Vol. I to III*, Anmol Publication, Delhi, 2008.

Index

H

I

L

M

N

O

P

Q

R

S

T

U

V

W

X